Diversifying Digital Learning

Tech.edu

A Hopkins Series on Education and Technology

Diversifying Digital Learning

Online Literacy and Educational Opportunity

EDITED BY

WILLIAM G. TIERNEY,

ZOË B. CORWIN,

AND

AMANDA OCHSNER

Johns Hopkins University Press

Baltimore

Johns Hopkins University Press
2715 North Charles Street
Baltimore, Maryland 21218-4363
www.press.jhu.edu

Library of Congress Cataloging-in-Publication Data

Names: Tierney, William G., editor. | Corwin, Zoë B., 1971–, editor. | Ochsner,
Amanda, 1986–, editor.
Title: Diversifying digital learning : online literacy and educational opportunity /
edited by William G. Tierney, Zoë B. Corwin, and Amanda Ochsner.
Description: Baltimore : Johns Hopkins University Press, 2018. | Series: Tech.edu :
a Hopkins series on education and technology | Includes bibliographical
references and index.
Identifiers: LCCN 2017016320| ISBN 9781421424354 (hardcover : alk. paper) |
ISBN 9781421424361 (electronic) | ISBN 1421424355 (hardcover : alk. paper) |
ISBN 1421424363 (electronic)
Subjects: LCSH: Educational technology—Social aspects—United States. |
Internet in education—Social aspects—United States. | Youth with social
disabilities—Education—United States. | Computer literacy—United States. |
Digital divide—United States. | Educational equalization—United States.
Classification: LCC LB1028.3 .D583 2018 | DDC 371.33—dc23
LC record available at https://lccn.loc.gov/2017016320

A catalog record for this book is available from the British Library.

*Special discounts are available for bulk purchases of this book. For more information,
please contact Special Sales at 410-516-6936 or specialsales@press.jhu.edu.*

CONTENTS

Over the past two decades, the Pullias Center for Higher Education has conducted research on college access and completion for historically underrepresented students. More recently, we have turned our attention to how digital tools interface with the field of college access. We are deeply appreciative of the following organizations for funding the research that informed the creation of this book: University of Southern California Office of the Provost, TG, the Rosalinde and Arthur Gilbert Foundation, the Bill & Melinda Gates Foundation, the US Department of Education's Institute for Education Sciences (award R305A110288), and the US Department of Education's Fund for the Improvement of Postsecondary Education, First in the World grant (award P116F140097). The text does not reflect the views of these organizations.

We are tremendously grateful to Suneal Kolluri, Tattiya Maruco, and Antar Tichavakunda for their time and expertise in helping prepare a high-quality manuscript—and to Diane Flores and Monica Raad for their stellar administrative support.

It is our hope the chapters that follow will advance an agenda of digital equity for all young people in the United States.

CHAPTER ONE

Mapping the Terrain
Youth and Digital Media

WILLIAM G. TIERNEY AND SUNEAL KOLLURI

Young people today make sense of their world in ways different from their counterparts of only a generation ago. The manner in which youth interact with one another, their families, their teachers, and strangers, and how they experience their neighborhoods, schools, and youth-based organizations are inevitably framed by technologies that were nascent at the turn of the century (boyd, 2014; Palfrey & Gasser, 2013; Thomas & Brown, 2011). Our increased understanding of young people as active consumers and producers of knowledge calls for us to reconceptualize teaching and learning not only in how it is done but also where and when it is done. Individuals are able to access information with the click of a mouse or simple perusal of their iPhone or iPad. As we shall discuss, technology has become common in schools, and to an even greater extent, what students learn has extended well beyond the formal setting of the classroom.

A challenge, of course, is that youth experience their social worlds in ways that are circumscribed by larger social and economic forces that privilege some and marginalize others (DiMaggio, Hargittai, Celeste, & Shafer, 2004; Hargittai & Hsieh, 2013). The "digital divide" creates an additional layer of challenge to students already facing inadequate services in their schools and communities. Consensus exists among academics and practitioners that this challenge is not only about access to computers and broadband but also about learning opportunities related to digital literacies in formal and informal contexts (Becker, 2000; DiMaggio & Hargittai, 2001; Helsper & Eynon, 2010; Lu & Straubhaar, 2014; Putnam, 2015; Warschauer & Matuchniak, 2010). We know that the social context of learning matters, but we know relatively little about the context of online use and video game play for low-income children and children of color. Accordingly, this book is structured to provide a framework for understanding how marginalized youth most effectively engage with technology—and how social organizations help or hinder growth of digital literacies. The chapters that follow provide multifaceted portrayals of how students, teachers, counselors, mentors, parents, and other stakeholders engage with digital technologies and how multiple online contexts affect such engagement.

The Pew Institute estimates that the vast majority of high school youth play games on social media (84% of boys and 59% of girls) and that 95% of teens belong to at least one social networking site (Lenhart, 2015). A Kaiser Family Foundation study reported that children between the ages of 8 and 18 spend an average of 7.5 hours per day using computers and/or MP3 players, or watching some sort of video programming (Rideout, Foehr, & Roberts, 2010). Unfortunately, most educational systems and programs have yet to catch up with how youth are making use of social media (Jenkins, 2006). To be sure, some schools and afterschool programs are technologically well equipped, but many schools and programs in low-income neighborhoods lag in the sorts of resources that those in middle- and upper-income neighborhoods have. More importantly, how children from different social classes use technology and social media differs as well (Attewell & Winston, 2003; Lenhart, 2015; Zhang, 2015). Thus, the authors in this book discuss the sorts of problems that exist, identify successful strategies that have proven effective, outline the opportunities that need to be created, and consider what different organizations and constituents might do to jump-start the idea of digital equity. Our assumption, then, is that digital equity does not yet exist but a more equitable digital landscape is possible.

At times, it seems as if society suffers from digital amnesia—as if what exists today has always been with us. We forget that websites have been ubiquitous for little more than a generation; that MySpace predated Facebook; and the user base of Facebook has morphed from one largely composed of youth to one that is now predominantly the terrain of adults, while teenagers and young adults have migrated to Instagram, Snapchat, and elsewhere (Murphy et al., 2017). New terminology arrives—"texting," "friending," and the like—and old terms lose their meaning: "sounding like a broken record" and "he has a rolodex," to name but a few. Our intent is not so much to document what exists today as if what we were describing were a historical artifact but instead to try to get a lay of the digital land in order to understand the changing terrain.

In what follows, we begin with an overview of how we are thinking theoretically about technology; we then outline the changes in technology over the past two decades and what sorts of inequities exist between low-income and middle- or upper-income youth. We describe the sorts of technologies individuals have, as well as how different individuals and groups make use of social media. Our purpose here is to offer a platform for the subsequent chapters' delineation of various aspects of digital inequities and the strategies the authors consider to overcome or to restructure those inequities.

Cultural and Social Capital as a Framework for Understanding Digital Equity

The sociological literature has explicated various forms of capital. *Economic capital*, of course, pertains to those resources related to money—property, equity in stocks and bonds, and the like. In a digital framework, economic capital would include the ownership of computing technologies such as laptops and tablets. *Human capital*, as discussed by Gary Becker and others (Becker, 1962; Dean, 1984; Welch, 1970), concerns those skills that individuals acquire, usually through formal schooling. *Digital human capital* would entail the capacity of individuals to employ digital technologies for the purposes of economic advancement. A more recent notion, *social capital*, has been discussed by many theorists including Pierre Bourdieu (1986) and James Coleman (1990). The assumption here is that one accrues social networks and connections that provide valuable access to privilege and power. A related term, *cultural capital*, concerns cultural resources and artifacts that enable and promote social and educational advancement (Bourdieu, 1986). As Sablan and Tierney (2014) note, "These resources are not just material resources such as books or computers, but can also exist in more subtle forms, such as the dispositions of upper classes. Their properties explain the perpetuation of the privileged class's advantage" (pp. 155–156). Theories of social and cultural capital, therefore, would encourage a more robust analysis of digital equity, beyond a mere accounting of who has access to what technology.

Obviously, there are interrelationships among these forms of capital. Pierre Bourdieu (1973), in particular, has focused on how economic inequality is perpetuated. The assumption is that "hard work" alone does not bring about a transformation of economic realities. Instead, the purpose of studies that focus on these alternative versions of capital is to try to understand how the more invisible structural and cultural aspects of society privilege some and disable others. Human capital, of course, puts a premium on educational opportunity. If the skills one acquires amount to economic success, then the policy implications are clear: a society concerned with economic equality needs to ensure that all individuals have equal access to the same sorts of schooling. Those proponents of human capital will acknowledge that poor children are at an educational disadvantage. Low-income youth come from families that do not have the material resources of their well-off counterparts. Poor families lack access to many goods and services that allow children from wealthier families to get ahead, such as reliable Internet connections and state of the art technology. To be sure, individuals need to work hard and demonstrate initiative, but most observers will acknowledge that society has different levels of access to educational opportunity. The challenge, and onus, however, for those who subscribe to human capital is that, if one works hard and society provides the resources, then individuals will succeed.

In many respects, the policies and regulations put forward by proponents of the Great Society (Jacob, Kapustin, & Ludwig, 2014; Karoly, 2001) follow from the idea that human capital is essential in improving the lives of the poor. Busing, desegregation, affirmative action, Head Start, and an array of federal and state initiatives have had three explicit premises informed by the idea of human capital. First, individuals can succeed in the United States if they work hard in school. Second, education is a primary vehicle for moving individuals out of poverty. Third, society must provide programs that ensure that schools, and increasingly postsecondary institutions, enable success. Human capital, then, enables economic capital.

This logic, however, assumes the absence of more subtle structural forces that may impede an individual's capacity to take full advantage of such educational opportunities. Structural interpretations of social and cultural capital that are deterministic take a very different perspective than those from the lens of human capital (Bourdieu, 1986; Putnam, 1993). Social capital investigates the structure of relationships across social groups (Portes, 2000). Bourdieu (1986) provides a definition of social capital as "the aggregate of the actual or potential resources which are linked to a possession of a durable network of more or less institutionalized relationships of mutual acquaintance and recognition—or in other words, to membership in a group—which provides each of its members with the backing of the collectivity-owned capital, a 'credential' which entitles them to credit, in the various senses of the word" (p. 249).

The connections that an individual accrues account for one's social capital. Social capital, however, is not something that can simply be changed by well-intentioned social engineering. For Bourdieu, social capital contributes to the advantage of some and the marginalization of others. Rather than the ability to break out of one's economic class, social capital ensures that social reproduction will occur (Bourdieu, 1977). Thus, nonfinancial resources create networks in which additional privilege will accrue. Rather than promoting educational equity, from this perspective, schools, social organizations, and even digital networks mask how inequality gets reproduced.

Burton Clark's analysis of community colleges is a useful example of how reproduction occurs. In 1960, the state of California developed a Master Plan that ostensibly ensured a place in higher education for all of the citizens who graduated from high school and wished to attend college. Community colleges are purportedly a gateway from which one might attend college and then transfer to a four-year institution. However, to use Clark's well-worn phrase, community colleges "cool out" (Clark, 1960) the aspirations of those who attend. That is, community colleges ostensibly admitted students to a postsecondary education, but their aspirations for a four-year degree were not effectively fostered and the students "cooled out." The result is that economic disadvantage is perpetuated. Bourdieu and others (Bourdieu, 1977, 1986; Loury, 1977; Sandefur, Meier, & Campbell, 2006) look on such a point as evidence of how reproduction occurs.

Another example pertains to the children of those who have attended the University of California. They will have more networks available to them than those whose parents have never attended college. The children of alumni assume they will go to college because of the networks in which they naturally reside. First-generation students have no such networks. With respect to technology, use does not happen in a vacuum, and social networks can have profound effects on how young people interact with and learn from digital media (Hargittai & Hinnant, 2008; Hargittai & Hsieh, 2013; Putnam, 2015; Selwyn, 2004). As Corwin and Tichavakunda discuss in chapter 4, educators can play an integral role in cultivating social capital through digital media.

Cultural capital is distinct from, but related to, social capital. *Cultural capital* refers to those cultural resources that have a concealed exchange value (Bourdieu, 1986). Material resources, such as books, and access to computers and technology, are one form of cultural capital. Facility with language and knowledge about ideas that have been deemed important enable one not only to have cultural capital but also create the conditions to acquire more cultural capital. In the digital age, cultural capital in the form of technological skill and socialization into "techno-cultures" can enhance one's ability to exploit digital technologies (Selwyn, 2004). The expanded capacity to engage meaningfully in digital environments can in turn build more capital. In this sense, cultural and social capital are not unlike economic capital. Access to resources creates more resources. Lack of resources makes it harder to acquire additional resources, much less attain as much as those who began with more.

Attendance at a classical concert, then, not only provides an understanding about classical music, it also facilitates entry into social groups in a way that knowledge about Nas, Kendrick Lamar, or J. Cole, for example, does not. Thus, Beethoven's Ninth Symphony is not just an example or artifact of cultural capital because it is a cultural good (classical music). Beethoven's Ninth is a cultural resource because of the value placed on classical music in society (Sablan & Tierney, 2014). Having the knowledge, linguistic ability, and resources to decode the distinct value placed on these cultural goods represents one's cultural capital (Bourdieu, 1973). The tangible resources themselves supply those who hold them with cultural capital, as material goods convey symbolic meaning.

Cultural capital also exists in more subtle forms, such as the dispositions of the upper class. Children receive cultural resources from their families and communities. The simplest examples are the array of books that exist in middle- and upper-class homes but are often absent in lower socioeconomic status (SES) homes (Bourdieu, 1986). Similarly, children from the upper class are afforded opportunities to travel, attend afterschool activities, go to summer camps, interact with the latest technologies, and pursue other enrichment activities that develop a cultural literacy that is foreclosed to those who come from poor families. Although all social and economic classes have cultural capital (Carter, 2003), the rich develop among their children the most societally valued forms, in effect generating cultural capital: "the knowledge that elites value yet schools do not teach" (McDonough, 1997, p. 9). The result is that the properties of cultural capital help explain the pernicious perpetuation of the privileged class's advantage (Bourdieu, 1986). Indeed, from a deterministic standpoint, proponents of cultural and social capital interpret the idea of human capital as simply another way to justify inequality. If human capital has called for educational opportunity, and significant resources have been provided to create that opportunity, then when inequality continues to exist, the accusation is that it must be the fault of those who are poor. Simply stated, because the government has provided financial resources to a generation of low-income Americans, if one is poor, it is because he or she has not worked hard enough, and therefore is culpable in his or her inability to rise in a meritocracy.

A less deterministic interpretation, and the view ascribed to by the authors in this book, is that although social and cultural capital certainly disable some and empower others, the conditions for empowerment can be created so that agency exists for individuals to overcome inequality. From this perspective, these various forms of capital are interrelated. However, the assumption is that social organizations such as schools can help create networks that teach cultural capital and allow all individuals, regardless of social class, to accrue social capital. We certainly acknowledge that the children of the upper class begin from an advantaged position simply because of their economic wealth. However, the poor bring to their situation great stores of cultural wealth based on their community's racial and ethnic backgrounds (Carter, 2003). The challenge is not to assume that one's economic situation is caused by one's own identity or cultural background. Instead, we turn that idea on its head. The idea of cultural integrity (Tierney, 1999) assumes that one's standpoint provides potent areas of strength that, if tapped correctly, will foment and enable opportunity. These opportunities occur not only in social organizations such as schools, colleges, and universities but also in an array of community agencies and associations. Thus, social and cultural capital have the potential to both constrict and limit human and economic capital and to enable human capital and develop economic capital.

Technology is another form of capital that has direct and telling implications for cultural and social capital. Technology, as with books, or membership in particular social groups, is a form of capital rather than capital itself. We raise this point insofar as we need to be clear that it is individuals and groups who give meaning to different forms. Current types of music, for example, have emanated from different racial and social groups but do not lend themselves to the sorts of reproductive capabilities discussed above until the upper class appropriates them. Hip-hop, rap, and other culturally rich artistic forms do not offer the capacity for social mobility in a capitalistic economy until those in power acquire them and interpret them in a manner that creates class distinctions (Sablan & Tierney, 2014). Thus, African art was seen as "primitive" until artists such as Pablo Picasso appropriated it. Our point here mirrors the work of others who are investigating how technology is being used to equip or disable individuals and groups (Garrison & Bromley, 2004; Hargittai & Hinnant, 2008; Lu & Straubhaar, 2014; Peck et al., 2015). The massive technological changes that are occurring, both inside and outside of the classroom, are ripe areas for analysis. What makes investigations particularly compelling is that technology and social media are not only changing so quickly, but education and technology policies are shaped by whether policymakers prioritize economic, human, social, or cultural capital.

Some individuals have implicitly adopted a human capital perspective and tried to attend to what has been perceived as technological inequality. The ill-fated plan by then-superintendent of the Los Angeles Unified School District, John Deasy, for example, worked on the assumption that poor children lacked access to quality software. The result was a $1 billion initiative to provide every child in the district an iPad equipped with Common Core–aligned software. A *Los Angeles Times* report indicated that the high costs of the Apple tablets, minimal technological training for teachers, and poor internal communication about the initiative ultimately doomed the project (Blume, 2015). To be sure, there is a certain degree of legitimacy to Superintendent Deasy's assumption. If technology enables some and disables others, then access to quality equipment certainly needs to be addressed. One also ought not to reduce a well-intentioned effort like this one to a simplistic interpretation that Deasy, or any other educator who invests in technology, does so under the assumption that buying materials alone can overcome inequality. And yet, many critics of Great Society initiatives point to precisely such expenditures as wastes of public resources (Higgs, 2011). They point out that the individuals for whom such equipment has been intended did not benefit from these outlays: dropout rates remain the same; access to higher education has not increased; literacy and math rates have remained flat. The conclusion that such critics draw is that public monies have been wasted because the onus, ultimately, rests with the individual and his or her desire to achieve.

From the perspective advanced here, we certainly acknowledge the need for equity with regard to resources such as iPads and laptops. But when one works from a framework that calls upon social and cultural capital, we also recognize the shortcomings, and even danger, of reducing educational inequity to material goods and services. Instead, investigations need to be made about how individuals and groups utilize technology in ways that are more or less "capital enhancing" (Hargittai & Hinnant, 2008). Accordingly, we wish to consider the differences in technological capacities based on social class, as well as gender and race, not only from what groups have or lack, but also how such capacities are employed. Prior to such a discussion, however, it is fruitful to touch on why these differences matter.

The Landscape of Educational Opportunity in the Twenty-First Century

Although the changes in technology and social media are impacting all aspects of our lives, the focus here pertains to education, writ broadly. The United States always has made a commitment to increase the education of its citizenry, and that commitment has implied more formal schooling. Horace Mann, in the early nineteenth century, spoke about the need for free public education so that all children could attend school. During the depths of the Civil War, Abraham Lincoln passed the Land-Grant Act to establish free public higher education. By the turn of the twentieth century, attendance in elementary school—from grades 1 through 8—became mandatory for all states admitted to the Union. The GI Bill enabled returning veterans to attend postsecondary institutions. "Dropout" came into the lexicon in the 1950s, because the assumption was that all children needed to attend and graduate from elementary and high school. The Master Plan that we referenced above enabled all of California's citizens to attend a postsecondary institution if they so desired.

The rationale for America's infatuation with formal schooling lies in the goals that have been outlined and the outcomes that have occurred. From the early nineteenth century, when the United States was a relatively poor country, until today, the reasoning for formal education has largely focused on two issues: citizenship and skill development for economic participation. The first assumption has been that the more schooling children had, the better prepared they would be to participate in a democracy. This assumption has reason in fact. A variety of studies have demonstrated a strong causal link between education and political engagement (La, Lake, & Huckfeldt, 2012; Nie, Junn, & Stehlik-Barry, 1996; Wolfinger & Rosenstone, 1980). As people become more educated, they acquire social capital, critical thinking skills, and political knowledge that enable them to more easily access opportunities for political and civic engagement. Digital media has been shown to supplement in-school democratic education by enhancing knowledge of current events (Tewksbury, Weaver, & Maddex, 2001), exposing young people to diverse perspectives (Kahne, Middaugh, Lee, & Feezell, 2012), and encouraging civic engagement such as volunteering or signing petitions (Hargittai & Shaw, 2013; Wellman, Hasse, Witte, & Hampton, 2002).

The second argument pertains to the economic gains attributed to one's education. Over time the data has been conclusive that the more education one has, the more likely it is that one will earn more than those who have a lesser degree. Most recently, the argument has been made about the importance of attendance at a postsecondary institution. Carnevale, Rose, and Cheah (2011) have concluded that, over a lifetime, a college graduate earns nearly double that of a high school graduate. Further, multiple reports (e.g., Matthews, 2012) continue to point out that in the future, about 60% of all workers will need some form of postsecondary degree—a certificate, AA, or BA degree. The Georgetown Center on Education and the Workforce, the Public Policy Institute of California, the Lumina Foundation, the Gates Foundation, and the Obama administration all have argued for increased college-going and graduation rates (The Executive Office of the President, 2014; Johnson & Sengupta, 2009; Lumina Foundation for Education, 2015).

During the most recent recession, for example, although those with a college degree faced hardship, those with only a high school degree or less were even worse off (table 1.1). In 2014, the unemployment rate for individuals with less than a high school diploma was 9.0%; the unemployment rate for individuals with a high school diploma was 6.0%; and the unemployment rate for individuals with a bachelor's degree and higher was 3.2% (US Bureau of Labor Statistics, 2014).

A number of studies have suggested that student facility with digital technologies may play an important role on educational attainment measures such as test scores (Attewell & Battle, 1999), high school graduation rates (Beltran, Das, & Fairlie, 2008), and efficacy in college (Goode, 2010; Head & Eisenberg, 2011). Additionally, adults who use the Internet experience greater wage gains than adults who do not, and those who have more experience doing so see their wages grow even more rapidly than less experienced users (DiMaggio & Bonikowski, 2008).

TABLE 1.1
Unemployment Rates by Educational Attainment

Education Attained	Unemployment Rate in 2014 (%)
Bachelor's degree and higher	3.2
Associate's degree	4.5
Some college, no degree	6.0
High school diploma	6.0
Less than a high school diploma	9.0

Source: US Bureau of Labor Statistics, Current Population Survey, 2015.

Higher earnings benefit workers and their families and are also beneficial to the state and country. Increased income generates increased buying power, which generates revenue and additional tax dollars for a capitalist economy (Bowles & Boyer, 1995). In a country that relies on innovation and entrepreneurship, there is also evidence that a well-educated citizenry is more likely to create technological and scientific breakthroughs (Nelson & Phelps, 1966). To be sure, the American educational system is beset with problems and inequities. However, the argument can be made that for over two centuries, schooling has been a key driver in the success of the United States. At a time when our goods and services face serious global competition and, as some will argue, traditional industries such as manufacturing are in decline (Charles, Hurst, & Notowidigdo, 2013; Pierce & Schott, 2012), American higher education continues to import more students than any other country in the world (Choudaha & Chang, 2012).

The reason that students come to the United States for a postsecondary education is that America's view of education is largely the view of the rest of the world as well. Education is seen as a major way to enable a country's citizens to improve their economic livelihood. For over a century, we have seen elementary education increase throughout the world. In the more developed countries a high school degree has become a necessity, and in the industrialized world, a postsecondary credential is as important as in the United States. As Gradstein and Nikitin point out: "The last several decades have witnessed a remarkable expansion of schooling around the world. The increase in various measures of schooling in particular, at the primary and secondary level, has been rapid and steady. In particular, the average years of schooling for the adult population (15 years and above) grew from 3.7 years in 1960 to 5.0 in 1980 and 6.3 in 2000" (2004, p. 1).

Until recently, the consensus has been is that if a country's citizens wished to prosper, then the populace needed the skills that were taught primarily in formal venues such as schools—literacy, mathematics, and the like. Although the assertion that a better-educated workforce is beneficial to the workers and the country has remained steadfast, changes in technology and social media have created a slightly different conversation. Some have begun to question if learning needs to take place only, or primarily, in schools, colleges, and universities (Collins & Halverson, 2010; Tucker, 2007). Does technology create the possibility of learning without the formal structure of a teacher in front of every classroom? Today massive open online courses (MOOCs), Internet-based learning modules like Khan Academy, and "blended" classrooms are challenging traditional modes of education, for better or worse. As many authors suggest in the chapters that follow, although formal educational structures such as classrooms and campuses are likely to continue, at least in the near future, the advent of technological reform opens up many opportunities for learning that heretofore did not exist. We turn, then, to a discussion of the technological terrain and how it is being defined and traversed.

The Cartography of Technology and Digital Media

A framework that calls upon social and cultural capital looks on technology from at least two perspectives. Although we argued above that simply providing iPads or laptops is insufficient to overcome inequities, the converse also would be fallacious. A severe lack of technology in schools and communities certainly cannot benefit learning; hence the first part of our discussion addresses those structural inequities that exist. We turn then to what the literature says about how low-income, first-generation youth use technology—addressing both the "first-" and "second-level" digital divides—and then offer a short overview of the rest of the book.

Structural Inequalities

By some accounts, the digital divide has all but disappeared, and American youth now share the online landscape as equals regardless of race or social class. This argument contends that anyone born into a world of widespread computer use is inherently a "digital native," fluent in the language of technology in ways that older generations are not (Palfrey & Gasser, 2013; Prensky, 2001; Roberts, 2005). This narrative does have some credibility. Digital technology has become less expensive and thus more accessible to youth from historically marginalized groups. African American teens are now more likely than White teens to own smartphones and both African American and Latina/o students report going online more often than their White classmates. While African American and Latina/o teens are slightly less likely to own computers, their rates of tablet ownership are about the same as White youth (Lenhart, 2015). Furthermore, young people of all races visit social media pages at similar rates, and low-income teenagers are actually more likely to use social media platforms (Lenhart, 2015). These current trends are in stark contrast to digital realities from the turn of the century, when White households had twice the rate of Internet access as Black and Latina/o households (Fairlie, 2007). Also, Wells, Lewis, and Greene (2006) report that in-school technological gaps have nearly disappeared. On some measures, the United States has certainly made progress toward digital equity for its youth.

These numbers, while a cause for celebration, obscure stubborn techno-logical disparities between groups. First, when the data is disaggregated by socioeconomic status, as opposed to race, the numbers are particularly sober-ing. Teens from low-income households are 17% less likely to own a smartphone than those from middle- to high-income households and 14% less likely to own computers (Lenhart, 2015). As of 2010, 57% of very low-income households, making less than $25,000 a year, had no computer at all (US Census Bureau, 2010).

Additionally, many apparent gains in racial equity are more tenuous than they seem, likely caused by the intersections between race and class in America. Though Black and Latina/o youth go online as frequently as White teens, the devices they use to do so suggest disparities in financial resources available for technology. Black and Latina/o young adults are more than three times as likely to only have a smartphone for online access and are more than twice as likely to have their mobile service cut off because of the financial burden of monthly phone bills. Low-SES youth of all races also face substan-tial gaps in Internet access (Smith & Page, 2015). In addition, African American and Latina/o youth are more likely to report that their home computers lack Internet capability (Fairlie, 2007). This trend is in line with that of low-income teens, who are thirteen times more likely than high-income youth to be "smartphone dependent" in their Internet accessibility (Smith & Page, 2015). The nature of available data clouds how class and race each play distinct roles in the digital divide, but the discrepancies in access remain significant across both dimensions. Ultimately, the lack of robust, sustained home tech-nology usage for any young person can significantly hinder the development of technological skill (Facer, Furlong, Furlong, & Sutherland, 2003).

There are other factors beyond race and social class that act as barriers to access. With respect to language, Lopez, Gonzalez-Barrera, and Patten (2013) find that Spanish-dominant individuals are nearly 30% less likely to use the Internet than English speakers. It is contended by boyd (2007) that significant numbers of young people are absent from the digital world for more personal reasons—their parents have denied them access to social media or they are "conscientious objectors" who protest the excesses and frivolities of typical teenage online interactions. Whatever the cause of their absence from digital communities, a number of young people are not engaging with technology at the rates of their peers. A focus on inequities of access views technology as primarily an issue of economic capital. In the next section, we turn to how the ways in which youth use technology are circumscribed by issues of human, social, and cultural capital.

Tech-Use Inequalities

Access to digital tools is just one element of the digital divide. Selwyn (2004) makes the case that information and communications technology (ICT) access is a necessary but not sufficient condition for digital equity. This "second" digital divide (Hargittai, 2002), which focuses on how youth from different backgrounds use technology differently, is the new scholarly focus regarding digital inequity. DiMaggio and Hargittai (2001) describe this second level as having four components: autonomy of use, skill, social support, and the types of activities for which the technology is utilized. As will be outlined here, youth of different racial backgrounds and socioeconomic statuses endure gaps on these measures in school, at home, and with respect to future opportunities.

Research has uncovered significant inequity of technology use in schools for low-SES students. Teachers of low-income students report less access to digital resources and more barriers to digital instruction, such as web filters and school mobile phone policies, when compared with teachers of middle- and high-income students (Purcell, Heaps, Buchanan, & Friedrich, 2013). Although low-SES students report about as much in-school computer use as high-SES students, their use is mostly geared toward drills and memorization, as opposed to activities that develop higher-order thinking (Warschauer & Matuchniak, 2010; Wenglinsky, 2005). Garrison and Bromley (2004) describe how, at one urban magnet school, new technology mandates result in defensive teaching strategies during computer use that rigidly emphasize control over inquiry and exploration. In a qualitative study, Attewell and Winston (2003) notice how low-income students adeptly use the Internet as a form of entertainment but struggle to engage intellectually online because of challenges with literacy. For example, in a project designed to get students thinking about future careers, a student who thinks she might want to open a bakery, types "bakry" into a search engine and gets frustrated with the lack of results. Wealthier students, meanwhile, are able to nimbly access the Internet for academically enriching activities such as political research and media development. That particular skills are necessary for meaningful exploitation of technology implies a human capital framework is an important lens through which to investigate digital equity. Though perhaps sitting in front of the same types of technology, low- and high-SES students appear to be engaging in very different learning experiences in their schools.

Social and cultural capital can also play a significant role in how disparities in tech use arise, and studies of computing and race/ethnicity bear this out. DiSalvo and colleagues (2011) argue that African American male youth often view computing as outside of their social identities. They find that an extra-curricular program that actively seeks to align African American male identity with computing can counteract technological aversions that develop along racial lines. Unfortunately, few African American students experience such programs. Also, an ethnographic study of the "computer science pipelines" at Los Angeles area high schools shows how racialized technological aversion is reinforced by school structures. In this study, a school that primarily enrolls Black and Latina/o students offers no computer programming courses. While another high school with a more diverse student body has a computer science AP (Advanced Placement) class, but it is made up of almost entirely young White men (Margolis, Estrella, Goode, Holme, & Nao, 2008). The research implies that few schools actively interrupt racial patterns of technology engagement. That technology seems to reproduce, rather than counteract, entrenched inequities corroborates what Cuban (1986; 2001) has argued over decades: technology does not revolutionize education; schools merely incorporate new media into traditional practices that maintain historical inequality. Similar to Bourdieu's (1973) explanation of social reproduction, schools are thus complicit in processes that ensure students from dominant cultural groups maintain their position in the social hierarchy.

Inequalities also stem from the cultural milieu of lower- and working-class homes. When low-income youth log on at home, their online experiences further diverge from those of their more economically privileged peers. Zhang (2015) demonstrates positive correlations between high socioeconomic status homes and visits to the Khan Academy webpage, and between low socioeconomic status homes and visits to the Cartoon Network website, suggesting disparities in benefits from online educational resources. Admittedly, this study does not determine what individuals do on the websites, and it may be the case that students use the Cartoon Network site in a more engaged and creative fashion than students use the Khan Academy site. Indeed, some studies have found that commercial media designed purely for entertainment can be a catalyst for learning (Squire, 2011; Steinkuehler, 2008). For example, video games such as *Lineage* and *Civilization III* provide youth with ample opportunity to engage with challenging intellectual tasks (Squire, 2006; Steinkuehler, 2006). Unfortunately, low-income youth appear to engage in cognitively demanding, strategic game play less often than their more privileged counterparts. Andrews (2007) finds that many low-SES students are less likely to play games that include significant amounts of strategy and simulation and are also less likely to play in groups online. Finally, opportunities to "geek out," by engaging with robust, creative, and cognitively challenging uses of digital media, can be constrained within home ecologies that make frequent and concerted technological use challenging for low-income youth (Ito et al., 2010). Thus, the overall opportunities for low-SES youth to learn digital fluency in their homes may be constrained by the types of websites they visit, the games they play, and the limited capacity of their available technology.

At-home and in-school technological inequities carry over from high school into the technology-rich college setting. Goode (2010) uses a mixed-methods study to find that students who did not have access to robust ICT in their childhood homes struggle upon arrival to technology-minded college campuses. Lu and Straubhaar (2014) find that, among Latina/o students, a lack of "techno-capital" and "techno-dispositions" both significantly correlate with their struggle to adjust to college classes wherein professors expect high levels of technological capability. A study of college students at the library during finals week shows how some students gain an academic edge by cleverly incorporating technology into their study habits (Head & Eisenberg, 2011). In the modern age, digital fluency seems inextricably linked to college success.

Limited practice with digital media in one's youth also appears to impact career options. Scholars Trilling and Fadel (2009) develop a blueprint of necessary skills for success in the twenty-first-century job market that seem to significantly correlate with the types of digital opportunities experienced by privileged students. When technological experiences nurture critical thought and creativity, self-directed learning, collaboration, and digital fluency—the qualities that Trilling and Fadel argue are highly valued in today's job market—digital advantages can turn into financial rewards in the form of professional opportunities. These divergent technological experiences can also lead directly to inequities in technological fields. Black and Latina/o students enter into computing majors at significantly lower rates than their White and Asian classmates (Warschauer & Matuchniak, 2010). Subsequently, laborers from historically marginalized groups do not fill the high-status jobs within the technology industry. According to the US Census Bureau (Landivar, 2015),

Black and Latina/o workers make up just 9% of American software developers, despite being more than 25% of the entire workforce. The data thus suggests that technological ability can be a form of cultural capital that plays a role in social reproduction. The digital divide that begins in the childhood homes and schools of marginalized youth clearly lingers through adulthood.

A Roadmap for the Book

This text is intended to expand the way we think about digital equity across diverse educational, cultural, and socioeconomic contexts. Chapters' foci range from large-scale educational reform efforts to microlevel examples of how individuals are making sense of digital technologies. Authors address digital use in K–12 school systems as well as technology in higher education. In the following two chapters, authors explore wide-scale efforts to create more equitable access to, and effective use of, technology in schools.

In chapter 2 authors Joseph Kahne, Christina Evans, Erica Hodgin, and Young Whan Choi highlight the role digital media can play in encouraging youth engagement in participatory politics. The authors draw on a nationally representative survey of 15- to 25-year-olds. Their work discusses a formal initiative for expanding opportunities for civic learning for students in Oakland. They explore what educators might do to support youth's participation in civic life. The authors begin by documenting the nature of changes with regard to civic practices and the distribution of varied practices across socioeconomic status and among members of varied racial and ethnic groups. They argue that educators have an important role to play if youth are to receive high-quality and equitable support for engaging thoughtfully and effectively in civic and political life in the digital age.

In chapter 3, Joanna Goode, Julie Flapan, and Jane Margolis delve into inequities found in computer science education. The chapter presents a framework for large-scale educational reform that explicitly centers equity in computer science. Using data from a case study of California computer science educational reform, the authors contend that political, technical, normative, and pedagogical issues must be attended to simultaneously in order to broaden participation in computing. The chapter highlights the value of microlevel practices that take students' unique lived experiences into account and macrolevel state policies that provide resources for high-quality computer science teaching.

In chapter 4, Zoë B. Corwin and Antar A. Tichavakunda expand on this introduction's exploration of social capital as a lens for understanding digital inequities by focusing on the role of educators. They consider the types of support students need to utilize online resources and how teachers can be more effective in using technology inside and outside of the classroom. Corwin and Tichavakunda propose a theoretical approach for understanding the intersection among digital tools, educators, and school context—and share data from a large-scale federal study to illustrate key concepts.

The overlap between S. Craig Watkins's and Amanda Ochsner's chapters 5 and 6 is purposeful. In both cases, assumptions and biases that are deeply ingrained in educational institutions ultimately deter certain types of students from pursuing trajectories associated with the design of technology and digital media.

Watkins covers how schools inadvertently deter low-income students from pursuing STEM. Ochsner's chapter covers how individuals and broader social trends discourage girls and young women from pursuing expertise in games and technology.

Watkins's chapter is based on data and findings from a one-year ethnographic study of a high school game design class. He argues for a game-based civic-centered approach to education where schools create opportunities for students to engage in production-centered learning activities and to participate in the civic life of their communities. Chapter 5 also contributes to the discussion of challenges that resource-constrained schools and communities face when they attempt to connect students to digital tools and resources outside of the classroom.

Ochsner also investigates opportunities for learning beyond the classroom. She discusses what she calls "digital clubhouses," such as game communities, and considers how they might be less exclusionary and more open to learning for all groups, especially those that have a reputation for being exclusionary cultures. Drawing from research on the learning trajectories and professional pathways of women in the game industry, chapter 6 offers suggestions for how stakeholders in education and research can contribute to diversifying these digital clubhouses.

In chapter 7, Crystle Martin explores the role of coding in fostering career aspirations in technology fields. Through interview data, Martin depicts entry points into coding, barriers to engagement, and the types of support useful to cultivating positive digital participation. Martin uses a connected learning framework to explain the complexity of interest-driven learning. Her work emphasizes the importance of creating nurturing, technology-rich learning environments for underrepresented students.

Chapters 8 and 9 investigate how online technologies might provide social, emotional, economic, and academic support for frequently marginalized students of color in postsecondary institutions. In chapter 8, Lynette Kvasny and Fay Cobb Payton examine the use of Tumblr as a tool for students seeking mental health support from their peers. In the following chapter, David J. Leonard and Safiya Umoja Noble explore how Black students are challenging institutional inequities through the use of social media campaigns. These chapters present students as active participants in efforts of digital activism. Both chapters suggest that informal support mechanisms have the potential to do much to aid students' persistence in schools and universities. Both chapters zero in on digital spaces to document activism that occurs among millennials of color. Focusing on the use of online technologies as a tool of organizing and of offering counternarratives, as a mechanism of community building, the authors argue that today's students are actively challenging educational inequity. The chapters highlight the power and potential of new media technologies in shaping and transforming the struggles of the twenty-first century.

The conclusion returns us to this introduction, and we consider how the framework of cultural and social capital enables us to think about technological capacities in a way that hopefully moves discussions away from simplistic analyses of the lack of goods and services, toward frameworks for understanding challenges and opportunities. We explore what we might learn from the examples the authors have provided, bringing things back around to how educators and other stakeholders can participate to increase the scale of practices such as these. Our intent, then, is not so much to offer a cookbook of solutions about how to overcome digital inequity, as if simplistic recipes are waiting for us to develop and deliver. Instead, we offer a provisional cartography of the landscape of today and how to reshape it for tomorrow.

REFERENCES

Andrews, G. G. (2007). *A tale of two game worlds: Comparing the literacy practices of low- and high-socioeconomic status (SES) students surrounding video games.* Unpublished master's thesis, Teachers College, Columbia University, New York.

Attewell P., & Battle, J. (1999). Home computers and school performance. *Information Society* 15, 1–10.

Attewell, P., & Winston, H. (2003). Children of the digital divide. In P. Attewell & N. M. Seel (Eds.), *Disadvantaged teens and computer technologies* (pp. 117–136). Münster, Germany: Waxmann.

Becker, G. S. (1962). Investment in human capital: A theoretical analysis. *Journal of Political Economy, 70*(5), 9–49.

Becker, H. J. (2000). Who's wired and who's not: Children's access to and use of computer technology. *The Future of Children, 10*(2), 44–75.

Beltran, D. O., Das, K. K., & Fairlie, R. W. (2008). Are computers good for children? The effects of home computers on educational outcomes. *Centre for Economic Policy Research,* ANU. Retrieved from http://pandora.nla.gov.au/pan/10580/20081212-0026/cepr.anu.edu.au/pdf /DP576.pdf.

Blume, H. (2015, January 13). IPad program plagued from outset; lack of resources and inadequate planning hurt LAUSD plan, federal review says. *Los Angeles Times.* Retrieved from http://search.proquest.com.libproxy1.usc.edu/docview/1644569417?accountid=14749.

Bourdieu, P. (1973). Cultural reproduction and social reproduction. In Richard Brown (Ed.) *Knowledge, education, and cultural change* (pp. 71–112). London, UK: Tavistock.

———. (1977). Cultural reproduction and social reproduction. In J. Karabel & A. H. Halsey (Eds.), *Power and ideology in education* (pp. 487–511). Oxford, UK: Oxford University Press.

———. (1986). The forms of capital. In J. G. Richardson (Ed.), *Handbook of theory and research for the sociology of education* (pp. 241–258). New York, NY: Greenwood Press.

Bowles, S., & Boyer, R. (1995). Wages, aggregate demand, and employment in an open economy: An empirical investigation. *Macroeconomic policy after the conservative era* (pp.143–171). Cambridge, UK: Cambridge University Press.

boyd, d. (2007). Why youth (heart) social network sites: The role of networked publics in teenage social life. In D. Buckingham (Ed.), *MacArthur Foundation series on digital learning—Youth, identity, and digital media* (pp. 119–142). Cambridge, MA: MIT Press.

———. (2014). *It's complicated: The social lives of networked teens.* New Haven, CT: Yale University Press.

Carnevale, A., Rose, S. J., & Cheah, B. (2011). The college payoff. *Rep. Georgetown University Center on Education and the Workforce, 5,* 1.

Carter, P. L. (2003). "Black" cultural capital, status positioning, and schooling conflicts for low-income African American youth. *Social Problems, 50*(1), 136–155. Retrieved from http://doi.org/10.1525/sp.2003.50.1.136.

Charles, K. K., Hurst, E., & Notowidigdo, M. J. (2013). *Manufacturing decline, housing booms, and non-employment. NBER Working Paper no.18949.* Cambridge, MA: National Bureau of Economic Research.

Choudaha, R., & Chang, L. (2012). *Trends in international student mobility.* New York, NY: World Education Services.

Clark, B. R. (1960). The "cooling-out" function in higher education. *American Journal of Sociology, 65*(6), 569–576.

Coleman, J. S. (1990). Social capital. In *Foundations of Social Theory* (pp. 300–321). Cambridge, MA: Harvard University Press.

Collins, A., & Halverson, R. (2010). The second educational revolution: Rethinking education in the age of technology. *Journal of Computer Assisted Learning, 26*(1), 18–27.

Cuban, L. (1986). *Teachers and machines: The classroom use of technology since 1920.* New York, NY: Teachers College, Columbia University.

———. (2001). *Oversold and underused: Computers in the classroom.* Cambridge, MA: Harvard University Press.

Dean, E. (Ed.). (1984). *Education and economic productivity.* Cambridge, MA: Ballinger Publishing.

DiMaggio, P., & Bonikowski, B. (2008). Make money surfing the web? The impact of Internet use on the earnings of US workers. *American Sociological Review, 73*(2), 227–250.

DiMaggio, P., & Hargittai, E. (2001). *From the "digital divide" to "digital inequality": Studying Internet use as penetration increases.* St. Louis, MO: Federal Reserve Bank of St Louis.

DiMaggio, P., Hargittai, E., Celeste, C., & Shafer, S. (2004). Digital inequality: From unequal access to differentiated use. In K. Neckerman (Ed.), *Social inequality* (pp. 355–400). New York, NY: Sage.

DiSalvo, B., Yardi, S., Guzdial, M., McKlin, T., Meadows, C., Perry, K., & Bruckman, A. (2011, May). African American men constructing computing identity. In *Proceedings of the SIGCHI conference on human factors in computing systems* (pp. 2967–2970). Vancouver, BC: Association for Computing Machinery.

The Executive Office of the President. (2014, January). *Increasing college opportunity for low-income students promising models and a call to action.* Retrieved from https://obamawhitehouse.archives.gov/sites/default/files/docs/increasing_college_opportunity_for_low-income_students_report.pdf.

Facer, K., Furlong, J., Furlong, R., & Sutherland, R. (2003). *Screenplay: Children and computing in the home.* London, UK: Routledge Falmer.

Fairlie, R. W. (2007). Explaining differences in access to home computers and the Internet: A comparison of Latino groups to other ethnic and racial groups. *Journal of Electronic Commerce Research, 7,* 265–291.

Garrison, M., & Bromley, H., (2004). Social contexts, defensive pedagogies, and the (mis)uses of educational technology. *Educational Policy, 18,* 589–613.

Goode, J. (2010). Mind the gap: The digital dimension of college access. *Journal of Higher Education, 81*(5), 583–618.

Gradstein, M., & Nikitin, D. (2004). *Educational expansion: Evidence and interpretation* (vol. 3245). Washington, DC: World Bank Publications.

Hargittai, E. (2002). Second-level digital divide: Differences in people's online skills. *First Monday, 7*(4). Retrieved from http://firstmonday.org/article/view/942/864.

Hargittai, E., & Hinnant, A. (2008). Digital inequality differences in young adults' use of the Internet. *Communication Research, 35*(5), 602–621.

Hargittai, E., & Hsieh, Y. P. (2013). Digital inequality. In W. H. Dutton (Ed.), *Oxford handbook of Internet studies* (pp. 129–150). Oxford, UK: Oxford University Press.

Hargittai, E., & Shaw, A. (2013). Digitally savvy citizenship: The role of Internet skills and engagement in young adults' political participation around the 2008 presidential election. *Journal of Broadcasting & Electronic Media, 57*(2), 115–134.

Head, A. J., & Eisenberg, M. B. (2011). Balancing act: How college students manage technology while in the library during crunch time. *SSRN Electronic Journal.* Retrieved from https://www.researchgate.net/publication/272300698_Balancing_Act_How_College_Students_Manage_Technology_While_in_the_Library_During_Crunch_Time.

Helsper, E. J., & Eynon, R. (2010). Digital natives: Where is the evidence? *British Educational Research Journal, 36*(3), 503–520.

Higgs, R. (2011). Economic analysis and the great society. *Freeman, 61,* 25–26. Retrieved from http://search.proquest.com.libproxy1.usc.edu/docview/869890235?accountid=14749.

Ito, M., Baumer, S., Bittanti, M., boyd, d., Cody, R., Herr-Stephenson, B., . . . & Tripp, L. (2010). *Hanging out, messing around, and geeking out: Kids living and learning in new media.* Cambridge, MA: MIT Press.

Jacob, B., Kapustin, M., & Ludwig, J. (2014). *Human capital effects of anti-poverty programs: Evidence from a randomized housing voucher lottery. Reisman Working Papers Series in Housing Law and Policy, 19.* National Bureau of Economic Research. Retrieved from http://chicagounbound.uchicago.edu/cgi/viewcontent.cgi?article=1034&context=housing_law_and_policy.

Jenkins, H. (2006). Confronting the challenges of participatory culture: Media education for the 21st century. An occasional paper on digital media and learning. *John D. and Catherine T.*

MacArthur Foundation. Retrieved from https://www.macfound.org/media/article_pdfs
/JENKINS_WHITE_PAPER.PDF.

Johnson, H., & Sengupta, R. (2009). *Closing the gap: Meeting California's need for college graduates.* San Francisco, CA: Public Policy Institute of California. Retrieved from http://www.ppic.org/content/pubs/report/R_409HJR.pdf.

Kahne, J., Middaugh, E., Lee, N. J., & Feezell, J. T. (2012). Youth online activity and exposure to diverse perspectives. *New Media & Society.* Retrieved from http://doi.org/10.1177
/1461444811420271.

Karoly, L. A. (2001). Investing in the future: Reducing poverty through human capital investments. In S. H. Danziger & R. H. Haveman (Eds.), *Understanding poverty* (pp. 314–356). New York, NY: Russell Sage Foundation.

La, R., Lake, D., & Huckfeldt, R. (2012). Social capital, social networks, and political participation. *Political Psychology, 19*(3), 567–584.

Landivar, L. C. (2015). Disparities in STEM employment by sex, race, and Hispanic origin. *US Census Bureau.* Retrieved from https://www.census.gov/prod/2013pubs/acs-24.pdf.

Lenhart, A. (2015). Teens, social media & technology overview 2015. *Pew Research Center.* Retrieved from http://www.pewinternet.org/2015/04/09/teens-social-media-technology-2015/.

Lopez, M. H., Gonzalez-Barrera, A., & Patten, E. (2013). *Closing the digital divide: Latinos and technology adoption.* Washington, DC: Pew Hispanic Center. Retrieved from http://www
.pewhispanic.org/files/2013/03/Latinos_Social_Media_and_Mobile_Tech_03-2013_final.pdf.

Loury, G. (1977). A dynamic theory of racial income differences. *Women, minorities, and employment discrimination, 153,* 86–153.

Lu, C., & Straubhaar, J. D. (2014). The influence of techno-capital and techno-disposition on the college-going processes of Latina/o college students in Central Texas. *Learning, Media and Technology, 39*(2), 184–198.

Lumina Foundation for Education. (2015). *A stronger nation through higher education: Ten-year time horizon brings goal 2025 into sharp focus.* Retrieved from https://www.luminafoundation
.org/files/publications/A_stronger_nation_through_higher_education-2015.pdf.

Margolis, J., Estrella, R., Goode, J., Holme, J., & Nao, K. (2008). *Stuck in the shallow end: Education, race, and computing.* Cambridge, MA: MIT Press.

Matthews, D. (2012). A stronger nation through higher education: How and why Americans must achieve a big goal for college attainment. A Special Report from Lumina Foundation. *Lumina Foundation for Education.* Retrieved from http://files.eric.ed.gov/fulltext/ED531139.pdf.

McDonough, P. M. (1997). *Choosing colleges: How social class and schools structure opportunity.* Albany: SUNY Press.

Murphy, E., Regan, N. M., Olson, M., Meyers, S., & Kemp, S. (2017). Piper Jaffray 33rd semi-annual taking stock with teens survey, spring 2017. *Piper Jaffray Companies.* Retrieved from http://www.piperjaffray.com/private/pdf/TWST-Spring-2017-Infographic.pdf.

Nelson, R. R., & Phelps, E. S. (1966). Investment in humans, technological diffusion, and economic growth. *American Economic Review, 56*(1/2), 69–75.

Nie, N. H., Junn, J., & Stehlik-Barry, K. (1996). *Education and democratic citizenship in America.* Chicago, IL: University of Chicago Press.

Palfrey, J., & Gasser, U. (2013). *Born digital: Understanding the first generation of digital natives.* New York, NY: Basic Books.

Peck, C., Hewitt, K. K., Mullen, C. A., Lashley, C., Eldridge, J., & Douglas, T. R. M. (2015). Digital youth in brick and mortar schools: Examining the complex interplay of students, technology, education, and change. *Teachers College Record, 117,* 1–40.

Pierce, J. R., & Schott, P. K. (2012). *The surprisingly swift decline of US manufacturing employment. NBER Working Paper no.18655.* Cambridge, MA: National Bureau of Economic Research.

Portes, A. (2000). Social capital: Its origins and applications in modern sociology. In E. Lesser (Ed.), *Knowledge and social capital* (pp.43–67). Boston, MA: Butterworth-Heinemann.

Prensky, M. (2001). Digital natives, digital immigrants, part 1. *On the Horizon, 9*(5), 1–6.

Purcell, K., Heaps, A., Buchanan, J., & Friedrich, L. (2013). How teachers are using technology at home and in their classrooms. *Pew Research Center.* Retrieved from http://www .pewinternet.org/files/oldmedia//Files/Reports/2013/PIP_TeachersandTechnologywithmet hodology_PDF.pdf.

Putnam, R. D. (1993). The prosperous community: Social capital and public life. *The American Prospect, 13*(Spring). Retrieved from http://prospect.org/article/prosperous-community -social-capital-and-public-life.

———. (2015). *Our kids: The American dream in crisis.* New York, NY: Simon and Schuster.

Rideout, V. J., Foehr, U. G., & Roberts, D. F. (2010). *Generation M2: Media in the lives of 8- to 18-year-olds.* Menlo Park, CA: Henry J. Kaiser Family Foundation. Retrieved from https://kaiserfamilyfoundation.files.wordpress.com/2013/01/8010.pdf.

Roberts, G. (2005). Technology and learning expectations of the net generation. In D. G. Oblinger & J. L. Oblinger (Eds.), *Educating the net generation* (pp. 3.1–3.7). Boulder, CO: Educause.

Sablan, J. R., & Tierney, W. G. (2014). The changing nature of cultural capital. In M. Paulsen (Ed.), *Higher education: Handbook of theory and research* (pp. 153–188). Dordrecht, Netherlands: Springer Netherlands.

Sandefur, G. D., Meier, A. M., & Campbell, M. E. (2006). Family resources, social capital, and college attendance. *Social Science Research, 35*(2), 525–553.

Selwyn, N. (2004). Reconsidering political and popular understandings of the digital divide. *New Media & Society, 6*(3), 341–362.

Smith, A., & Page, D. (2015). US smartphone use in 2015. *Pew Research Center.* Retrieved from http://www.pewinternet.org/2015/04/01/us-smartphone-use-in-2015/.

Squire, K. (2006). From content to context: Videogames as designed experience. *Educational Researcher, 35*(8), 19–29.

———. (2011). *Video games and learning: Teaching and participatory culture in the digital age.* Cambridge, MA: Teachers College Press.

Steinkuehler, C. A. (2006). Massively multiplayer online video gaming as participation in a discourse. *Mind, Culture, and Activity, 13*(1), 38–52.

———. (2008). Cognition and literacy in massively multiplayer online games. In J. Coiro, M. Knobel, C. Lankshear, & D. Leu (Eds.), *Handbook of research on new literacies* (pp. 611–634). Mahwah, NJ: Erlbaum.

Tewksbury, D., Weaver, A. J., & Maddex, B. D. (2001). Accidentally informed: News exposure on the World Wide Web. *Journalism and Mass Communication Quarterly, 78*(3), 533–554.

Thomas, D., & Brown, J. S. (2011). *A new culture of learning: Cultivating the imagination for a world of constant change,* 219. Lexington, KY: CreateSpace.

Tierney, W. G. (1999). Models of minority college-going and retention: Cultural integrity versus cultural suicide. *Journal of Negro Education, 68*(1), 80–91.

Trilling, B., & Fadel, C. (2009). *21st century skills: Learning for life in our times.* New York, NY: John Wiley & Sons.

Tucker, B. (2007). Laboratories of reform: Virtual high schools and innovation in public education. *Education Sector Reports.* Retrieved from https://static.newamerica.org /attachments/9973-laboratories-of-reform/Virtual_Schools.46190ca70e684105b967e0e444a6 afda.pdf.

US Bureau of Labor Statistics. (2014). *Employment status of the civilian noninstitutional population 25 years and over by educational attainment, sex, race, and Hispanic or Latino ethnicity.* Retrieved from http://www.bls.gov/cps/cpsaat07.pdf.

US Census Bureau. (2010, October). *Current population survey school enrollment and internet use supplement.* Retrieved from http://www.ntia.doc.gov/files/ntia/publications/exploring _the_digital_nation_computer_and_internet_use_at_home_11092011.pdf.

Warschauer, M., & Matuchniak, T. (2010). New technology and digital worlds: Analyzing evidence of equity in access, use, and outcomes. *Review of Research in Education, 34*(1), 179–225. Retrieved from http://doi.org/10.3102/0091732X09349791.

Welch, F. (1970). Education in production. *Journal of Political Economy, 78*(1), 35–59.

Wellman, B., Hasse, A. Q., Witte, J., & Hampton, K. (2002). Capitalizing on the Internet: Social contact, civic engagement and sense of community. In B. Wellman and H. Haythornthwaite (Eds.), *The Internet in everyday life* (vol. 45, pp. 436–455). Oxford, UK: Blackwell.

Wells, J., Lewis, L., & Greene, B. (2006). *Internet access in US public schools and classrooms: 1994–2005.* Washington, DC: National Center for Educational Statistics.

Wenglinsky, H. (2005). *Using technology wisely: The keys to success in schools.* New York, NY: Teachers College Press.

Wolfinger, R. E., & Rosenstone, S. J. (1980). *Who votes?* (vol. 22). New Haven, CT: Yale University Press.

Zhang, M. (2015). Internet use that reproduces educational inequalities: Evidence from big data. *Computers and Education, 86,* 212–223.

CHAPTER TWO

Equitable Education for Democracy in the Digital Age

A District-Wide Approach

JOSEPH KAHNE, CHRISTINA EVANS, ERICA HODGIN, AND YOUNG WHAN CHOI

Young people's use of digital media has the potential to help create a more participatory and more equitable democracy. Realizing this potential requires that educators provide all youth with high-quality digital literacy and civic-learning opportunities. In the first part of this chapter we explain the reasoning behind these claims by drawing both on recent scholarship and on an analysis of data from the nationally representative Youth and Participatory Politics national survey. With this foundation laid, the second part of the chapter assesses the on-the-ground work of the Educating for Democracy in the Digital Age initiative (EDDA, the "Initiative") in Oakland, California, through examination of survey, observational, and interview data. This district-wide initiative aims to promote expanded and equitable access to high-quality opportunities for digital literacy and civic learning for all students in Oakland high schools. Our broad goal for the chapter is to highlight the potential of digital media to support youth engagement in participatory politics as a means of confronting larger political inequalities and the critical role schools can play in addressing the digital inequities that stand in the way of achieving that potential.

Youth Engagement in Participatory Politics

Digital media is expanding opportunities for a set of practices that we refer to as *participatory politics*. These practices differ from institutional politics in that they are peer-based and interactive. The "participatory" aspect of participatory politics is rooted in Henry Jenkins's concept of participatory culture, in which participation is peer-based, interactive, nonhierarchical, and social (Jenkins, Purushotma, Clinton, Weigel, & Robison, 2009). Similarly, youth engaged in participatory politics often employ social networks and are not guided by deference to traditional elites or institutions; though, of course, they often aim to influence and engage institutions (Kahne, Middaugh, & Allen, 2015). For example, youth learn about issues in ways that are mediated by their peers' online postings and comments; they start or join online groups to address political issues; they engage in dialogue with their peers via social networking platforms; they produce, remix, and circulate compelling blogs or other content; and they work to mobilize their social network to support a cause. Such engagement can be local and small scale, but it can also expand to include on-the-ground actions and can mobilize widespread activity and attention, as have the DREAMer and Black Lives Matter movements.

National survey data also indicate that online participatory politics provides a promising means of promoting democratic engagement and democratic equality for youth. Indeed, though youth are marginal players in traditional institutional politics and participate at much lower rates than do adults, the opposite is true online. Specifically, 39% of all adults engaged in some online political activity in 2012, in contrast to 67% of those aged 18 to 24. And this engagement is growing rapidly. In 2008, 13% of 18- to 24-year-olds posted or circulated political news on a social networking site. Four years later, that portion more than doubled to 32% (Smith, 2013). In addition, unlike traditional forms of political engagement, engagement in participatory politics is distributed relatively equitably across race, ethnicity, and income (Cohen, Kahne, Bowyer, Middaugh, & Rogowski, 2012). At the same time, as discussed below, the relatively equitable engagement in participatory politics does not erase the digital divides related to access, skills, and supports that most often impact low-income youth, youth of color, and those in underresourced communities.

Youth Participatory Politics and Political Inequality

The magnitude of political inequality within the United States is immense. We are not suggesting that youth engagement with participatory politics will, on its own, bring about political equality. Gilens (2012), for example, examined thousands of proposals to change national policy. He found that when the policy preferences of low- and middle-income Americans diverged from those of the affluent, the preferences of low- and middle-income groups had almost no impact on policy outcomes. In addition, political inequality has multiple roots, ranging from the ways that congressional districts are designed, to the nature of campaign finance laws, to the distribution of income and wealth. Clearly, youth engagement with participatory politics cannot fully offset such powerful structural factors.

For those committed to fostering greater political equality, however, a premise of this chapter is that supports for youth engagement with participatory politics have the potential to help. Specifically, such supports can help youth foster the capacities, sense of agency, and commitments to express their voice on issues, to circulate information and perspectives, and, at times, to help mobilize others for change. Sometimes these efforts are local and function to highlight and address community concerns. But the combined efforts of youth (often in partnership with others) can also prompt substantial shifts in public consciousness and policy. For example, 40 policing laws changed in 24 states in the year following protests in Ferguson, Missouri (Lieb, 2015). Furthermore, youth participation, both digitally and on the ground, has been central to the battle for immigration reform at both state and federal levels (see Nicholls, 2013).

Building the Participatory Political Capacity of Youth through Digital Civic Learning Opportunities

Educational institutions have long been charged with preparing youth for productive engagement in democratic life. In the digital age, this agenda must respond to new forms of participation enabled by the affordances of digital media. In particular, it is important to combine opportunities to develop digital literacies (such as capacities to find, assess, use, share, and create media) with civic learning opportunities (such as opportunities to learn about and work to address societal problems). Early studies indicate that this combination, which we refer to as *digital civic learning opportunities,* can meaningfully augment both the quantity and the quality of youth civic and political engagement (Hobbs, 2007; Kahne, Feezell, & Lee, 2012).

It is also important for educational institutions to prepare youth to productively grapple with the numerous risks and challenges that confront individuals and groups hoping to leverage the power of social media and digital production toward civic ends. Youth, for example, must consider the risks of echo chambers, think about the digital afterlife of postings, and learn to productively handle contentious online exchanges (Metzger, 2007; Soep, 2014).

While these opportunities and challenges are relevant to all school contexts, they are particularly important to address in low socioeconomic status (SES) schools. Hargittai (2010) finds that Internet skill level increases correspondingly with students' SES. If efforts to promote participatory politics are to foster greater digital and political equality, supports must reach youth in underresourced schools and communities. Moreover, these pursuits require much more than youth being able to tweet, circulate messages, or use the camera on their phone. All youth must be supported in developing the capacities, sense of agency, and commitments needed to pursue desired civic and political goals.

Although we lack nationally representative data related to digital civic learning opportunities, studies of more broadly focused civic learning opportunities create cause for concern. Long-valued civic learning opportunities such as engagement in discussions of controversial issues, simulations of government processes, and service learning are inequitably distributed. Youth from upper-income families, those who are White, and those who are high achieving academically tend to receive far more of these learning opportunities than others (Kahne & Middaugh, 2008). Thus, schools, rather than helping to narrow political inequality, may often reinforce it.

In addition, exposure to digital learning opportunities appears to be both inequitable and low overall. With respect to equity, Gray, Thomas, and Lewis (2010) found that educators of high-income youth are significantly more likely to require use of educational technology to prepare written text or media presentations, whereas those teaching low-income youth are more likely to require use of educational technology for practice tied to basic skills. Moreover, schools are only just beginning to support teachers and prepare youth for the digital age. For instance, a district-wide survey conducted in Oakland, California, in 2013 found that 93% of teachers believe that technology is essential but that 63% reported not having had *any* technology-related professional development (OUSD, 2013). Similarly, in the Youth and Participatory Politics national survey, only 14% of high school age respondents reported experiencing more than just a few class periods related to judging the credibility of online information. In order to respond to these shortcomings, schools and teachers will need both improved infrastructure and additional professional development.

The Educating for Democracy in the Digital Age Initiative

In what follows, we examine the EDDA initiative—a partnership between Oakland Unified School District (OUSD, the "District"), Mills College, and the National Writing Project (NWP). EDDA has worked to leverage Web 2.0 tools and best practices in civic education to provide all high school students in Oakland with increased, equitable, and high-quality digital literacy and civic learning opportunities. Drawing on interviews and surveys of teachers and students as well as on observational data, we assess three core elements of the Initiative's theory of action. In doing so, we identify strategies that both aided and constrained the implementation and equitable spread of civic learning opportunities, with particular attention paid to digital civic learning opportunities. In addition, drawing both on a focused study of a particular group of teachers and on a district-wide high school exit survey, we also assess the impact of these learning opportunities on youth's digital civic literacies and school engagement.

We hypothesized that a district-wide approach that sought to serve all Oakland high school students would promote more equitable preparation for democracy in two ways. First, we hypothesized that expanding digital literacy and civic learning opportunities in a district that serves a large number of low-income students of color would promote their capacities for and commitments to participate and, thereby, lessen political inequality (see Gilens, 2012). Second, at the national level, youth of color, low-income youth, and lower-academic-achieving youth are much less likely to receive high-impact civic learning opportunities, such as service learning, simulations, and discussion of controversial issues (Kahne & Middaugh, 2008). Hence, we hypothesized that EDDA could counter this driver of political inequity by supporting all teachers in Oakland to provide these opportunities to all students.

In addition, it is important to note that while the Initiative has focused attention on digital forms of participation, EDDA has worked to promote civic learning opportunities even when they lack a digital component. This reflects EDDA's overarching goal to provide equitable preparation for civic and political life broadly. Indeed, a great deal of scholarship indicates that digital forms of civic and political engagement are best understood as part of broader civic and political repertoires (Kahne, Middaugh, & Allen, 2015).

Finally, from the standpoint of strategy, it is worth noting that adoption of a systemic district-wide approach for civics is unique. Indeed, while district-wide attention to math, science, and English competencies as well as college and career readiness is ubiquitous, school district policies rarely aim to prepare all students for civic and political life in a democratic society; they rarely target significant resources and policies to pursue this goal; and they rarely assess the degree to which students receive desired civic learning opportunities or attain desired civic capacities and commitments. It is telling that a report from the National Campaign for the Civic Mission of Schools, designed to identify schools and districts that prioritized civic learning, focused on just eight schools and three districts—and all of the districts were small, with only one high school (Nuxoll, 2010). Few school districts have made a systematic commitment to promoting civic education, which greatly limits access to the civic and political learning opportunities needed to address political inequality in the digital age. Hence, we are concerned that many low-income youth and youth of color will not have the experiences that prepare them to participate fully in democratic life. For this reason, our study examines the potential of a district-wide strategy for promoting equitable exposure to digital civic learning opportunities as well as the impact of implementing such strategies.

Methods

We assess this effort using a theory-driven approach to evaluation (Chen, 1990). Rather than focusing on broad outcomes, this approach assesses core assumptions in EDDA's theory of action. The aim is to examine the factors influencing the reform's impact, to generate insights regarding modifications that may help the reform become more effective, and to share insights with others working on or considering similar efforts. This theory of action is detailed in a separate section below.

It is also important to highlight that the authors were positioned as "insider-researchers" (Unluer, 2012), in that we have been heavily involved in shaping this Initiative. We wrote the grant that funded the project, developed the reform strategy in partnership with OUSD and NWP, and formulated the assumptions that make up the theory of action. We have been sharing findings and observations on an ongoing basis with those implementing the Initiative. Moreover, one author of the chapter, Young Whan Choi, is the civic engagement coordinator leading the District's effort.

Data

Our ongoing assessment of EDDA reflects our synthesis of themes from more than 30 interviews and focus groups with teachers, just over 70 individual interviews and focus groups with students, triannual teacher feedback surveys, and over 150 observations of classrooms and professional development sessions. Data collection and synthesis from 2012 to 2014 was led by co-principal investigator Ellen Middaugh. The teacher and student experiences and perspectives reported on in this chapter are drawn from case studies we conducted of particular curricular efforts by small groups of teachers. Although interview questions were structured to fit the particular curricula, we reexamined the qualitative data to assess the particular assumptions under consideration—factors that shaped the spread of the EDDA agenda and the degree to which the curriculum appeared to have its intended effects.

We also share findings from the OUSD Senior Exit Survey designed by Ellen Middaugh, which was administered annually in classrooms between 2012 and 2014 to a largely representative group of high school seniors (sample sizes varied from 860 to 1,020). (For detailed analyses of these data, see Middaugh, 2015a.) These surveys focused principally on the nature and extent to which students received civic and digital learning opportunities and students' levels of engagement in school and in civic and political life. Finally, we draw on system-wide teacher surveys conducted by the District that asked about teacher engagement with digital media and about their overall satisfaction with professional development experiences, including EDDA.

Context

OUSD enrolls 9,193 students in 15 high schools ranging in size from just over 100 students to over 2,000 students. OUSD's diverse student body is 30% African American, 14% Asian, 1% Filipino, 39% Latino, 0.5% Native American, 1% Pacific Islander, 12% White, and 2.5% not specified. Seventy-three percent of OUSD students qualify for free or reduced lunch, and 50% speak a language other than English at home. The graduation rate was 67% in 2012–13 compared with a statewide graduation rate of 80%.

A number of factors highlight the challenging context in which this reform took place. First, the District went bankrupt in 2003 and was under state control until 2009. The budget pressures of this period led to some of the lowest teacher salaries in the region. Teachers worked without a contract for several years and with no cost of living raises. In addition, for each of the first three years of the Initiative, the District had a different superintendent. Moreover, after the first year of EDDA, the principals of the six largest high schools were all let go or reassigned to other positions within the District, and multiple schools were threatened with closure.

The timing of the Initiative also coincided with a transition regarding technology use and access in OUSD. An infusion of capital from a local bond measure and one-time funding from the state of California enabled infrastructure and hardware upgrades needed to meet Common Core testing requirements. While the upgrades to infrastructure, hardware, and a recent rollout of Google apps district-wide began addressing issues of access, there continued to be a need for professional development that supported teachers to leverage these new digital resources in ways that move beyond testing.

The Theory of Action Guiding EDDA

Our theory of action includes the three core assumptions that structure our assessment of EDDA's district-wide effort to promote the equitable provision of digital civic learning opportunities. First, one might assume that a district-wide strategy would imply a broad systemic approach—the District would specify goals, implement shared assessments, align the agenda with other district-level reforms, and create professional learning communities (PLCs) at the school level that reflect a uniform set of priorities. As Fullan (2010) and others have noted, these kinds of systemic strategies have proved effective in a number of contexts, though are often difficult to implement. In this instance, a systemic district-wide approach was both politically and technically infeasible.

While stakeholders were generally supportive of EDDA's broad goals, neither the superintendent, nor the principals, nor even social studies teachers wanted to mandate participation or institute uniform curricula related to this agenda. Indeed, before the Initiative began, two district curriculum specialists and several teacher leaders told us that uniform curricula come and go with various educational trends and passing leadership. They cautioned that top-down mandates fuel distrust of the central administration. Moreover, they described several specific efforts to spread a particular curriculum—none of which were sustained after the initial startup funds ended.

The challenges of promoting this agenda district-wide were substantial. The District lacked resources to provide support across all the high schools as well as consensus regarding priorities and ways to pursue them. These limitations were particularly significant with respect to digital civic learning opportunities. Few teachers had experience with such strategies, the technology infrastructure had many shortcomings, and, other than a small number of individuals hired through the EDDA grant, there were few in the District who could support this work.

At the same time, EDDA leadership believed that earning teachers' respect and building teacher commitment to this agenda was key to the Initiative's success. Therefore, EDDA adopted a hybrid strategy that coupled district-wide goals and supports with teacher-led initiatives. While EDDA leadership worked to legitimize civic priorities at the district level, teacher leaders worked to integrate EDDA priorities throughout the District from the ground up. EDDA is facilitated through the District, but teacher participation is optional and teachers have not been given a set curriculum. Rather, teachers opt into themed PLCs, where they work individually and in small groups to craft their own curricular efforts. This hybrid model is reflected in the first two assumptions we consider in this chapter:

Assumption #1: A district-wide commitment to promoting civic priorities will enable coherent, effective, and more equitable provision of learning opportunities.

Assumption #2: Having teachers play a central role in shaping both the goals and the strategies of the EDDA agenda will strengthen and expand its spread.

The third assumption focuses on the impact of the digital dimensions of the EDDA initiative.

Assumption #3: Integrating attention to digital literacy will make civic and political learning opportunities more relevant, compelling, and valuable for students.

Assumption #1

To guide EDDA efforts, the grant funded a civic engagement coordinator. He advocated for the inclusion of civics in District priorities. For example, he gave input into the development of the District's Graduate Profile, which articulates the desired attributes of OUSD graduates. His contribution was amending the phrase "Our graduates are college and career ready" to read, "Our graduates are college, career, *and community* ready." The coordinator then convened a group of seven teachers to articulate the learning goals associated with becoming community ready—a formulation which integrated in concern for digital forms of civic engagement.

This addition to the District's Graduate Profile appeared to legitimize and help institutionalize civics from the standpoint of district leadership.

Indeed, almost all of the senior district leadership turned over in the course of the Initiative's first three years, and incoming leadership took the inclusion of "community ready" as a given. To cite one important consequence, the new deputy chief of post-secondary readiness identified the District's commitment to "community ready" as the rationale for having the District pay for the civic engagement coordinator position once the three-year grant ran its course.

An assumption was that increased legitimization of civics and digital learning would enable the civic engagement coordinator to align and integrate EDDA's priorities into other major district efforts. This assumption held in a variety of ways. For example, the District expanded its focus on academic discussion to include discussion of controversial issues, created a district-wide writing assessment for economics that focused on a current policy question regarding the minimum wage, and modified the Senior Project to include an emphasis on civic engagement. To provide a sense of the potential and some constraints on such efforts to institutionalize EDDA priorities, we describe one relatively successful and one less successful effort.

The District's Senior Project

At the start of the Initiative, both district leaders and teachers expressed concern that the Senior Project was not achieving its potential. While the Senior Project was a graduation requirement by Board Policy, in an informal survey of nine high schools conducted in 2012, only four schools reported that this requirement was enforced consistently across their school. The head of high schools expressed the hope that explicit attention to civic engagement might help strengthen the quality of the projects and students' interest in them. An opportunity to advance this agenda occurred when the Linked Learning Office (LLO) in OUSD received a grant to develop a set of more coherent criteria for the Senior Project. Linked Learning is a nation-wide initiative that aims to connect rigorous academic work to high-quality career-technical education. The civic engagement coordinator joined the leadership team of the LLO grant, and using the Graduate Profile and the "community ready" language, worked with teachers to develop common criteria that enabled greater attention to civic priorities.

In the first year, 15 teachers from four high schools created or modified their Senior Project assignments to incorporate these criteria. In the second year, 30 teachers from 10 high schools were involved. They agreed to use the same rubrics across school sites. The teachers were enthusiastic about this work. As one 12th grade teacher reported, "This doesn't feel like reinventing the wheel. It just feels supportive and I think the [Senior Project] rubrics are *much* clearer than the ones that were developed at the school level." Although the reform of the Senior Project is still a work in progress, teacher participation is growing and many more OUSD students are asked to do high-quality senior projects that have a civic focus.

In addition, increased attention to the Senior Project highlighted the need to teach digital research, since students increasingly undertook digital research when completing their projects. EDDA has been able to meet this need by providing learning opportunities for teachers and disseminating teacher-created materials related to digital research. By integrating civics and digital literacies into an existing graduation requirement, the Initiative increased students' opportunities to learn to do digital research.

The Common Core State Standards' Focus on Digital Literacy

The EDDA leadership team assumed that the strong connection between digital literacy skills and the Common Core State Standards (CCSS) for English language arts at the 9th to 12th grade levels would lead to support for digital literacy from both teachers and the District. The standards state that students should be able to "use technology, including the Internet, to produce, publish, and update individual or shared writing products in response to ongoing feedback, including new arguments or information" (National Governors Association, 2010). EDDA leadership saw these skills as ones that could be used in a civic context and hoped alignment would bring civic engagement under the umbrella of District priorities. The District's priorities regarding technology, however, primarily focused on upgrading the wireless infrastructure and getting enough Chromebooks into the schools to prepare for CCSS testing. Comprehensive and much-needed professional development on digital media was not available to teachers outside of EDDA.

While EDDA leadership believed that the District's move to implement the Common Core would support the expansion of digital literacy, the technical challenge of implementing mandatory testing took precedence over improving students' digital literacy. We do not view this outcome as a sign that aligning with district priorities is the wrong strategy. Rather, we view District leaders' choice not to focus District resources on supporting teachers to provide digital literacy learning opportunities as a reflection of the challenges they faced when balancing competing priorities. Nonetheless, this outcome is an important reminder of the limits of a district-wide approach.

Assumption #2

The other component of the hybrid strategy assumed that if teachers played a central role in shaping the Initiative, they would be motivated to continue to participate and further spread EDDA throughout the District. In turn, we assumed that by increasing the number of teachers in EDDA that the number of students with access to digital literacy and civic learning opportunities would also increase.

The Initiative started with 28 teachers in Year 1. It grew to 52 in Year 2 and 82 in Year 3. By the fourth year, just over 100 teachers from 11 of the 15 District high schools were engaged in the Initiative. One 11th-grade English teacher shared, "I'm really grateful to the EDDA project for pushing me to do this work, because it's not something that comes naturally to me, it is not something that was already in my skill set. Civic engagement was not what I was thinking about at the time until [the civic engagement coordinator] invited me to be part of this. But it's been a really big part of my growth as a teacher and I really appreciate being pushed, and now I can't imagine not having done it." Analysis of teacher survey and interview data revealed that teachers felt the opportunities to pursue their interests and grow in their practice were motivating factors for their continued participation in EDDA.

EDDA professional development trainings and PLCs were organized around various themes, such as academic discussion, research and publication in the digital age, and integrating civic engagement into core content areas like world history. When asked about her experience at one of the EDDA professional developments, an 11th-grade English teacher shared, "A huge part of why I continue with this group is that I feel like this professional development is driven with the philosophy that if you give teachers the tools and the support, they will take it and make good things happen." An OUSD survey (n=1,078) in 2014 also highlighted teacher satisfaction with EDDA. Teachers rated EDDA in the top 3 out of 16 professional development initiatives. Ninety-three percent of respondents rated the program positively, and 64.5% gave it the highest rating. In short, data indicated that EDDA created a supportive space for teachers to identify civic learning possibilities in their curriculum, explore digital tools, and collaborate with one another.

The Freedom and Flexibility of the Teacher-Led Approach

The teacher-led approach resulted in tremendous instructional variation that had some benefits, but it also created some challenges. On the positive side, teachers were able to design and implement learning opportunities that aligned with their interests and were relevant to their students and their school contexts. Thus, the freedom and flexibility of the model led to a wide range of civic projects, including, for example, working on electoral campaigns, developing a school-wide recycling project, and producing and circulating infographics about living on the minimum wage.

On the other hand, the variation made it difficult for teachers to collaborate and, at times, this made the PLCs less productive. For example, on a mid-year feedback survey one teacher noted that the "somewhat scattered collection of issues" teachers were focused on made her PLC less helpful than it might have been. The range of projects also made it difficult to spread curricular resources and develop common measures that could easily be adopted by teachers throughout the District.

Finally, the freedom and flexibility of the model meant that teachers helped identify priorities within EDDA and, therefore, only some of the PLCs emphasized digital media. In Year 1, there were 12 teachers in a digital research and literacy group supported by NWP and OUSD's instructional technologist. In Year 2, seven teachers were part of a PLC focused on research in the digital age. This PLC expanded in Year 3 to explore research and publication and grew to 17 teachers. Teachers in other PLCs, in some instances, also expanded their instruction to incorporate digital civic learning opportunities. Yet, interviews revealed that some teachers were not comfortable using digital media and others were limited by technological constraints at their school.

Lack of Equitable Exposure to Digital Civic Learning Opportunities

Despite increases in teacher participation, many students in OUSD, including many EDDA students, did not have access to digital civic learning opportunities. Baseline data indicated that there was a great need throughout the District. For example, 82% of graduating OUSD seniors reported they were expected to use the Internet to find information, but just 67% received support for assessing the credibility of online information, and only 53% received support for searching more effectively (Middaugh, 2015a).

Research suggests that there are more robust digital learning opportunities in schools that have more resources and a higher concentration of high-SES youth (Gray, Thomas, & Lewis, 2010). However, this was not the case with EDDA. The highest concentration of EDDA teachers implementing digital projects was at two high schools, in which 83% and 93% of students received free and reduced lunch. Teachers at these schools were implementing digital civic projects such as conducting in-depth online research, learning how to code, as well as blogging about social issues and engaging in online dialogue with other students from across the country. Thus, while digital civic learning opportunities did not reach all students, these opportunities were not disproportionately provided to youth from higher-SES backgrounds.

In sum, we found that teacher-led reform efforts may increase teacher participation and retention, but they may only draw teachers interested in expanding their practices in ways that align with the reform. In addition, while the freedom of such a model may enable curricula to be responsive to students, schools, and communities, it may not lead to equitable exposure to robust digital civic learning opportunities. Complementary district-wide structures and supports, like the Senior Project or the district-wide History Writing Task (HWT), may be necessary to bolster a teacher-led approach in order to ensure that all students have access to digital civic learning opportunities. In short, our findings highlight the need for both a teacher-led approach that can ensure alignment with teachers' priorities and district-wide efforts that can help the reform reach all students.

Assumption #3

When asked to describe one of the most important things he learned during the 2014–15 school year, Tony, a 12th-grade EDDA student, responded, "I think one of the most important things would be that you could create something [using technology] that can help your community out." In addition to teaching coding languages in her EDDA classroom, Tony's teacher exposed students to ways coding could be used for civic action, both in and out of class, and provided concrete examples of ways technology might address problems impacting his school and community. At the end of the year, Tony participated in a school-based hackathon that brought students at the school together to "hack" or find tech-based solutions to civic issues confronting them. Based on interest, students organized themselves into groups, each with a tech industry and a teacher mentor, to develop prototypes of smartphone apps that addressed issues like police response times in their neighborhoods, access to bathrooms at school, and students' need for professional mentors. Tony and his group developed an app to improve graduation rates at his school. "We were trying to create a place where students could interact with each other and get tutored without needing to go outside of their house."

Tony and his classmates not only learned coding and concrete ways to use technology to address personally relevant issues but also expanded what Evans (2016) has described as their digital civic imagination—their capacity to imagine tech-based strategies and solutions using personal technology like smartphones to address civic issues. Tony's teacher noted that her students now understand how programming you do on the back end of a smartphone app shows up on the front end of their smartphones.

Similarly, a teacher whose students blogged about personally relevant social issues on the school-based social networking site, Youth Voices, reported "the platform did provide students with a regularly accessible authentic audience, which added a lot to their level of engagement and to the overall quality of their work. Each time students logged on to Youth Voices, at least one student in the room would shout, 'Hey! Someone commented on my work who I don't even know!'" These students' enthusiasm about using technology in civic ways was reflected in interview data from other EDDA students and teachers.

The Emergence of Digital Civic Literacy Learning Opportunities

EDDA teachers created a range of digital literacy learning opportunities responsive to student needs, interests, and contexts. The digital civic literacy framework that emerged from studying these projects describes a constellation of important new literacies—Search (students investigate civic issues), Credibility (students determine trustworthiness of online civic information), Collaboration (students use networked tools to collaborate with others), and Going Public (students use digital tools and networks to share their perspectives on civic issues) (Middaugh & Evans, 2016). One teacher, for example, progressively integrated an online research component into her civil rights unit, which included using Advanced Google Search, assessing credibility of online sources, and producing media. Students had opportunities to collaborate in small groups on issues they viewed as the new civil rights issues—including police violence, access to healthy food, and youth economic opportunity—and did extensive online research on their topics. They then went public, sharing a personal commentary on Youth Voices, where students from across the country were able to engage them in dialogue on these topics.

The Promotion of Digital Literacies and Increased School Engagement

Analysis of survey data finds that students who were in EDDA classrooms and had access to digital civic literacy learning opportunities developed digital civic literacies around, for example, online search. The Initiative's Digital Civic Literacy study led by Ellen Middaugh compared Senior Exit Survey responses of OUSD seniors who had not participated in EDDA with juniors who had, and it found that the EDDA students showed increased efficacy around doing online searches. EDDA students were more likely than non-EDDA students to report that they: (1) try to get more than one source, (2) can enter the right search terms, and (3) can sort through many results (Middaugh, 2015a). In addition to increased efficacy, Middaugh and Evans (2016) found that the in-depth technology integration moved EDDA students from the application of rigid rules to employing more nuanced strategies for search and for assessing credibility of online sources. They further found that students in these classrooms developed skills related to online collaboration that enhanced their ability to connect to communities online and off, as well as to express their civic voices online.

More broadly, we saw evidence that access to these kinds of digital literacy learning opportunities increased student engagement in school: "63% of students reporting high levels of exposure to digital media learning opportunities agreed their 'school work' is meaningful and relevant," compared to 39% of those with low levels of access to such opportunities. Moreover, these differences were all found to be statistically significant, even with controls in place for student demographics and level of academic achievement (Middaugh, 2015b).

Digital Inequity and the Obstacle of Structural Inequality

To the extent that EDDA students received support for developing digital literacies, this likely helped narrow the digital divide between these students and those in more privileged settings. However, even for students who received exceptionally supported digital literacy learning opportunities like those Tony and his classmates experienced, looming structural inequities influenced both the starting point and ongoing shape of those digital learning experiences. Many students were not academically or emotionally equipped to take full advantage of those opportunities. A classmate of Tony's, for example, reported that his EDDA class "dropped by half. I would say most of them gave up because they said that it was hard and that they couldn't even do it because they're not good at it." Tony's teacher described what was for her a particularly crushing experience of a student who dropped out of the class. The student read at "a fourth or fifth grade level, and her math skills, I mean like basic division and things like that were really hard. So programming was . . . adding an extra layer of anxiety to think about on top of these other things." The crushing part of the experience for this teacher was that the student had the intellectual potential to do the work. "She was the first person to get . . . the idea behind" a complex coding concept, for example.

Most of the digital literacy teachers, however, were not focused on coding but on developing foundational digital literacies related to activities such as online research and expressing civic voice through blogging. These teachers met students where they were in terms of their online search skills, interests, and academic preparation. While their work began to address digital and participation divides shaped by the underlying structural inequalities, it did not level the playing field. Responding to the structural disadvantages her students faced, an EDDA teacher concluded that their digital skill levels were "not even close" to those of her own relatively advantaged children. She reported that her son "did an internship here [at the high school where she teaches] . . . and he was in the [computer] lab, showing them [her students] how to use, and access, and do things that was a complete mystery to them." OUSD students, like students in other low-resourced districts, are confronted daily with the structural inequalities that build the digital divides related to access, production, and participation (Gray, Thomas, & Lewis, 2010; Hargittai, 2010; Schradie, 2011). Many teachers were motivated to provide digital literacy instruction both as a means of responding to these divides and because they believed that such instruction was a fundamentally important means of promoting academic, professional, and political access. In the words of one 11th-grade EDDA teacher: "For my students, online research is a human right—an empowering tool, if students can learn to use it to dig up new information. Empowerment does not look like using 'Yahoo Answers' as one's main source, or finding only cursory, basic info. Empowerment looks like using the Internet for discovery, self-education, and choice. It looks like joining new communities and discourses. My participation in EDDA has helped me to see online research as a form of civic engagement."

While the EDDA survey and qualitative data found that engaging students with technology is a powerful way to leverage student skills and interests to make both civic engagement and school more relevant, structural inequalities continue to be powerful obstacles. Our evidence suggests that the steps the Initiative had taken toward bridging the many divides—digital, educational, and otherwise—while critically important, were not sufficient.

Conclusion

In high school graduation speeches across the country, it is common to remind youth to draw on their talents to make their communities and the world a better place. It is far less common for high schools to consciously organize their efforts to prepare youth for making the world a better place. Moreover, low-income youth, youth of color, and those in underresourced communities are far less likely to get such supports and opportunities. Absent reform to address these digital and civic learning opportunity gaps, schools may well enlarge, rather than redress, political inequality.

It is too soon to fully judge Oakland's effort to equitably prepare all high school students for civic and political life in the digital age, but districts committed to digital equity and to equitable access to civic learning opportunities can learn a great deal by assessing the strategies employed during the Initiative's first few years. While reformers will need to grapple with tensions and challenges, we see promise in EDDA's hybrid strategy. Supporting urban districts (and other districts serving low-income students and students of color) to adopt a district-wide commitment to providing civic learning opportunities appears to offer a way to move civic education from the margins and to make equitable provision of these learning opportunities a priority. Indeed, the integration of "community readiness" in the District's Graduate Profile led the District to fund the civic engagement coordinator position and a variety of professional development activities—further enabling both spread and institutionalization. Moreover, this shift prompted the integration of civic priorities into many district-wide efforts, such as the Senior Project and the History Writing Task. These requirements reach all students at a given grade level and, therefore, promote more equitable exposure to important learning opportunities.

Coupling this district-wide approach with teacher-led initiatives also appears valuable. The district-wide components of the Initiative were all shaped in large part by teams of teachers who collectively determined, for example, the meaning of "community ready" and the rubrics used to assess the civic elements of the Senior Project. In addition, the Initiative provided teachers with the flexibility to shape the ways they integrated digital literacy and civic learning opportunities, which, in turn, was central to enabling the growth in participation and the dedication, creativity, and commitment of so many teachers to this effort (i.e., growing from 28 teachers in Year 1 to more than 100 by the start of Year 4). Indeed, enabling teachers to join PLCs tailored to their interests led many teachers to experiment, often for the first time, with using technology in their teaching. Reformers hoping to promote teachers' engagement with curricula tied to digital media and civic learning would likely benefit from developing structures that enable teacher leadership, innovation, and collaboration.

Perhaps most importantly, interviews with and surveys of students and teachers revealed that the digital literacy and civic learning opportunities provided by EDDA promoted greater capacities and commitments to engage in civic and political life. This supports the assertion that such learning opportunities can help narrow the participation divide. Students who had these opportunities also reported finding school overall more engaging. In particular, we believe that a solid foundation of digital civic skills, civic agency, and civic commitments is especially important for students in Oakland and other under-resourced communities. Such opportunities enable them to leverage digital tools and networks for efficacious civic and political engagement.

In short, the reform strategies and the curricular efforts EDDA employed hold promise. There is still much to learn. The EDDA reform, however, does appear to employ potentially powerful strategies for addressing inequities—digital and otherwise—through expanded learning opportunities that prepare all youth to be civic and political actors in the digital age.

REFERENCES

Chen, H. (1990). *Theory-driven evaluations.* Newbury Park, CA: Sage.

Cohen, C., Kahne, J., Bowyer, B., Middaugh, E., & Rogowski, J. (2012). *Participatory politics: New media and youth political action* [YPPSP Research Report]. Retrieved from http://ypp.dmlcentral.net/publications/107.

Evans, C. (2016). *iImagine: Building digital civic imagination in urban classrooms.* Manuscript in preparation.

Fullan, M. (2010). *All systems go: The change imperative for whole school reform.* Thousand Oaks, CA: Corwin Press.

Gilens, M. (2012). *Affluence and influence: Economic inequality and political power in America.* Princeton, NJ: Princeton University Press.

Gray, L., Thomas, N., & Lewis, L. (2010). *Teachers' use of educational technology in US public schools: 2009 (NCES 2010-040).* Washington, DC: National Center for Education Statistics, Institute of Education Sciences, US Department of Education.

Hargittai, E. (2010). Digital na(t)ives? Variation in Internet skills and uses among members of the "Net Generation." *Sociological Inquiry, 80*(1), 92–113.

Hobbs, R. (2007). *Reading the media: Media literacy in high school English.* New York, NY: Teachers College Press.

Jenkins, H., Purushotma, R., Clinton, K., Weigel, M., & Robison, A. J. (2009). *Confronting the challenges of participatory culture: Media education for the 21st century.* [Occasional paper on digital media and learning.] Chicago, IL: John D. and Catherine T. MacArthur Foundation.

Kahne, J., Feezell, J., & Lee, N. (2012). Digital media literacy education and online civic and political participation. *International Journal of Communication, 6,* 1–24.

Kahne, J., & Middaugh, E. (2008). *Democracy for some: The civic opportunity gap in high school* [CIRCLE Working Paper 59]. Retrieved from http://www.civicyouth.org/PopUps /WorkingPapers/WP59Kahne.pdf.

Kahne, J., Middaugh, E., & Allen, D. (2015). Youth, new media, and the rise of participatory politics. In D. Allen & J. S. Light (Eds.), *From voice to influence: Understanding digital citizenship in the digital age* (pp. 35–55). Chicago, IL: University of Chicago Press.

Lieb, D. A. (2015, August 3). Ferguson spurs 40 new state measures; activists want more. *AP The Big Story.* Retrieved from http://bigstory.ap.org/ article/2cd834a26ad146cebo4ba6f2655 66ec5/ferguson-spurs-40-new-statemeasures-activists-want-more.

Metzger, M. J. (2007). Making sense of credibility on the Web: Models for evaluating online information and recommendations for future research. *Journal of the American Society for Information Science and Technology, 58*(13), 2078–2091.

Middaugh, E. (2015a). *Digital civic literacies in Oakland high schools* [EDDA Research Summary No. 2]. Retrieved from http://eddaoakland.org/wp-content/uploads/2015/07/EDDA _Research-Brief_Digital-Literacy_R.pdf.

———. (2015b). *Supporting school engagement in Oakland high schools* [EDDA Research Summary No. 3]. Retrieved from http://eddaoakland.org/wp-content/uploads/2015/06 /EDDA_Research_Student-Engagement_030715.pdf.

Middaugh, E., & Evans, C. (2016). *From theory to practice: Fostering digital civic literacy in urban classrooms.* Manuscript in preparation.

National Governors Association Center for Best Practices, Council of Chief State School Officers. (2010). *Common core state standards for English Language Arts and literacy in history/social studies, science, and technical subjects.* Washington, DC: National Governors Association Center for Best Practices, Council of Chief State School Officers. Retrieved from http://www.corestandards.org/wp-content/uploads/ELA_Standards1.pdf.

Nicholls, W. J. (2013). *The DREAMers: How the undocumented youth movement transformed the immigrant rights debate.* Palo Alto, CA: Stanford University Press.

Nuxoll, K. (Ed.). (2010). *No excuses: Eleven schools and districts that make preparing students for citizenship a priority, and how others can do it, too.* Washington, DC: Campaign for the Civic Mission of Schools.

Oakland Unified School District (OUSD). (2013). *OUSD smarter balanced readiness survey report.* Oakland, CA: Instructional Technology Department.

Schradie, J. (2011). The digital production gap: The digital divide and Web 2.0 collide. *Poetics, 39*(2), 145–168.

Smith, A. (2013). *Civic engagement in the digital age.* Washington, DC: Pew Research Center's Internet & American Life Project. Retrieved from http://pewinternet.org/Reports/2013/Civic -Engagement.aspx.

Soep, E. (2014). *Participatory politics: Next-generation tactics to remake public spheres.* Cambridge, MA: MIT Press.

Unluer, S. (2012). Being an insider researcher while conducting case study research. *The Qualitative Report, 17*(58), 1–14.

CHAPTER THREE

Computer Science for All

A School Reform Framework for Broadening Participation in Computing

JOANNA GOODE, JULIE FLAPAN, AND JANE MARGOLIS

Computer science is currently experiencing an educational renaissance in public schools. Following President Barack Obama's 2016 final State of the Union address prioritizing computer science education, he launched a Computer Science for All initiative, calling on states and the nation's school districts to design five-year plans to ensure that all students have access to computer science education. The president's call, which addresses how computer science is driving innovation, is important for *all* students to learn, and makes an appeal to Congress to pass a bipartisan budget to expand educational opportunities in all schools (The White House, 2016).

Having worked on the issue of broadening participation in computing and educational equity for over two decades or more, along with many other teachers and researchers across the country, we applaud the increased commitment to computer science education by the White House. Yet, at the same time, we urge a word of caution. Even with the call for "CS for All," it could be too easy for computer science to scale but still remain a largely tracked and segregated subject. It could be too easy for courses to be introduced into the schools but still leave students without the necessary scaffolding and preparation they need.

The legacy of computer science education includes ongoing pervasive gender and racial inequities between those students who typically have access, encouragement, and social capital to study computer science and those who do not (Goode, Estrella, & Margolis, 2006; Margolis, Estrella, Goode, Holme, & Nao, 2008). Though many educators working toward reforming computer science education center their efforts on diversifying computer science, a cohesive and scholarly framework has rarely been used to guide these multiple efforts. This chapter will present a framework for large-scale educational reform that explicitly places inclusion, equity, and broadening participation in computer science at the center. We will describe how multiple forces must be simultaneously attended to—including political, technical, normative, and pedagogical issues—in order to ensure that equity remains a priority as local districts, states, and the federal government support expansion of CS for All.

Inequity in Secondary Computer Science Education

The discipline of computer science has a history of deep inequities in access and participation to robust learning spaces. Our prior research documents how our education system has reproduced these inequalities and segregation in computer science education (Margolis et al., 2008; Goode et al., 2006).

Current data on participation and achievement rates in AP computer science among students disaggregated by race/ethnicity illustrates this continuing divide (Martin, McAlear, & Scott, 2015). Students of color have low rates of participation in the AP computer science course, the only nationwide computing course that has been operating for decades (College Board, 2015) (table 3.1). Partly because of a widespread lack of course availability in low-income schools (Margolis et. al, 2008), students of color are severely underrepresented in this course. Table 3.1 shows that even as the course exam participation has surged from 29,555 students to 46,344 in just two years, a 57% expansion, the participation rates of students of color in this course have shown little growth (College Board, 2013, 2014, 2015). Simply increasing overall student participation in computer science clearly does not lead to broader participation from students of color.

As shown in table 3.2, an examination of the passing rate data reveals disparities that fall along racial and gender lines. Together, Latinos, African Americans, and Native American students account for only 8.5% of students who received a passing score on the 2015 AP computer science exam, though they make up 13% of the course population. This achievement gap across racial

TABLE 3.1.
Participation of Students in AP Computer Science Exams, by Race/Ethnicity, 2013–2015

	2013	2014	2015
African American / Black	4%	4%	4%
Latino	8%	9%	9%
Native American	0.4%	0.4%	0.4%
Asian	29%	30%	29%
White	54%	52%	52%
Female	19%	20%	22%
TOTAL	29,555	37,327	46,344

Source: College Board, 2013, 2014, 2015.

TABLE 3.2.
Participation and Pass Rates of Students in 2015 AP CS Exam, by Race/Ethnicity

	Participation Rate	Pass Rate	Percentage of Total Passing Students
African American / Black	4%	38%	2%
Latino	9%	41%	6%
Native American	0.4%	53%	0.3%
Asian	29%	72%	33%
White	52%	66%	53%

Source: College Board, 2015.
Note: Percentages do not add up to 100 because not all students provided demographic information to the College Board.

groups highlights that course access in itself is not enough to eliminate inequities in computing education (Howard, 2010).

Further, if we apply an intersectional lens to the historical lack of gender diversity in computer science, we can see that overall rates of female participation in this course inched up in 2015 to 22% after an 18% participation rate hovered for years, while exceptionally low participation rates of girls in this course, especially girls of color, persist. As table 3.3 shows, African Americans and Latinas pass the AP CS exam at less than half the rate of their white and Asian peers. Overall, pass rates in every racial group are lower for female students than male students. Taken together, the AP CS data suggests that not only are there disparities in which students have access to this course but also in which students succeed in this course. Broadening participation in computing, then, requires both increasing the availability of courses to more students but also an examination of the teaching and learning in schools and classrooms that lead to more equitable, diverse, and supportive learning spaces.

TABLE 3.3.
Participation and Pass Rates and Gender in 2015 AP CS Exam, by Race/Ethnicity

	% Female Participants in Racial Group	Pass Rate for Females	Pass Rate for Males
African American / Black	25%	31%	40%
Latino	24%	30%	44%
Native American	24%	48%	55%
Asian	29%	71%	72%
White	17%	62%	67%
TOTAL	22%	61%	65%

Source: College Board, 2015.

Computer Science Education Reform: A National Movement

With a deep and long-term commitment from the National Science Foundation (NSF), the academic field of K–12 computing education has begun to expand in recent years, along with an explicit focus on broadening participation in computing. As part of this effort, the NSF has helped sponsor the development of two new high school courses focused on attracting and supporting more diverse students: Exploring Computer Science (ECS) and Advanced Placement Computer Science Principles (AP CSP). These are the two high school courses that are among those described by the White House and the Department of Education as part of President Obama's Computer Science for All initiative (The White House, 2016).

To accompany these courses, researchers and educational leaders have developed curricula, rigorous teacher professional development programs, informed educational policies supporting computer science, and designed and conducted accompanying educational research (Brown & Briggs, 2015a, 2015b; Goode, Chapman, & Margolis, 2012). In the past few years, both of these courses have scaled nationwide, even though the AP Computer Science Principles course is in pilot mode and will not be formally assessed by the College Board as an AP course until the 2016–17 school year. Exploring Computer Science, co-created by two of the authors of this paper, is currently being taught in the seven largest urban school districts in the country (Margolis, Goode, & Chapman, 2015).

Both of these new courses, ECS and AP Computer Science Principles, are notable for their intentional instructional design that is intended to draw a more diverse population of students into computing (Margolis et al., 2012; Astrachan, Osborne, Lee, Beth, & Gray, 2014). Moving away from a programming-centric approach to learning CS, these two courses provide a broader view of computing that includes programming as just one of many key topics in the course. This more comprehensive approach includes a set of six computational practices that underlies the social engagement related to *doing* computer science. These practices include:

- Connecting computing to society and people
- Creating computational artifacts
- Applying abstractions and models
- Analyzing problems and artifacts
- Communicating about computing
- Collaborating on computing activities

In addition to the curriculum design, these courses emphasize the importance of rigorous, long-term professional development programs for teachers. The ECS professional development is 14 days, over the course of two years, and focuses on building the capacity of teachers to incorporate inquiry and equity-based pedagogies in their classrooms (Goode, Margolis, & Chapman, 2014).

Using California as a case study in this chapter, we describe the complex and interactive roles of curriculum development, teacher preparation, policy, and belief systems about who should study computer science. Borrowing from Oakes (1992), we describe these reform efforts under the categories of *technical, normative,* and *political.* Additionally, because of the importance of addressing educators' teaching practices that include the cultural and political dimensions of teaching, we also include a fourth category—*pedagogical.* As computer science continues to expand in schools nationwide, we hope this framework provides a guide for researchers, educational reformers, and other educators to ensure that reform efforts provide new opportunities for low-income students and students of color to learn computing.

The Context of Schooling: Detracking Computer Science

This chapter examines the recent K–12 computer science education reform efforts from an equity lens. While innovative programs to introduce kids to computer science exist in a variety of informal spaces (museums, camps, etc.), we have committed to bringing learning opportunities into the school curriculum, as school is where all students are. This commitment brings with it the necessity to reckon with systemic inequality that plagues our educational system. School tracking and the impact it has on educational opportunity for all kids is one poignant example.

High schools often track students by "ability levels," which often leads to two available pathways: college-preparatory or career technical education

(CTE) (Oakes, 1985). Students and courses are often assigned in one of these two categories, and students rarely have much input in these tracking decisions. Particularly in STEM (science, technology, engineering, and math), stark inequities by race, social class, and gender exist and pose a particularly negative impact on low-income, African American, and Latino students resulting in unequal access to STEM courses (Oakes, 1989). As a result, equity-minded computer science education reform must grow and establish a deep-rooted presence in schools, while simultaneously working to detrack computing classes from any ability grouping mechanisms. In computer science high school education, this means that CS classes should encourage both CTE and college-prep students to enroll. By detracking, we refer to disrupting the phenomenon in which schools organize the distribution of learning opportunities that lead to differences in students' daily experiences associated with these practices (Rubin & Noguera, 2004).

To better understand and change the larger school dynamic that organizes around tracking, Oakes proposes attending to three dimensions that influence this social organization. As Oakes argues, "Viewing schools from technical, normative, and political lenses allows traditional school practices to be examined in the context of the beliefs, values, relationships, and power allocations that keep them in place" (Oakes, 1992). By *technical*, Oakes refers to the structure of curriculum differentiation—including the curriculum, systems of differentiation to determine tracks of students, and the existence of college-preparation and non-college-preparation tracks at a school site. The *normative* dimension includes the web of cultural assumptions about what is true and "normal" and what constitutes appropriate action, given these belief systems. The *political* dimension includes how labels, status differences, and the significance of these systems are codified in schooling policies that influence opportunities for academic and occupational attainment. Oakes notes the political dimension captures the ongoing struggle for individuals and groups to raise their own relative advantage in the distribution of school resources and opportunities through the development of policies that determine who receives fiscal and human resources that sustain quality effective teaching and learning.

Taken together, Oakes contends that these overlapping dimensions must all be understood and addressed to disrupt the problematic phenomenon in tracking. Given the achievement gap in computer science education, we also propose that access to an engaging and inclusive *pedagogy* must also be considered as an essential ingredient when framing reform initiatives that broaden participation in computing.

Data Sources

The sources for the data presented in this chapter primarily come from three associated NSF-sponsored research projects that the authors have been involved in over the last decade. Taken together, these varied data sources are deeply situated in school spaces and go beyond identifying barriers in CS education to providing a multilayered approach for expanding opportunities in CS for low-income communities and students of color.

The first source draws from a UCLA-based research project, "Out of the Loop," that involved a three-year ethnographic study of high school computer science education across three Los Angeles public schools, each serving a different student population. Using a variety of data to investigate the question, *why are there so few students of color and females studying computer science in high school?*, data sources included 185 student interviews, educator interviews, dozens of classroom observations, and relevant school and district policy artifacts collected from 2000 to 2004. While much of this data is presented and analyzed in detail in *Stuck in the Shallow End: Education, Race, and Computing* (Margolis et al., 2008), this chapter uses these findings to highlight the technical and normative considerations that must be addressed today to broaden participation in computing.

The second source of data includes a more recent study focused on cataloguing the classroom instruction of ECS classroom teachers. ECS is a college-preparatory course designed specifically to engage all students, especially historically underrepresented students, with an engaging, culturally relevant instruction to computing. With a focus on broadening participation embedded in the curriculum and professional preparation for ECS teachers, this study examined how teachers enact pedagogy and equity with their students. This study took place over an academic school year (2011–12) and included 219 weekly observations, teacher interviews, student pre- and postsurveys, and teacher surveys.

Finally, the political dimension of this report is drawn from the very recent work of the Alliance for California Computing Education for Students and Schools (ACCESS), a statewide policy organization that informs—and is informed by—local district implementation and California legislation and regulations that govern who teaches computer science, how it counts toward graduation and college admissions, and where it fits in the curriculum. This effort is part of an NSF "Expanding Computing Education Pathways" project aimed at building state capacity to provide computer science education to K–12 students. The collection of these approaches to policy provides a robust lens into the rapidly moving space of computer science education. Further, they include important levers for broadening participation in computing.

A Framework for Computer Science Educational Reform

The analysis of these data sources reveals that broadening participation in computing is a dynamic interrelated process and thus requires ongoing stewardship to assure that equity goals are being met. Decisions made by policymakers have a profound influence on course availability and classroom-level instruction, while current teaching and curricular practices continue to inform and shape policy decisions. Conversely, normative belief systems influence and are influenced by policy and practice. An analysis of the data sources points to an interconnected and reciprocal relationship between the macro- and microdimensions of computer science educational reform. We forward a framework for broadening participation in K–12 computer science that simultaneously attends to these four interrelated dimensions of reform: technical, normative, pedagogical, and political.

Technical Dimension

Findings from data presented in *Stuck in the Shallow End* highlight the importance of attending to the technical dimension of computing reform (Margolis et al., 2008). While most of these technical dimensions take place at the school site, they are closely linked with district- and state-level policies and normative beliefs about students' technology abilities and potential.

Technical dimensions involve course availability, access, and sufficient resources to teach the course. Ensuring that the course exists on the school master schedule with a prepared CS teacher assigned to teach the course is a necessary first step in distributing more opportunities for students to learn computer science within a school site, yet this step by itself is insufficient.

Building Course Access and Teacher Capacity

The field of computer science has historically reached only a small portion of the population, predominantly white and Asian males in more resourced schools. Schools are facing numerous challenges to increase access and achievement in the Common Core, and students are overwhelmed by existing general education requirements. Although there is heightened interest in accessing technology across subjects, schools are pressured to focus more on core subjects that are assessed by high-stakes tests. The lack of nationally accepted computer science standards contributes to its exclusion from the curriculum. Determining where computer science "fits" in the curriculum and who is qualified to teach it contributes to how school leadership prioritizes computer science education, and for which students (ACM Education Policy Committee, Kaczmarczyk, & Dopplick, 2014).

One of the largest obstacles to broadening participation in computing is the availability of well-prepared computer science teachers who have sufficient content knowledge and effective pedagogical instructional skills. Few teacher preparation pathways include coursework or pedagogical preparation for teaching computer science. Only a handful of states offer teaching certificates in computer science (Lang et al., 2013). Furthermore, the dynamic nature of computer science requires computing educators to update their knowledge more frequently than many academic disciplines.

The isolation teachers often experience is exacerbated in computer science, where a given teacher may be the only computing teacher at the school site. As a result, computer science teachers typically take on the essential role as the unofficial department head for CS, ensuring courses are available on each year's master schedule, recruiting students, aiding counselors in placing students in the class, and ensuring instructional resources and technology infrastructure are in place for the class. This course sustainability work goes beyond what most subject-area teachers must do for other courses in schools.

Though teacher advocates might engage in recruitment efforts for computer science classes, ultimately, a combination of teacher and counselor decisions determines student placement. At some schools, teachers must grant permission to students before they are enrolled in a course. Many schools rely on guidance counselors to use their professional judgment to steer students toward computing courses. Yet, teachers and guidance counselors often reinforce biased belief systems about who belongs and doesn't belong in computer science.

Take, for example, this conversation with a student in a low-resourced and overcrowded school in East Los Angeles, with a predominantly Latino/a population:

Interviewer: Okay. So, tell me about the floristry class. How did you get in there?

Sandy: Cause it's a technical art. You need a technical art in order to graduate and the computer class was taken and there's no more room for me, so.

Interviewer: What do you mean computer class is taken? It was filled. It was filled up?

Sandy: Yeah.

Interviewer: If you had a choice to satisfy this technical art requirement and you had to choose between that and another semester of programming to fulfill that requirement . . .

Sandy: I would have.

Interviewer: You would have done programming?

Sandy: Yeah.

Interviewer: Instead of the floristry one?

Sandy: Yeah. I. I don't. I'm not really a girly girl, so the flower thing's not really me.

Interviewer: Did your counselor put you in that class?

Sandy: Yeah cause it was either that, or I would have taken service again.

Though Sandy had previously taken programming and would have preferred more computing to service (administrative office work and errands for school) or floristry, the lack of space in programming did not allow her to pursue a computing course. Having course availability and enough seat space for all interested students is absolutely essential for building learning opportunities for students (Margolis et al., 2008, p. 34).

Normative Dimension of CS Educational Reform

Computer science is one of the fields most defined by stereotypes and belief systems that undercut the participation of African Americans, Latinos, females and other underrepresented groups. An important normative perspective in computing education is the concept of "preparatory privilege," a phenomenon in which childhood enrichment experiences and familial social capital are mistaken by educators for "innate" ability and suitability for studying more computing (Margolis et al., 2008). Students without such experiences, including low-income students, students of color, and girls, are then labeled as not being able or suitable for even introductory computer science courses.

This complex set of belief systems, values, and attitudes drives both policy and practice in schools. For example, during our study of the computing curriculum across three demographically diverse schools in Los Angeles, only one of these schools offered AP computer science. This school was located in a white, wealthy community, and though students were bused to the school from over a hundred zip codes across the city, the majority of students in AP CS were white and middle class. The teacher, who formerly worked as a software engineer, was the de facto gatekeeper to student enrollment, personally selecting which students would be permitted to learn AP CS material. Her beliefs exemplified preparatory privilege, mentioning that when it comes to computer science, students "have it or don't have it." Further, when referring to the most knowledgeable, male students in the classroom, she noted that they possessed "an aptitude" for computing that made them "prone to know" CS.

This attitude did not escape the attention of her students, particularly those who were not in this category. As one of the only female students noted, "[The teacher] felt if you don't get it, you don't get it, you know? You have to have the mind to do well in this class and just—you get it like that, basically. That's how she was, and she told me plenty of times" (Margolis et al., 2008).

Yet, interviews with these so-called techie students revealed a common lifelong legacy of exposure to robotics kits, computer camps, prior learning experiences, and adults in their lives who worked as software engineers. These students did not have natural ability; they had extreme preparatory privilege in CS. The teacher's assessment of her students was not identifying ability as much as the social capital and material privileges that only a small set of students, "the techies," were provided before they ever walked into a high school classroom. These normative perspectives can maintain and reproduce unequal opportunities for students of color and girls by perpetuating a "common sense" belief about who belongs, and who doesn't belong, in computer science (Margolis et al., 2008, p. 84).

Pedagogical Dimension of CS Education Reform

Though educational reform movements often include instructional considerations as part of a technical dialogue of reform, our classroom data highlights how CS pedagogy has a dramatic influence on the actual engagement and learning that takes place, especially for underrepresented students. Considering pedagogy as its own unique dimension in school reform redefines notions of "access" to include access to culturally relevant instruction in the classroom setting that fosters learning for all students.

Inquiry and Equity Instructional Practices
in Computing Classrooms

Classroom data gathered over the course of a year (2011–12) in nine computer science classrooms, all taught by teachers who had attended ECS professional development sessions, documented the frequency and type of instructional practices that have been shown to be equitable and effective for rigorous and active learning (Darling-Hammond, 2008; National Research Council, 2000). Analysis revealed the following most common teaching practices observed across classrooms that teachers used to enact equity and inquiry (Margolis, Goode, & Chapman, 2014).

Most frequent equity-based teaching practices:
• Teachers use culturally responsive teaching that connects computer science learning to students' personal experiences and the social and political contexts relevant to students, their families, and their communities.
• Teachers encourage collaboration and validate multiple perspectives through peer-to-peer learning, small group work, and in-depth whole class discussions.

Most frequent inquiry-based teaching practices:
• Teachers use guided inquiry: carefully designing, facilitating, and assessing learning opportunities so that students engage in active learning.
• Teachers support exploration, autonomy, risk-taking, and creativity by resisting "giving" students immediate solutions and encouraging students to make projects uniquely their own.

Taken together, these instructional strategies show that teachers are moving beyond a direct approach to computing education and instead are serving as facilitators of dynamic and diverse student learning. Yet, this data also reveals that not all practices are utilized in computing classrooms with the same frequency. In observations, teachers were most likely to connect CS to equity and everyday issues, encourage collaboration, and employ guided inquiry methods. However, of all practices observed, teachers rarely used journal writing as a way to make connections between lessons, nor did they comfortably differentiate instruction between students with varying needs. Another pedagogical issue that showed variation was the practice of deeper cognitive questioning. Not having horizon content knowledge, or knowledge of the field of computer science beyond introductory topics presented in the curriculum, limited teachers' ability to ask more probing questions of students about particular topics. Not having fluency with inquiry-based pedagogy led to teachers retreating to more direct instruction approaches in teaching CS. With so few teachers having a background in CS and/or inquiry-based pedagogy, these results point to the need to deepen ongoing professional development support for CS teachers.

Student Outcomes: Belonging and Learning

Belief systems about who belongs and does not belong in CS classrooms remain deeply entrenched in computer science education reform efforts. Recognizing preparatory privilege and the opportunities it provides some students can disprove the prevailing assumption that one can identify early on whether students have the innate ability or capacity to learn computing. Well-intentioned efforts that aim to identify the existing talent of who should be funneled into computer science courses must be eschewed in favor of a true CS for All perspective, which relies on inclusive pedagogy inside the classroom. Effective teaching pedagogy does more than improve students' understandings of content, it also intentionally shapes student learning opportunities that build a sense of belonging within a field of knowledge.

According to Dweck (2008), many fields adhere to a "fixed mindset"—a static view of intelligence that negatively impacts educators' attitudes toward students, as well as students' internalized views about their capabilities and school performance. The "growth mindset," on the other hand, is based on the belief that "although people may differ in every which way—in their initial talents and aptitudes, interests, or temperaments—everyone can change and grow through application and experience" (p. 7).

Across 25 ECS classrooms, analysis of over 1,000 students' pre- and post-course surveys demonstrate the significance of pedagogy that promotes a growth mindset rather than a fixed mindset approach to computer science. Rather than misidentifying preparatory privilege with a fixed ability to do computing, growth mindset educators note that abilities and skills are built with hard work, access to content experts, and resiliency. As figure 3.1 shows, ECS students were asked, "What does it mean to think like a computer scientist?" at the beginning and again at the end of the course. Student responses were clustered into two discourse groups:

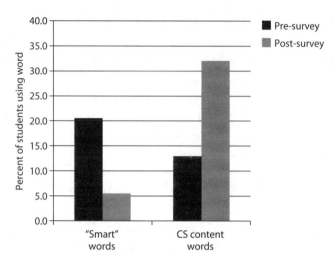

Figure 3.1. Pre- and Post-Test Occurrences of Using at Least One "Smart" or "CS Content" Word in Response

1. Smart words: "smart," "talented," "brilliant," "genius"
2. CS Content/Computational Practices words: "analyzing," "problem-solving," "programming"

At the beginning of the course, students were more likely to use smart words to describe the thinking of computer scientists. After the course, they more frequently used language to describe the computational practices that underlie CS. This movement away from smart/innate and fixed-mindset language was most pronounced among female students.

These shifts in students' own beliefs about computer science reflect the type of teaching strategies that emphasize problem solving, critical thinking, and computational practices. Further, they demonstrate how teachers do not just teach CS content but introduce students to the ways of knowing and doing in a whole new discipline (Margolis, Goode, & Binning, 2015).

Political Dimension of CS Educational Reform

Decades of research on school reform reminds us of the importance of this interrelated web of structural, normative, and political dimensions that operate simultaneously. These changes at the political level overlap with the biased beliefs, the sorting of students, and the availability of teachers and classrooms that have been discussed previously. This section will focus on the policy changes that must occur to institutionalize computer science learning beyond a teacher, classroom, school, or district so that structural changes are supported as part of a long-term equitable and sustainable approach to computer science education.

While many computer science expansion efforts have primarily focused on increasing the overall numbers of students in CS education, a mindful policy strategy is required to ensure these efforts are equitable, high quality, and sustainable.

Transforming our education system to provide access and equity in computer science education relies on a reciprocal relationship between changes at the local school/district level in the near term and a coordinated statewide policy strategy that sustains systemic changes over the long term. Our experience piloting ECS in the Los Angeles Unified School District and emerging pilot sites across California has taught us that the challenges we face at the district level are not only local but also stem from statewide policies governing teachers, standards, and curricula.

Recognizing the importance of how a statewide policy strategy can both inform—and be informed by—local computer science education equity efforts, ECS leadership was instrumental in forming a steering committee of computer scientists, educators, and professionals across institutions to develop a statewide policy strategy in California. In partnership with ECS leadership, this steering committee now leads ACCESS. This statewide group is dedicated to advocating for high-quality K–12 computer science education in California and ensuring its accessibility to all students, specifically underrepresented students, including girls, students of color, and low-income students. As an organization that is dedicated to building capacity of key decisionmakers, many initiatives focus on legislation, regulatory changes, and other policy changes to existing political systems. Examples of some of the most pressing policy issues impacting broadening participation in computing are described below.

Computer Science Standards

Not surprisingly, our test-based accountability system forces schools to prioritize courses for which they are held accountable based on the performance measures for their students. These measures are based upon standards typically found in either the Common Core or Next Generation Science Standards. California does not recognize CS as an autonomous discipline and currently does not have its own standards to support it. Statewide standards would specify what students should know and be able to do in computer science. Having state standards in California will help establish expectations for students in computer science, and they will also help align the teacher qualifications needed for those who teach it.

In an effort to promote CS as an integrated discipline with those already found in the core curriculum, ACCESS has been instrumental in advocating for inclusion of computer science principles into the Next Generation Science Standards and leveraging existing legislation that encourages the state to consider developing CS standards.

Teacher Credentialing

As there are no uniform standards for computer science education, there are no uniform requirements for teacher credentialing in computer science (Lang et al., 2013). Teacher credentials vary from state to state, some requiring credentials in math, others in science, and some in business. In California, teachers with single subject-matter credentials in math, business, industrial technology education, and career technical education (CTE) are authorized to teach computer science. Teachers outside of these authorizations are eligible to pursue further coursework and obtain the Computer Science Supplementary Authorization as an add-on credential. ACCESS leadership recognized that an older version of the authorization was outdated and contributed to the development of a new statewide authorization that was more reflective of what teachers would need to know in order to teach computer science. ACCESS recognizes the value of high-quality professional development for all teachers, regardless of credential, and supports policies that help build the capacity of all teachers to teach computer science.

Getting CS to "Count"

High school students are already burdened with numerous graduation requirements that leave them college and/or career ready. It's understandable that students prioritize courses that "count" toward graduation and college admission. Research reveals that when courses count toward graduation and college admission, students are more likely to take them. For that reason, ACCESS is advocating for CS to count as a fourth-year mathematics or science course so that students are incentivized to take it. As part of its outreach strategy, ACCESS is working in partnership with representatives of higher education to ensure that the higher education community recognizes the value in computer science education.

ACCESS also advocates for computer science to enroll both CTE and college-preparatory students. However, the classification of the course often determines the teaching credential required. Some schools are incentivized to place the course in a CTE pathway in order to be eligible for additional funding from the Perkins Act distributed from the federal to state and local levels. ACCESS is instrumental in attending to the various political dimensions of equitable computer science expansion in order to support changes in the normative and technical aspects of school change.

Funding

In order for teachers to be able to offer a computer science course, principals and other school administrators must provide learning spaces, professional development support, and fund a portion of a teacher's salary to teach the course. In a time of strapped school budgets, administrative support strongly influences the existence and sustainability of a secondary school course.

A persistent challenge to course access is funding to provide students with robust CS educational experiences. Students must have access to working computers with high-speed Internet access, even when computer labs are being used for school-wide testing. Courses often encourage students to apply their computing knowledge to interactive devices, such as robots. These types of hands-on devices cost money to purchase, maintain, and update. And, some CS high school curricula and professional development cost schools thousands of dollars.

As a collective, these technical dimensions provide an inventory of key structures and supports that should be available at each school to provide opportunities and access to students. While these technical elements are discussed above as a pragmatic list of school structures, it is important to examine the trends in distribution of these supports across low-income schools and for schools serving large numbers of students of color. This then becomes another policy dimension that impacts the equity of computer science learning for all students.

Growing Political Momentum

ACCESS helps build the capacity of our legislature, staff, and key decision-makers to develop a coherent system that responds to the challenges of CS education expansion. These statewide efforts have also helped elevate the public discourse about computer science education. Highlighting the issue of computer science education and centering equity in all deliberations, ACCESS helps garner attention among key decisionmakers, business leaders, the media, educators, parents, and students to increase demand for computer science education. As the political momentum is increasing, our state policy goals will be supported by a more informed public to ensure these changes are institutionalized in order to expand teaching and learning opportunities in computer science. As this political momentum grows, we can expect that CS education may get pitted against other subjects such as the humanities and the arts in the schools. It is simply tragic that schools and districts, because of lack of funds or teachers, face pressures and decisions to cut critical subjects. This most frequently occurs in schools in underserved communities. We strongly believe that policymakers must ensure that equitable distribution of all learning opportunities (including computer science as well as the humanities and the arts) occurs.

How Will We Measure Success?

As the momentum for CS for All expands across the country, we must pause and ask ourselves what CS for All really means and what specific outcomes are most desirable. From our own experience, we have witnessed how "access-only" too often results in courses being offered in the schools, while only a narrow band of students enroll or are successful in the course. College Board pass rates on the AP exams are a disappointing example of how increased access does not always translate to equal outcomes. As computer science gets scaled, how can we increase numbers, attend to high-quality coursework, and ensure equitable access for teaching and learning opportunities?

The critical question pressing the Computer Science for All agenda is: are good things happening for *all* computer science students inside learning spaces, especially those from groups that have been traditionally underrepresented in the field? Here again, numbers are not a sufficient indicator. We must go beyond numerical counts of "access" to measure the success of the broadening participation in computing effort. As we ensure efforts to increase participation in computing, we must be careful not to further widen the achievement gap that already exists in high school computing courses.

Rather, how do we know if students who have been traditionally underrepresented in the field are engaging with and understanding the relevance and meaningfulness of computer science for their lives (Margolis et al., 2015)? Measuring numbers of students in computer science needs to be paired with measuring student outcomes such as engagement and interest as well as the depth of learning computer science knowledge and skills.

Thus, just as scaling and simultaneously detracking computer science education requires attention to the technical, normative, pedagogical, and political aspects of computing education, measuring the impact of the Computer Science for All initiative must go beyond simple quantitative analyses of enrollment counts or a tally of policies passed. Rather, researchers must be diligent in observing how the confluence of these four reform dimensions simultaneously shape the distribution of opportunities for students to engage in deep, culturally relevant learning in computer science.

Conclusion

Over 10 years ago we began an investigation into why so few African American, Latino, and female students are learning computer science. That research identified the ways in which computer science is a window into how fields become segregated and how inequality produces and reproduces itself. The research also identified the interlocking constellation of dynamics that are addressed in this chapter, which need to be addressed.

This framework for computer science educational reform in K–12 education as presented in this chapter illustrates the complex and interrelated elements that must be considered when working toward expanding opportunities for historically underrepresented students to study computer science. While attending to the technical issues required to successfully maintain computer science courses at the school level is important, reformers need to also consider how normative perspectives about who belongs in computer science shape the status of the course, the distribution of opportunities between schools, and the experiences of students in these courses. Once inside computing classrooms, students need teaching that draws on their own lived, cultural experiences. Relatedly, state policies must support the organization of resources and procedures that ultimately support powerful teaching and learning for all students in computer science.

As we conclude this chapter, President Obama recently spoke to the importance of computer science education in his final State of the Union address, noting that one of his priorities for the final year of his presidency is "helping students to write computer code" and "offering every student the hands-on computer science" classes that prepare them for participation in the economy. We applaud this increased commitment to computer science education, and yet we urge a word of caution: without explicit commitment to expanding diversity with initiatives in state and school district policies and practices, without attention to the teaching and learning and the quality of students' experiences in the classrooms, increases in CS education will still not be equally available for all American students.

ACKNOWLEDGMENTS

The authors would like to acknowledge the support of the National Science Foundation, grants #0090043, #1228352, and #1241284.

REFERENCES

ACM Education Policy Committee, Kaczmarczyk, L., & Dopplick, R. (2014). *Rebooting the pathway to success: Preparing students for computing workforce needs in the United States.* New York, NY: Association for Computing Machinery.

Astrachan, O., Osborne, R. B., Lee, I., Beth, B., & Gray, J. (2014). Diverse learners, diverse courses, diverse projects: Learning from challenges in new directions. In *Proceedings of the 45th ACM technical symposium on computer science education* (pp. 177–178). New York, NY: Association for Computing Machinery.

Barton, A. C., & Tan, E. (2010). We be burnin'! Agency, identity, and science learning. *Journal of the Learning Sciences, 19*(2), 187–229.

Brown, Q., & Briggs, A. (2015a). The CS10K initiative—part 1: Progress in K–12 through exploring computer science. *ACM Inroads, 6*(3), 52–53.

———. (2015b). The CS10K initiative—part 2: Progress in K–12 through computer science principles. *ACM Inroads, 6*(4), 56–57.

College Board (2013). *AP program participation and performance data* [Data file]. Retrieved from http://media.collegeboard.com/digitalServices/pdf/research/2013/National_Summary_13.xls.

———. (2014). *AP program participation and performance data* [Data file]. Retrieved from http://media.collegeboard.com/digitalServices/pdf/research/2014/National_Summary.xlsx.

———. (2015). *AP program participation and performance data* [Data file]. Retrieved from http://media.collegeboard.com/digitalServices/misc/ap/national-summary-2015.xlsx.

Cuny, J. (2015). Transforming K–12 computing education: AP® computer science principles. *ACM Inroads, 6*(4), 58–59.

Darling-Hammond, L. (2008). *Powerful learning: What we know about teaching for understanding.* San Francisco, CA: Jossey-Bass.

Dweck, C. (2008). *Mindset: The new psychology of success.* New York, NY: Ballantine Books.

Goode, J. (2007). If you build teachers, will students come? Professional development for broadening computer science learning for urban youth. *Journal of Educational Computing Research, 36*(1), 65–88.

Goode, J., Chapman, G., & Margolis, J. (2012). Beyond curriculum: The exploring computer science program. *ACM Inroads, 3*(2), 47–53.

Goode, J., Estrella, R., & Margolis, J. (2006). Lost in translation: Gender and high school computer science. In W. Aspray & J. M. Cohoon (Eds.), *Women and information technology: Research on underrepresentation* (pp. 89–113). Cambridge, MA: MIT Press.

Goode, J., Margolis, J., & Chapman, G. (2014). Curriculum is not enough: The educational theory and research foundation of the exploring computer science professional development model. In *Proceedings of the 45th ACM technical symposium on computer science education* (pp. 493–498). New York, NY: Association for Computing Machinery.

Howard, T. C. (2010). *Why race and culture matter in schools: Closing the achievement gap in America's classrooms.* New York, NY: Teachers College Press.

Lang, K., Galanos, R., Goode, J., Seehorn, D., Trees, F., Phillips, P., & Stephenson, C. (2013). *Bugs in the system: Computer science teacher certification in the US.* New York, NY: Computer Science Teachers Association.

Margolis, J., Estrella, R., Goode, J., Holme, J., & Nao, K. (2008). *Stuck in the shallow end: Education, race, and computing.* Cambridge, MA: MIT Press.

Margolis, J., Goode, J., & Binning, K. (2015). Exploring computer science: Active learning for broadening participation in computing. *Computing Research News, 27*(9).

Margolis, J., Goode, J., & Chapman, G. (2014). That classroom "magic." *Communications of the ACM, 57*(7), 31–33.

Margolis, J., Goode, J., & Chapman, G. (2015). An equity lens for scaling: A critical juncture for exploring computer science. *Inroads Magazine, 6*(3), 58–66.

Margolis, J., Ryoo, J. J., Sandoval, C. D., Lee, C., Goode, J., & Chapman, G. (2012). Beyond access: Broadening participation in high school computer science. *ACM Inroads, 3*(4), 72–78.

Martin, A., McAlear, F., & Scott, A. (2015). *Path not found: Disparities in access to CS courses in California schools.* Oakland, CA: Level Playing Field Institute.

National Research Council. (2000). *Inquiry and the national science education standards: A guide for teaching and learning.* Washington, DC: National Academies Press.

Oakes, J. (1985). *Keeping track* (2nd ed.) New Haven, CT: Yale University Press.

———. (1989). Tracking in mathematics and science education: A structural contribution to unequal schooling. In L. Weis (Ed.), *Class, race, and gender in American education* (pp. 106–125). Albany: State University of New York Press.

———. (1992). Can tracking research inform practice? Technical, normative, and political considerations. *Educational Researcher, 21*(4), 12–21.

Rubin, B. C., & Noguera, P. A. (2004). Tracking detracking: Sorting through the dilemmas and possibilities of detracking in practice. *Equity & Excellence in Education, 37*(1), 92–101.

The White House. (2016). *Fact sheet: President Obama announces Computer Science for All initiative.* Retrieved from https://www.whitehouse.gov/the-press-office/2016/01/30/fact -sheet-president-obama-announces-computer-science-all-initiative-0.

CHAPTER FOUR

Facilitating Digital Access

The Role of Empowerment Agents

ZOË B. CORWIN AND ANTAR A. TICHAVAKUNDA

Journalists, policymakers, practitioners, and scholars have adopted the term "digital native" to describe youth who are growing up accustomed to digital technology (e.g., Gu, Zhu, & Guo, 2013; Koutropoulos, 2011). Because of the near ubiquity of technology in modern society, digital natives are said to display more tech savvy than adults from earlier generations (Prensky, 2001). Other scholars have challenged the digital native theory, on account of a lack of empirical evidence and broad generalizations that assume digital fluency without careful examination of the context of computer use (Barron, Gomez, Pinkard, & Martin, 2014; Broos & Roe, 2006; Brown & Czerniewicz, 2010; Helsper & Eynon, 2010; Warschauer & Matuchniak, 2010). Physical availability of computer devices, context of use, socioeconomic status (SES), race, and gender are among the factors that have led to the so-called digital divide (Campos-Castillo, 2015; Hargittai & Hinnant, 2008; Margolis, Estrella, Goode, Holme, & Nao, 2010; Office of the Press Secretary, 2015; Selwyn, 2004). As a result of the digital divide, levels of digital fluency vary across different demographics. Understandings of the digital divide have thus expanded to include an emphasis on digital literacies and participation in learning opportunities related to digital media (Alston, Dias, & Phillips, 2015; Eastin, Cicchirillo, & Mabry, 2015; Lutz & Hoffmann, 2014; Selwyn, 2004; Warschauer, 2004).

Despite criticisms of the digital native theory, the fact that youth are using digital media and technology at unparalleled rates at earlier ages is indisputable (Common Sense, 2015; Kabali et al., 2015; Lenhart, 2015). Given the rapid pace of innovation in digital spaces, practitioners are challenged to integrate new technologies, including social media, into their pedagogical practices. Understanding how to evaluate and incorporate digital tools into curricula, however, is complex. Even the most tech-savvy practitioners are challenged to deal with the interface between students, technology, and the digital infrastructure of schools. These obstacles are often exacerbated in low-income schools, where educators report school technology rules, Internet filters, and limited professional development as barriers to teaching with technology (Purcell, Heaps, Buchanan, & Friedrich, 2013). These same educators are positioned to play an integral role in cultivating students' digital literacies, given varying access to digital hardware, wide discrepancies in digital knowledge and skills, and differing levels of interest in technology.

While schools have the potential to facilitate or deter access to digital resources through technology infrastructure and policies, we have chosen to focus on the role of individuals at school sites in this chapter. How teachers, counselors, or other staff harness the potential of technology tools has implications for the types of digital learning that can occur in classrooms and beyond (Ertmer, 2005; Gu, Zhu, & Guo, 2013). Given the highly connected nature of youth and the fact that students spend about seven hours a day in school, we take particular interest in the role of educators as participants in students' social networks—and how those educators make use of technology.

In chapter 1, Tierney & Kolluri point to the utility of social and cultural capital in making sense of digital equity. Goode, Flapan and Margolis, in chapter 3, highlight the importance of pedagogy in addressing how computer science teachers interface with their students. In what follows, we add to these theoretical discussions by examining the role of institutional agents—or adults employed by schools and other educational entities—in cultivating youth's ability to develop social capital. We are particularly interested in the interaction among institutional agents, students, and technology. We highlight educators for two main reasons: (1) their unique position to provide access to technology that students may not have at home and (2) their close proximity to students in a leadership capacity. It should be noted that our focus is not on computer science teachers as highlighted in chapter 3, but rather more broadly on any educator who is in the position to broker educational resources through digital venues.

This chapter is informed by a large-scale study examining the effects of technology on low-income students' college preparation (Corwin & Danielson, 2016; Corwin, Danielson, Ragusa, & Tierney, 2016; Pullias Center for Higher Education, 2016). Data-driven analysis is forthcoming; below we offer a theoretical exploration of educators' roles in facilitating technology use, with a particular focus on digital tools that broker social capital. We begin by discussing three concepts to explore how educators might promote digital equity: (1) the role of relationships in facilitating the growth of social capital; (2) the use of social media in cultivating social capital; and (3) the role of educators in cultivating digital identities. We then share educator-focused findings from a federally funded study designed to assess the effects of a game-based college access intervention on first-generation students' college-going. Our intention is to use examples from the field to highlight the theoretical concepts we outline in the first half of the chapter. We are particularly interested in exploring how school faculty and staff harness the power of technology to support students, given unique school structures, diverse student populations, and varying degrees of access to resources. In theorizing approaches to supporting students in growing their digital expertise, we outline the concept of a "digital empowerment agent." By examining the role of individuals who can potentially broker technology resources, we aim to further theoretical and practical understandings of social capital and digital equity.

Social Capital Theory: Selected Concepts

Social capital theory has gained traction in educational literature as a means to explain how students navigate educational institutions as well as how they make use of social relationships to varying degrees of effectiveness. In this chapter we focus on one particular facet of social capital theory: the role of institutional agents—individuals who occupy positions of high status and who have the potential to broker valuable resources (Stanton-Salazar, 2011).

The Role of Relationships

Social relations can be characterized by strength of ties. Strong ties are generally associated with close friends or family and derive from more closely knit networks. Within these close-knit networks, consistent contact and high levels of trust and/or expectations of reciprocity influence interactions. In contrast, weak ties are linked to acquaintances and stem from interactions with individuals in low-density networks where individuals are less likely to be socially involved with one another (Granovetter, 1983). For instance, a first-generation student who seeks guidance on applying for college scholarships might gain emotional support through relationships characterized through strong ties such as with parents or cousins. But he might not be able to ask those same members of his social network for advice on the application process. Through weaker ties found in school-based relationships or through social media, however, he has the potential to reach out to professionals or friends—or friends of friends—to find answers to his questions.

Strengths of ties appear to be influenced by mode of communication. Research conducted by Haythornthwaite (2002) emphasizes the interplay among strength of ties, adoption of digital tools, and communication—and contends that the relational context of digital use matters. When people communicate through new media, relationships are mediated differently than in offline environments (Haythornthwaite, 2002). In a study on distance learners that compared how students chose to communicate, Haythornthwaite found that more weakly tied participants used fewer mediums to communicate. Over time, however, participants activated latent ties (ties that exist but have not been activated) and communicated more actively.

An interesting tension exists, therefore, between strong tie relationships—here participants are more likely to support each other through exchange of resources due to higher frequency and intensity of interactions—and weak tie relationships that hold less motivation to be supportive but higher likelihood to facilitate access to resources beyond an immediate social circle. Given that strength of ties and composition of social networks are fluid and constantly changing, especially in online networks, it is more than likely that students will participate in a range of relationships characterized by weak and strong ties at any time. These distinctions are important with regard to the potential of social media and other digital tools to serve as viable resources to support low-income students.

Teachers and school staff have the potential to develop strong ties with students. They are also in a position to facilitate connections beyond a student's immediate social network, connections that would most likely be characterized by weak ties. As an example, a high school teacher we collaborate with often brings in speakers from the professional community to meet with her students and conduct mock interviews. Students share their resumes with speakers and are encouraged to follow up with thank you emails, thus creating weak ties with individuals outside of their closely knit family and peer networks. By creating this opportunity, the teacher has activated the creation of social capital between students and career professionals. This is an example of both social capital developed by face-to-face teacher-facilitation and digitally mediated (i.e., email, social media) social capital. Below we delve deeper into the unique role teachers play in students' social networks.

Educators as Empowerment Agents

High school students' social networks are constantly evolving and entail a wide range of participants, from parents, peers, coaches, administrators, college outreach staff, religious leaders, and extended family, among others. Educators, by way of their institutionalized position, tend to play a formal role in students' social networks. They consequently have the potential to impact students' ability to form, maintain, and grow social capital. As such, we view educators as *institutional agents*. Institutional agents have the potential to socialize adolescents in ways that reify mainstream norms (Ianni, 1989) or in ways that encourage youth to question the various forms of oppression in their lives and how they might engage in resistance (Stanton-Salazar, 2011). The latter approach of fostering a "critical consciousness" as conceptualized by Stanton-Salazar, leads to processes of empowerment.

The capacity of an institutional agent can be influenced by the structure and resourcefulness of his or her social network (Stanton-Salazar, 2011, p. 1068). Empowerment agents move beyond simply sharing resources by: (1) recognizing power-laden relationships; (2) tuning into unique identities and backgrounds of students; and (3) connecting youth with skills and information that cultivate those students' critical consciousness. When working at schools with limited resources or within institutional contexts that create challenges to accessing digital resources, this approach can prove transformative.

Through the research we (the chapter authors) have conducted in high school environments, we have become particularly interested in teachers' potential to empower students, and we contend below that institutional agents who are able to empower students are more likely to offer robust opportunities for learning in digital and traditional spaces. This theme resonates with findings shared in a white paper on brokering learning opportunities published by the HIVE research network (Mozilla's applied research collaboration), which argues that students benefit when they are connected to meaningful learning opportunities facilitated by robust social networks (Ching, Santo, Hoadley, & Peppler, 2015).

The proposition we are advancing in this chapter focuses on how teachers might become *digital* empowerment agents. Consider, for example, a classroom where all students are using laptops; teachers acting as digital empowerment agents will relinquish their authoritative control to mediate student, self-guided learning (Warschauer, 2007). This is in contrast to situations where teachers are suspicious or uncomfortable about students displaying advanced technological skills in the classroom, thereby discouraging innovative uses of technology (Fahser-Herro & Steinkuehler, 2009). Margolis and colleagues (2010) put forward a related concept: teachers as potential change agents—innovative, passionate, and informed teachers who are willing and able to develop strong computer science programs in schools serving low-income students. In this chapter, our discussion of *digital empowerment agents* aims to build onto the discussion of change agents by broadening the concept to include all teachers (not just computer science teachers) and incorporating an explicit focus on agents who approach their work with a critical consciousness as outlined by Stanton-Salazar (2011). In the section below, we clarify how digital resources serve as tools for empowerment agents, thus emphasizing the digital facet of what it means to be a digital empowerment agent.

The Potential of Digital Resources to Engender Social Capital

Digital mediums have added an element of complexity into how we understand social capital. In 2007, Ellison, Steinfield, and Lampe recognized the need to explore the role of social media on college persistence. In one of the earliest studies on the role of social media in college access and completion literature, they examined the role of Facebook on the development of college students' social capital and found that social media practices may have positive effects on the informational and support networks utilized by first-generation students in pursuit of postsecondary degrees. The authors argued that Facebook provides the social and technical mechanisms to convert latent ties into weak ties.

Later, Wohn, Ellison, Kahn, Fewins-Bliss, and Gray (2013), explored the role of social media on the college aspirations of first-generation students. Their research examined the role of family, peers, and broader social network participants in providing access to college and found that social media provided first-generation students access to different types of informational resources and thus boosted confidence in the college application process. For first-generation students, for example, having access to a broader online social network proved helpful in increasing knowledge about how to apply to college.

In a study examining the role of social media and games on students' abilities to navigate the financial aid process, Deil-Amen and Rios-Aguilar (2014) described 15 college-related games and mobile apps launched since 2010. Their analysis points out that the app/games made use of students' social networks in varied ways and thus enabled students to share their accomplishments and information with each other. The study outlined the potential of game and social media approaches to benefit students in building and strengthening their social networks through connecting with teachers, counselors, and college-going peers. Studies have also explored the effects of online resources on financial aid literacy, specifically how students seek information online about affording college (Corwin & Calderone, 2015; Tierney & Venegas, 2006).

In previous research, we have found that peers can serve as active participants in sharing college resources through online social networks—at times capitalizing on relationships with individuals inside of school, at others relying on relationships with people outside of school (Corwin et al., 2012). As an example, in schools where online social networking among students was supported by faculty, students actively shared information and offered support through online social networks. Students reminded each other about college and financial aid deadlines, posted helpful articles and posed questions to each other via Facebook and Edmodo (a school-based social network platform). Students also learned about college from peers, older siblings, and cousins who were currently in college. By viewing Facebook posts, students learned, albeit at a superficial level, about university life. For instance, students shared impressions that college seemed to involve lots of studying and lots of partying but could not provide details about college life from their impressions based on social media. Other students reached out to Facebook friends who were currently in college to ask specific questions or reached out directly to admissions or financial aid offices.

The Potential of Educators to Bolster Digital Identities

How might educators cultivate digital expertise in meaningful ways so that students are empowered to access digital resources and use those tools to enhance their own social capital? The structural barriers related to digital and participation divides mentioned in the beginning of the chapter—and throughout this book—play a key role in how students see themselves in relation to technology. Goode (2010) advocates for using a technology identity framework to determine if, and to what extent, a student considers him/herself a computer person. She lists four components of digital/technology identity: (1) belief about one's technology abilities; (2) belief about technology participation opportunities; (3) belief about the importance of technology; and (4) one's motivation to learn more about technology.

The digital identity framework is useful for understanding the digital/participation divide because it addresses individual and structural factors that impact digital participation. Expounding upon the multiple factors that foster one's technological identity, Goode explains, "the ideas of participation and cultural capital underlie how one's technology identity is built upon a psychological and sociological interplay between opportunity, knowledge, and attitudes about technology" (2010, p. 590). Drawing from Bourdieu's theory of cultural capital (1986), Goode suggests that part of becoming a "computer person" occurs through socialization processes that are grounded in one's familial, socioeconomic, cultural, educational, and geographical contexts. For example, if a student grows up in a working-class family that does not value technology, the student likely will have a negative disposition toward technology. Students need more than a positive attitude toward technology, however, to confidently participate in the digital realm. Prerequisites for using technology for learning include a positive disposition toward technology, physical access to digital resources, and knowledge about how to use technology tools.

How might educators play an active role in facilitating growth of students' technology identities? A teacher's ability to broker technological opportunities depends on various structures. Margolis and colleagues (2010), for example, explained how broader-level influences such as district policies, and even historical social forces such as racism, often influence decisions about school-level technology use. In some cases, teachers may understand the value of technology in the classroom yet be situated in places without structural capabilities to ensure that their students can access robust technology tools. Without convenient access to technology, technical support, administrative support, and/or a flexible curriculum that allows for digital integration, teachers cannot effectively act as digital empowerment agents for their students (e.g., Ertmer, 2005; Fahser-Herro & Steinkuehler, 2009; Hutchison & Reinking, 2011; Margolis et al., 2010).

The socioeconomic composition of schools also impact how teachers use technology in class. Warschauer, for example, found that students in majority low SES classrooms typically "were subjected to such drill-and-practice software, while high-SES students have more opportunities to use school technology for broader purposes of research, simulation, data analysis, and creative expression" (2007, p. 161). Depending on their pedagogical beliefs and technological self-efficacy, teachers may effectively integrate technology and digital media in their pedagogy to transform their classroom. Teachers who are comfortable using technology are most likely to provide students with opportunities for meaningful tech use and instruction (Ertmer, 2005; Gu, Zhu, & Guo, 2013; Hutchison & Reinking, 2011). Fahser-Herro and Steinkuehler (2009) found that, even with technological means such as laptops for every student, teachers often used technology only to supplement their teaching rather than to transform their pedagogy. In a later study, Herro (2015) discovered that some teachers, despite less than amenable conditions for technology use, acted as "mavericks" and led meaningful efforts of technology adoption in their classes and schools.

In our current thinking, we contend that for educators to serve as digital empowerment agents, and effectively use digital tools in supporting students, they: (1) act as participants in students' school-based social network and thus are able to broker institutionalized resources; (2) bring a critical consciousness to the work they do, that is, recognizing that students from varying backgrounds bring varying skills and digital identities to their schooling—and respond effectively to those unique characteristics; (3) make use of digital tools in meaningful ways; and (4) strive to foster positive student digital identities.

We conclude the chapter by sharing concrete examples of challenges and successes that begin to shed light on the concept of digital empowerment agents. These findings are not meant as an empirical assertion. Rather we share examples from the field to provide a foundation for future research and to stimulate discussion about practice.

Digital Empowerment Agents in Action: Examples from the Field

Given the challenges outlined above, how is it possible for educators to move beyond structural barriers and informal challenges to foster robust digital literacies among students? Since 2010, we have been conducting research with colleagues from the Pullias Center for Higher Education at the University of Southern California on the impact of games and social media on college access. The data shared below pertains to research funded by a US Department of Education Fund for the Improvement of Postsecondary Education grant (RA#P116F140097) where we have developed a randomized control trial study to assess the impact of a game-based social media intervention, the *Mission Admission* Challenge, on postsecondary outcomes in 60 low-income high schools across the state of California. The Challenge is centered around the *Mission Admission* online role-playing game, where students select an avatar and guide that character through a week of college and financial aid application activities. Beyond playing the game, Challenge activities included taking pre- and postplay surveys and exploring college-related resources (i.e., articles, quizzes, videos, and games) on the Get Schooled (a college access nonprofit organization with a strong online presence) social media platform. Schools facilitated initial access to the Challenge during a structured class period; subsequent game play was designed to take place outside of class. The grant was also intended to provide insight into how to best implement technology tools in school contexts.

Data collected during the first year of the intervention's deployment focused on understanding school context and documenting the process of implementing the game intervention in 30 Title I schools. Data shared in this chapter highlights findings from the educator component of the study and pinpoints instances that offer insight into what it means to effectively empower students through the use of digital tools. Data pertaining to educators derived from three sources: (1) 546 surveys administered to teachers; (2) 62 interviews conducted with teachers, counselors, and/or administrators at each school; and (3) fieldnotes from observations collected during project implementation at selected treatment schools. We begin by exploring challenges educators faced in their pursuit to use digital tools for learning.

Challenges to Facilitating Digital Empowerment

At the school level, researchers observed a number of challenges to implementing the *Mission Admission* Challenge, primarily related to students' access to computers. The month-long Challenge was designed to be launched in junior-level classrooms and then played outside of instructional class time. Schools agreed to involve all juniors and administer the "launch" during a singular week. They then were able to determine how and when students might have additional access to play during the school week. While the launch process worked smoothly in one-third of participating schools, the majority of schools struggled to make the program available to students because of problems in providing access to digital devices. Difficulties in ensuring access to computers or tablets at the school level fell into four categories: (1) prevalence of broken laptops/tablets on laptop/tablet carts; (2) inability to schedule classes into computer labs or to reserve laptop carts because of heavy use from other classes; (3) school schedules that did not allow ample time for students to visit computer labs or check out laptops from carts (i.e., short advisory or homeroom periods); and (4) weak broadband connection on campus. These institutional shortcomings represent first-level digital divide issues and greatly impacted educators' abilities to provide students access to digital tools, let alone ensure learning opportunities through use of the tools.

At the classroom level, researchers observed a wide range of approaches to supporting the implementation of the Challenge. A sizeable group of teachers met with administrators to plan out launch activities, read prelaunch materials, and take an active role in rolling out the Challenge. Several teachers relied on other adults or student leaders to come into their classes and launch the Challenge. Of the latter group, teachers tended to either play an active role in encouraging students to participate or remained disengaged from the activity. Engaged teachers circulated the room, offered extra credit for completing project milestones and spoke about the value of participating in a college-related activity. Disengaged teachers mostly remained at their desks and did not make attempts to learn about the project. In these cases, educators served as their own barrier to using digital tools for learning. Teacher engagement tended to vary within schools. On multiple occasions researchers observed a highly engaged teacher in one classroom and then a disengaged teacher in another classroom down the hall. The attitude of the teacher affected students' ability to check out devices (digital divide issue) and interact with the intervention (participation divide issue). Over the course of two months, researchers tracked school-level outcomes related to participation in Challenge activities. Schools with a cohesive technology structure and strong teacher engagement performed more positively in the Challenge overall.

Responses on two survey questions might offer insight into why teachers are less likely to implement technology in their classrooms. Of the 546 teachers surveyed, the majority indicated that they were more confident using technology at home than in the classroom. Notably, teachers were least comfortable with online games. This finding may have impacted the implementation of the Challenge, which was game based. Without strong digital

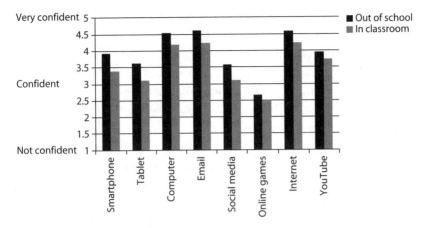

Figure 4.1. Teachers' Confidence with Technology. Y-axis numerals indicate teachers' self-reported levels of confidence on a 5-point Likert scale.

identities of their own, it is possible that educators lack the ability to positively influence students' technology identities.

Interview data emphasized student-level challenges of working with digital tools in low-income schools. Similar to what we documented during observations, teachers spoke about the difficulties their students had in accessing the Internet once they left campus. One veteran high school technology educator summarized the challenges she faces with regard to technology. She first outlined extraschool challenges that correspond with challenges related to the first-level digital divide: "They think they can do all their homework on a smart phone. They have one computer at home—shared among the entire household—so any family with multiple students has to share. When finances are tough—Internet is easily one of the first things to go for the month or more. No private space at home to work—one student slept in the living room with his brother—he had no personal space of his own, let alone a quiet place to work." Other challenges she explained are more related to habits of digital use and can be observed inside of school: "When doing work in the classroom, a strategy is not often discussed or established to provide sharing time; one student will take the machine and leave the others out. Discipline and time management—let's say you finally get your hands on a machine—it takes real discipline to get to work first versus playing games or watching videos. By the time students get around to working—they are too tired and unfocused to get much done."

In a different school, a teacher who serves as an information technology (IT) lead shared an anecdote that complicates the concept of digital natives and underlines the prevalence of a participation divide. She addressed the disservice done to students when making an assumption that all youth are proficient using technology: "I think the term digital native is nonsense [laughs]. Kids know how to upload images to Instagram, but in an educational setting we haven't taught them how to use the tools. And I use a silly example, when we give kids pens and pencils in Kindergarten & first grade, we teach them how to *use* them. If we don't, they will typically start using them as swords. We do the same thing with computers. If we don't teach them how to use [technology] properly, they use them for other purposes. They need to learn how to use [technology] as a learning tool." One teacher explained that her students did not know how to check emails properly (this had implications for corresponding with colleges) or how to forward test scores to postsecondary institutions. She underlined the need to support students in navigating the online nature of college applications and acceptances prior to making errors in online communications.

An educator who teaches computer programming addressed a more complex concern about educators' low expectations of students' abilities and lack of understanding about career possibilities. He argued that without a solid understanding of what a career in a technology field entails, teachers run the risk of dissuading students from pursuing postsecondary options that might lead to a fruitful career: "Adults at schools do kids a disservice because they don't know current stuff. They think students have to fit into a little box. And if you don't fit into that box, then college isn't for you. Teachers talk down to students and continue to oppress them. They say 'these people can't code, they can't speak English.' That's crazy. So there's institutionalized racism in the tech education space." While highlighting challenges encountered by students, this educator strongly illustrates a critical consciousness about the challenges his students face and an understanding of larger contextual digital equity issues. His understanding of the obstacles faced by low-income students provides a segue into exploring strategies of digital empowerment.

Strategies of Digital Empowerment

Over the course of the first year of data collection, we encountered several educators who stood out in their approaches to using technology in the classroom. While they varied in their pedagogical approach, personal background, and institutional position, their insights and strategies offer a starting point for defining and better understanding the potential of a digital empowerment agent to support the cultivation of students' digital identities and social capital. These educators conveyed: (1) an understanding of the potential of technology to positively impact students; (2) a critical consciousness or keen awareness of micro- and macrolevel challenges faced by students and educators; and (3) creativity in their approaches to ensuring that students had access to technology and support. In some cases, the teachers were situated in formalized technology roles within the school environment. In other cases, teachers did not have an explicit digital focus but incorporated technology into their practice.

One teacher explained, "technology provides a tool for students to showcase their skills, accomplishments and can be used to network and enhance their social capital." She offered four suggestions for ensuring that teachers maximize their impact on students through technology education: "Get the work done during school time; ensure that students graduate with skills and a portfolio—not just a diploma; keep students at the center of learning; and focus on the problem solving process that is integral in computer science and programming." This teacher clearly articulated a philosophy that centers students and recognizes the value of rigorously and realistically preparing students for life after high school.

Another teacher emphasized the value of instilling confidence in his students, especially for those who have come from schools where low expectations reign. "My philosophy," he explained, "is 'you be you and we'll help you get into tech.' I empower students with support, encouragement, belief, coaching. And then with tech, I can help you get there. It's a combination of belief and skills." This teacher was acutely aware of his potential to move beyond simple technology instruction toward empowering students.

In order to combat insufficient technology funds at school and in response to knowing that her students do not have reliable broadband access outside of school, another teacher maintained an open-door policy during lunch and before school. She employed a variety of strategies to teach students how to remember passwords, work around technology glitches, and seek support when needed. Her approach moved beyond simply assisting students with technology or providing help on schoolwork and/or college applications. Rather, she worked with students to make sure they could access digital resources in meaningful ways and was explicit about how to cultivate social relationships to support their goals. She refused to be intimidated by new approaches: "Some teacher will say, 'I don't know how to do that' but I just say, 'ok, let's try this.'" This teacher exemplified a creative approach to incorporating digital tools into her everyday activities. In response, her students actively and effectively engaged with technology.

Akin to the barriers HIVE collaborators found with regard to how educators brokered resources (Ching et al., 2015), we observed that educators teaching in underresourced schools faced complex institutional and individual challenges to providing robust learning opportunities through digital tools. Effective educators recognized challenges and acted in savvy ways to counteract institutional constraints. By recognizing students' interests and personal needs, educators were able to engage students in relevant and meaningful ways that made positive use of technology and helped students understand the value of technology in promoting positive learning outcomes.

Facilitating Digital Empowerment: Concluding Thoughts

We opened the chapter by discussing how teachers might contribute to the growth of their students' social capital and how they might use technology to facilitate the accumulation and maintenance of social capital and growth of digital identities. Through the implementation of an online, game-based intervention designed to boost college knowledge and college aspirations, we have learned that the space where teachers, students, and technology interact is complicated. Digital infrastructures vary tremendously between and within schools. Teachers' comfort levels with and knowledge of digital tools also differ substantially—this in turn affects teachers' abilities to effectively make use of technology in the classroom. When equipped with a critical consciousness pertaining to students' backgrounds, needs, and interests, as well as a solid understanding of the capacity of an institution's technology infrastructure to support learning, educators appear to be able to empower students through the use of digital tools. Accordingly, they have the capacity to build students' technology identities—and relatedly, their social capital through online networks.

Students' abilities to utilize digital tools well vary tremendously and are facilitated or hindered by access to computers/tablets and broadband outside of school. Our observations underlined the fact that the first-level digital divide as previously conceived (i.e., lack of access to computers) still persists. We also observed that a more nuanced participation divide (i.e., lack of access to higher-order skills via technology instruction) also poses challenges to students.

At the same time, we documented instances where teachers recognized challenges related to digital access, made students aware of those challenges, and worked with students to find work-around solutions. Despite structural factors in the school and limited resources, such educators served as a specific type of institutional agent—a concept we have put forward as digital empowerment agents. These educators manifested a critical consciousness about their work and a creative approach to working with students and digital tools. Consequently they were poised to broker resources in culturally and digitally relevant ways that made sense to students. As we continue to explore this concept further, we aim to identify ways to build the capacity of educators to use technology wisely and consequently expand high-quality digital learning opportunities for students.

REFERENCES

Alston, O., Dias, M., & Phillips, B. (2015). *Toward addressing the participation gap of the digital divide: A digital fluency perspective of millennials.* Paper presented at Americas' Conference on Information Systems: Adoption and Diffusion of Information Technology, Puerto Rico.

Barron, B., Gomez, K., Pinkard, N., & Martin, C. K. (2014). *The digital youth network: Cultivating digital media citizenship in urban communities.* Cambridge, MA: MIT Press.

Bourdieu, P. (1986). The forms of capital. In J. G. Richardson (Ed.), *Handbook of theory and research for sociology of education* (pp. 241–258). New York, NY: Greenwood.

boyd, d. (2014). *It's complicated: The social lives of networked teens.* New Haven, CT: Yale University Press.

Broos, A., & Roe, K. (2006). The digital divide in the Playstation generation: Self-efficacy, locus of control and ICT adoption among adolescents. *Poetics, 34*(4), 306–317.

Brown, C., & Czerniewicz, L. (2010). Debunking the "digital native": Beyond digital apartheid, towards digital democracy. *Journal of Computer Assisted Learning, 26*(5), 357–369.

Campos-Castillo, C. (2015). Revisiting the first-level digital divide in the United States gender and race/ethnicity patterns, 2007–2012. *Social Science Computer Review, 33*(4), 423–439.

Ching, D., Santo, R., Hoadley, C., & Peppler, K. (2015). On-ramps, lane changes, detours and destinations: Building connected learning pathways in HIVE NYC through brokering future learning opportunities. *Hive Research Lab.* Retrieved from http://www.kyliepeppler .com/Docs/2015_Peppler_Hive-WhitePaper_OnRampsLaneChanges.pdf.

Coleman, J. S. (1990). *Foundations of social theory.* Cambridge, MA: Harvard University Press.

Common Sense. (2015). *The common sense census: Media use by teens and tweens.* Retrieved from https://www.commonsensemedia.org/sites/default/files/uploads/research/census _researchreport.pdf.

Corwin, Z. B. (2009). The paper trail of Lily Salazar. In W. G. Tierney & J. E. Colyar (Eds.), *Urban high school students and the challenges of access* (2nd. ed., pp. 113–139). New York, NY: Peter Lang.

Corwin, Z. B., & Calderone, S. (2015). *Information-seeking in the digital age: Documenting the online financial aid knowledge pathways of low-income, students of color.* Paper presented at the American Education Research Association annual meeting, Chicago, IL.

Corwin, Z. B., & Danielson, R. (2016). Admission is the mission: How first generation students approach learning about college through games. In Y. B. Kafai, B. M. Tynes, & G. T. Richard (Eds.), *Diversifying Barbie and Mortal Kombat* (pp. 272–284). Pittsburgh, PA: Carnegie-Mellon Press.

Corwin, Z. B., Danielson, R., Ragusa, G., & Tierney, W. G. (2016). Can games facilitate access to college? In H. F. O'Neil, E. L. Baker, & R. S. Perez (Eds.), *Using games and simulations for teaching and assessment: Key issues* (pp. 230–250). New York, NY: Routledge Press.

Deil-Amen, R., & Rios-Aguilar, C. (2014). From FAFSA to Facebook: The role of technology in navigating the financial aid process. In A. Kelly & S. Goldrick-Rab (Eds.), *Reinventing financial aid: Charting a new course to college affordability* (pp. 75–100). Cambridge, MA: Harvard Education Press.

Eastin, M. S., Cicchirillo, V., & Mabry, A. (2015). Extending the digital divide conversation: Examining the knowledge gap through media expectancies. *Journal of Broadcasting & Electronic Media, 59*(3), 416–437.

Ellison, N. B., Steinfield, C., & Lampe, C. (2007). The benefits of Facebook "friends": Social capital and college students' use of online social network sites. *Journal of Computer-Mediated Communication, 12*(4), 1143–1168.

Ertmer, P. A. (2005). Teacher pedagogical beliefs: The final frontier in our quest for technology integration? *Educational Technology Research and Development, 53*(4), 25–39.

Fahser-Herro, D., & Steinkuehler, C. (2009). Web 2.0 literacy and secondary teacher education. *Journal of Computing in Teacher Education, 26*(2), 55–62.

Goode, J. (2010). The digital identity divide: How technology knowledge impacts college students. *New Media & Society, 12*(3), 497–513.

Granovetter, M. (1983). The strength of weak ties: A network theory revisited. *Sociological Theory, 1*(1), 201–233.

Greenhow, C., & Robelia, B. (2009). Old communication, new literacies: Social network sites as social learning resources. *Journal of Computer-Mediated Communication, 14*(4), 1130–1161.

Gu, X., Zhu, Y., & Guo, X. (2013). Meeting the "digital natives": Understanding the acceptance of technology in classrooms. *Educational Technology & Society, 16*(1), 392–402.

Hargittai, E., & Hinnant, A. (2008). Digital inequality: Differences in young adults' use of the Internet. *Communication Research, 35*(5), 602–621.

Haythornthwaite, C. (2002). Strong, weak, and latent ties and the impact of new media. *The Information Society, 18*(5), 385–401.

Helsper, E. J., & Eynon, R. (2010). Digital natives: Where is the evidence? *British Educational Research Journal, 36*(3), 503–520.

Herro, D. (2015). Sustainable innovations: Bringing digital media and emerging technologies to the classroom. *Theory Into Practice, 54*(2), 117–127.

Horrigan, J. (2015, April 20). The numbers behind the broadband "homework gap." *Pew Research Center.* Retrieved from http://www.pewresearch.org/fact-tank/2015/04/20/the-numbers-behind-the-broadband-homework-gap/.

Hutchison, A., & Reinking, D. (2011). Teachers' perceptions of integrating information and communication technologies into literacy instruction: A national survey in the United States. *Reading Research Quarterly, 46*(4), 312–333.

Ianni, F. (1989). *The search for structure: A report on American youth today.* New York, NY: Free Press.

Ito, M., Antin, J., Finn, M., Law, A., Manion, A., Mitnick, S., . . . & Horst, H. A. (2009). *Hanging out, messing around, and geeking out: Kids living and learning with new media.* Cambridge, MA: MIT Press.

Kabali, H. K., Irigoyen, M. M., Nunez-Davis, R., Budacki, J. G., Mohanty, S. H., Leister, K. P., & Bonner, R. L. (2015). Exposure and use of mobile media devices by young children. *Pediatrics, 136*(6), 1–7.

Koutropoulos, A. (2011). Digital natives: Ten years after. *Journal of Online Learning and Teaching, 7*(4), 525–538.

Lenhart, A. (2015). Teens, social media & technology overview 2015. *Pew Research Center.* Retrieved from http://www.pewinternet.org/2015/04/09/teens-social-media-technology -2015/.

Lutz, C., & Hoffmann, C. P. (2014, May 12). Towards a broader understanding of the participation divide(s). *Social Science Research Network,* 1–5.

Margolis, J., Estrella, R., Goode, J., Holme, J. J., & Nao, K. (2010). *Stuck in the shallow end: Education, race, and computing.* Cambridge, MA: MIT Press.

Office of the Press Secretary. (2015, December 10). *White House report: The Every Student Succeeds Act.* Retrieved from https://www.whitehouse.gov/the-press-office/2015/12/10/white -house-report-every-student-succeeds-act.

Prensky, M. (2001). Digital natives, digital immigrants part 1. *On the Horizon, 9*(5), 1–6.

Pullias Center for Higher Education. (2016). *Launching the Mission: Admission Challenge.* Retrieved from http://www.uscrossier.org/pullias/wp-content/uploads/2016/08/Launching _MA_FINAL-08.16.16.pdf.

Purcell, K., Heaps, A., Buchanan, J., & Friedrich, L. (2013, February 27). How teachers are using technology at home and in their classrooms. *Pew Research Center.* Retrieved from http://www.pewinternet.org/2013/02/28/how-teachers-are-using-technology-at-home-and -in-their-classrooms/.

Selwyn, N. (2004). Reconsidering political and popular understandings of the digital divide. *New Media & Society, 6*(3), 341–362.

Stanton-Salazar, R. D. (2011). A social capital framework for the study of institutional agents and their role in the empowerment of low-status students and youth. *Youth & Society, 43*(3), 1066–1109.

Tierney, W. G., & Venegas, K. M. (2006). Fictive kin and social capital: The role of peer groups in applying and paying for college. *American Behavioral Scientist, 49*(12), 1687–1702.

Warnath, C. F. (1973). The school counselor as institutional agent. *The School Counselor, 20*(3), 202–208.

Warschauer, M. (2004). *Technology and social inclusion: Rethinking the digital divide.* Cambridge, MA: MIT Press.

Warschauer, M. (2007). A teacher's place in the digital divide. *Yearbook of the National Society for the Study of Education, 106*(2), 147–166.

Warschauer, M., & Matuchniak, T. (2010). New technology and digital worlds: Analyzing evidence of equity in access, use, and outcomes. *Review of Research in Education, 34*(1), 179–225.

Wohn, D. Y., Ellison, N. B., Khan, M. L., Fewins-Bliss, R., & Gray, R. (2013). The role of social media in shaping first-generation high school students' college aspirations: A social capital lens. *Computers & Education, 63,* 424–436.

CHAPTER FIVE

Reimagining STEM

Catalyzing Digital Media and Learning for Civic Engagement

S. CRAIG WATKINS

Participation in the digital world continues to evolve in ways that are difficult to predict. For example, today black and Latino youth are just as likely as their white and Asian counterparts to go online (Rideout, Foehr, & Roberts, 2010). Moreover, black and Latino youth are increasingly likely to spend more time using social or mobile media (Lenhart, 2015). These are just two of the many trends that point to the remaking of the digital landscape. But even as a greater diversity of young people are using digital media than ever before, not all forms of digital media participation are equal. The media practices of black and Hispanic teens continue to be influenced by race/ethnicity, class, and schooling.

In this chapter, I focus on a specific feature of youth digital media culture: the opportunities to learn and develop a civic voice with technology in the formal schooling environment. Since 2005, computers and the Internet in US schools have expanded significantly. As a result, the media and technology lives of students from lower-income households have changed in some noteworthy ways. By 2005, students from economically disadvantaged homes were just as likely as students from affluent homes to attend schools with Internet access (Wells & Lewis, 2006). The diffusion of technology in classrooms raises important questions about the learning opportunities available to students.

Future-oriented narratives about schools and learning are overwhelmingly preoccupied with the challenges of preparing young people for the formal economy. Educators typically emphasize the cultivation of STEM (science, technology, engineering, and math) literacies. This is driven in large measure by economic forecasts that predict that the most robust employment opportunities in a knowledge-driven economy are in the STEM sector (Langdon, 2011). But as Keri Facer (2011) explains, "The idea that this is all that education should be concerned with, or even that preparation for the formal economy should be the pre-eminent function of education, is highly debatable" (p. 3). This chapter shifts the focus on learning and education to a different terrain—the civic education of young people and the development of their civic voice.

More specifically, the discussion below draws from an ethnographic study of a high school game design class that attempted to construct game creation as a pathway to new learning and civic futures. In addition to leveraging digital media and learning for economic opportunity, how can digital media and learning be catalyzed for civic opportunity? I also explore the challenges that resource-constrained schools encounter when they incorporate ideas and technologies that are intended to foster student creativity, digital literacy, and civic agency and voice.

Schools and the Civic Opportunity Gap

To frame my analysis of the game design class, I consider the work of education scholar Jeannie Oakes (2005). According to Oakes, the institutional practices developed by schools structure the opportunities that students have to learn. Importantly, these institutional practices vary by schools and the resources that are available to teachers and students. As more schools embrace technology and its presumed benefits as pathways to "21st century learning," a key question emerges: how do the institutional practices of schools shape digital media and learning opportunities? Not all opportunities to learn with digital media are equal. Thus, what students actually learn in their engagement with digital media varies significantly by the kinds of resources (e.g., curriculum, technical) that schools can provide.

Oakes situates her analysis of educational inequalities this way: "What happens if different kinds of classrooms systematically provide students with different kinds of learning experiences?" Further, she asks: "Do these differences mean that some students have greater opportunities to learn than others?" (2005, p. 94). When Oakes compared students in high-privileged and higher-track classrooms to students in low-privileged and lower-track class-rooms, she found that the former benefit from many factors (i.e., high-quality instruction, more time on task) that enhance their opportunities to learn. While Oakes focuses on opportunities to learn conventional academic content, her provocations open up a space to think about other forms of learning and development that schools facilitate, such as the opportunity to cultivate the civic knowledge and competencies of students.

Among the institutions that prepare young people for civic life, none may be more important than schools (Gibson & Levine, 2003). While schools are generally viewed as places for academic training, they can also be fertile terrain for cultivating civic knowledge, civic attitudes, and civic behaviors among adolescents (McLeod, Shah, Hess, & Lee, 2010). Schools provide civic education through formal and informal learning. In the formal learning con-text, schools promote the development of civic education and civic attitudes through academic courses and service-learning opportunities that encour-age community involvement. In the informal learning context, extracurricu-lar activities like student government embolden students to take an active role in the life and governance of their school.

Unfortunately, not all students have access to learning opportunities that support civic-mindedness and civic engagement (Corporation for National and Community Service, 2005). The educational disparities in the US educa-tional system are well documented (National Commission on Excellence in Education, 1983). These disparities, however, stretch far beyond the tradi-tional academic achievement gaps such as standardized test scores, enrollment in advanced classes, graduation rates, or four-year college enrollment. These disparities also limit the opportunities for many students to cultivate a wider variety of skills such as twenty-first-century literacies (Partnership for 21st Century Skills, 2008), new media literacies (Jenkins, 2009), and civic literacies (Youniss & Levine, 2009).

In their study of high schools, Joseph Kahne and Ellen Middaugh (2009) found that students who are academically successful and those with parents of higher social and economic status receive more classroom-based civic learning opportunities. Kahne and Middaugh write that, "rather than help-ing to equalize the capacity and commitments needed for democratic par-ticipation, [schools] appear to be . . . providing more preparation for those who are already likely to attain a disproportionate amount of civic and political voice" (2009, p. 43). In addition to lacking access to high-quality instruction (US Department of Education, 2002), rich curricula, and meaningful opportunities for academic-oriented learning, lower-income students may also lack access to the classes and extracurricular opportunities that develop civic competencies (Levinson, 2010). Researchers call this the "civic opportunity gap."

The effects of the civic opportunity gap are significant. Most measures of civic and political activity suggest that groups from higher social and economic standing are more likely to participate in civic and political activities (Levinson, 2010). Young people who participate in civic and community-related activities are more likely to participate in civic and political life as adults (Flanagan & Levine, 2010). They are also more likely to develop a greater sense of political efficacy, a key predictor of civic engagement (Levinson, 2010).

Youth from resource-constrained communities are not disinterested in civic life. A survey of older teens and young adults by Cathy Cohen and Joseph Kahne (2012) provides evidence that youth from diverse racial and ethnic backgrounds are involved in what they describe as "participatory politics." This is a reference to "interactive, peer-based acts through which individuals and groups seek to exert both voice and influence on issues of public concern" (Cohen & Kahne, 2012, p. vi). Examples of participatory politics include starting a new political group online, circulating political or civic-related information via a website, or forwarding a political video to one's social network.

Black youth, Cohen and Kahne report, were much more likely than their white, Asian, or Latino counterparts to have engaged in some form of civic activity in the form of online politics, institutional politics, or voting. While Latino youth may vote less than their counterparts, they may be especially engaged in informal civic activities related to improving their communities (Cohen & Kahne, 2012). Recent youth-driven civic initiatives like the DREAMers (Zimmerman, 2012) and Black Lives Matter (Kang, 2015) illuminate how Latino and African Americans are identifying alternative spaces and resources for catalyzing their civic voices and imagination beyond more conventional civic pathways.

Still, sustained forms of youth civic engagement usually occur in the context of institutions—schools, faith-based organizations, and youth groups (Eccles & Gootman, 2002). Schools, for example, are a unique and vital institution in the lives of resource-constrained communities. Schools connect students to an assortment of resources that may be difficult for them to access, such as technology, institutional forms of social capital, and enrichment activities (Watkins et al., forthcoming).

Schools and Youth Civic Voice

In this chapter, I consider some of the specific challenges that schools face in developing the civic voices of young people. Peter Levine defines political voice as "behavior that expresses a point of view" (2007, p. 50). A key aspect of this type of expression, Levine notes, is to assert some type of influence in the political or public sphere. Nick Couldry describes voice as the ability of humans to "give an account of themselves and of their place in the world" (2010, p. 1). But, Couldry warns, being able to speak or give an account of your life is not enough. In addition, how voice is valued or not valued is important. Couldry maintains that the landscape in which people speak also matters. Thus the sociology of voice, that is, the social structures and institutional practices that shape the making and recognition or unmaking and misrecognition of voices is important to understand.

Among the institutions that give both form and recognition to the voices of teens, none may be more important than school. In addition to teaching students basic literacy skills, schools are a laboratory for the cultivation of other kinds of skills, including civic. Schools can play a powerful role in fostering or inhibiting student voices. Historically, schools have rarely recognized the voices of students or the accounts that they give of themselves and of their place in the world. Students have typically been socialized to be quiet and acquiescent, and schools expect students to mute their voices in deference to institutional norms and authority. People's voices tend to count only when their bodies matter and are valued (Butler, 1990). Consequently, the institutional constraints that schools impose may be even more severe for those students who are stigmatized, for example, as "lower-income," "disadvantaged," or "at-risk." Students who are designated as "English language learners" may literally be rendered voiceless because of cultural and linguistic barriers.

One way of thinking about the implications of the civic opportunity gap in schools is how this specific institution recognizes and, as a result, enables and validates certain voices and not others. Couldry adds, "Having a voice is never enough. I need to know that my voice matters" (2010, p. 1). In our discussions with students who resided on the academic edge at Freeway High School, there was a sense that teachers did not believe that they were capable of high-level achievement or value their voice. Moreover, these students were not active in traditional school leadership organizations like student government or journalism. As I discuss below, our work with students was a unique effort to find a space (the games class) and a resource (digital media) to have their civic voice heard and recognized.

The Study Site and Research Methods: Freeway High School

This chapter is based on a yearlong ethnographic study that was conducted at Freeway High School, located in the suburban fringes of Austin's growing entrepreneurial and technology-driven economy (Straubhaar, 2012).[1] During our fieldwork more than 2,200 students attended Freeway. The student population was predominantly Latino (48%) and African American (24%), but Asian (13%) and white (11%) students were also represented. English language learners represented about 11% of the student population.[2]

The racial and ethnic academic achievement gaps at Freeway were consistent with longstanding patterns. For example, Asian (57%) and white (43%) students were more than twice as likely than Hispanic (20%) or black (15%) students to have taken at least one Advanced Placement or International Baccalaureate examination. White (71%) and Asian (66%) students were substantially more likely than Hispanic (39%) or black (38%) students to be college ready in English language arts and mathematics. English language learners (71%), Hispanic (83%), and black (88%) students were less likely to complete high school in four years than their Asian (93%) and white (91%) counterparts.

Our yearlong immersion in the school provided an opportunity to gain better perspective of the role that digital media plays in the formal and informal learning environments of teens in underresourced schools. Similar to a large percentage of schools across the United States, Freeway and its students had access to technology. Despite broader access to technology in US schools, the learning outcomes associated with technology vary. For example, students in lower-income schools are less likely to experience instructors and curricula that provide access to more cognitively rigorous tasks and computer-based skills (Margolis, Estrella, Goode, Holme, & Nao, 2008).

Our research team received approval to study three classes, which included two Advanced Game Design courses and a technology applications course. We used mixed-method ethnography that included participant observations, stakeholder interviews (e.g., educators, administrators, and parents), and in-depth interviews with students throughout the course of the academic year on a variety of topics, including, for example, use of social media, academic disposition, civic engagement, and home life (Hatch, 2002). In this chapter I focus on the field research that we conducted with one of the game design courses.[3] Finally, our research team asked for and received permission to get involved with the classes by coordinating a game design project that allowed us to work side by side with students. As a result, we were not simply onlookers in the classroom; we were also participants.

Doing Civic Engagement: Rethinking the Games and Learning Model

The interest in games as a viable resource for deeper and more engaged forms of learning is growing (Squire & Jenkins, 2004). A number of learning principles have been identified in the architecture of games. These include the ability of games to foster situated learning (Gee, 2004), engagement, experiential learning, hypothesis testing, and problem solving (Gee, 2007). As a result, games are perceived as a catalyst for the development of "21st century skills" such as critical thinking, communication, and innovation (Partnership for 21st Century Skills, 2008).

The growing emphasis on STEM encourages K–12 educators to embrace more future-oriented curricula, including the adoption of games. There are many definitions of game-based learning, but this definition by the Institute of Play (2014) is clear-eyed and consistent with the approach that we took with Freeway students: "A learning approach that emphasizes engagement, learning by doing, collaboration, reflection, iteration, frequent feedback and sharing. The approach structures learning activities around real-world or fictional challenges that compel learners to take on a variety of roles as they actively identify and seek out the tools and multi-disciplinary information they need to generate solutions."

The definition above suggests that game-based learning is not simply about mastering a specific technical (e.g., coding) or creative (e.g., art design) skill. Moreover, the definition suggests that making a playable game is not necessarily a main goal of game-based learning. Instead, robust game-based learning settings situate opportunities for the development of a wide range of competencies, including the ability to seek out the appropriate information, tools, expertise, and skills necessary to address challenges through innovation. Our team took a similar approach to game-based learning. While it was important that students developed media assets that could be translated into a game, the learning outcomes that we emphasized stretched beyond producing a game artifact.

In the discussion below I focus on one aspect of the Institute of Play definition: "the structuring of learning activities around real-world challenges that compel learners to take on a variety of roles as they actively identify and seek out the tools and multi-disciplinary information they need to generate solutions."

For instance, we believed that game design presented the opportunity to situate thinking about a real-world problem—we chose childhood obesity—in a unique context that invited students to develop a probing mind and take on multiple identities such as researcher, artist, and designer. Our goal, in many ways, was not so much about cultivating game makers but critical thinkers and civic innovators. The project was an opportunity for students to establish a point of view or "give an account of themselves and of their place in the world" on matters related to food and social justice.

The approach that we took to games and learning in our work with Freeway students emphasized community engagement and, further, reflects the medium's ability to engage a variety of social and human experiences. Game designer and scholar, Ian Bogost (2011) urges us to begin thinking about the many different uses of video games and, in his words, "how together they make the medium broader, richer, and more relevant" (p. 7). Games, Bogost claims, "have seeped out of our computers and become enmeshed in our lives" (p. 3). Bogost offers this intriguing probe: how to do things with video games. Accordingly, as games become more enmeshed in our schools, educators must carefully consider how to do education—academic and civic—in more dynamic ways with the medium.

There is growing consensus that games can serve as a pathway to engaging core academic literacies in STEM, but games also present unique opportunities to reimagine how young people develop civic voices and new ways to enact those voices. Insofar as game creation encourages designers to create distinct stories and storyworlds, it also establishes the opportunity to think about alternative civic futures.

At Freeway we established a learning environment that encouraged students to *do something* with games, such as using the game creation process to think deeply and critically about the health and well-being of their community through the design and production of civic media. Researchers at Emerson University's Engagement Lab define civic media as follows: "the technologies, designs, and practices that produce and reproduce the sense of being in the world with others toward a common good . . . the civic in civic media is not merely about outcomes, but about process and potential"

(Gordon & Mihailidis, 2016, p. 2). This definition captures key aspects of our work with students. First, our goal was for them to create game-based media that provided an instrumental benefit to their community such as greater cognitive awareness of their food environment. Second, the game-based assets that they created were not the end goals of the project. Finally, we viewed game creation in this instance as an opportunity for students to express their civic voice and also be heard in the context of an influential institution like school.

The Civic-Centered Design Classroom

As part of our work with Freeway students we decided to introduce them to some of the principles and techniques associated with design thinking to spark inquiry-driven and civically engaged game making. A growing number of design professionals and educators are making a case for bringing design thinking into the K–12 environment (IDEO, 2012). Chris Pacione, director of the LUMA Institute in Pittsburgh, believes that design should be as pervasive in our schools as reading, writing, and arithmetic. Pacione (2010) lays out the case for how design literacy or "pervasive competency in the collaborative and iterative skills of 'looking' and 'making' to understand and advance our world" could represent a breakthrough moment in the history of common literacy.

While the naming of the core design principles may vary across practitioners and educators, there are three main elements that best characterize the insertion of design thinking into the K–12 setting: Looking, Understanding, and Making (LUMA Institute, 2012). *Looking* involves a series of methods intended to facilitate the observation of some aspect of human behavior or experience. In our project with Freeway students, for example, we asked students to take a thorough look at their food environment. *Understanding* represents methods for synthesizing and summarizing knowledge through identifying patterns. After looking at their food environment we asked students to identify some of the salient trends and their impact on community health. Finally, *Making* is an especially important element and typically involves building prototypes that manifest ideas and future possibilities in tangible forms. We asked students to translate their understanding of the food environment into media content for their game that also met compelling community needs such as awareness, education, and behavioral change.

Drawing from a series of interviews with executives from the LUMA Institute, I modify their definition of human-centered design to propose what our team calls *civic-centered design* (LUMA Institute, 2012). More specifically, civic-centered design is "the discipline of generating solutions to community-based problems and opportunities through the act of making 'something' new, where the activity is driven by the needs, desires and context of the people for whom the design is intended to support or empower in some meaningful way."

The core elements of civic-centered design align with the idea that robust academic and civic outcomes are possible when civic education is inquiry-based not rote, hands-on rather than abstract, production-oriented rather than test and memorization heavy, and situated in a broader universe of experience and expertise rather than the four walls of a classroom. Many researchers in the domain of youth and civic engagement agree that young people best develop civic-mindedness through action-oriented activities (Eccles & Gootman, 2002). We subscribed to the view that by connecting game creation to their everyday lives the learning experiences of students would be more relevant and impactful.

The civic-centered design classroom differs from more traditional classrooms in several ways. In the traditional classroom learning is vertical and memory-driven. More specifically, knowledge and information are dispensed in a top-down fashion, insofar as teachers are positioned as the exclusive source of expertise in the classroom. By contrast, learning in the civic-centered design classroom is horizontal and inquiry-driven. That is, knowledge and information flow in multiple directions from teacher-to-student, student-to-student, and even student-to-teacher. In the traditional classroom learning is memory-driven. As a result, assessment is typically based on how well students can memorize classroom facts. In the civic-centered design classroom learning is inquiry-driven. Assessment is based on how well a student can probe a community-based challenge and develop innovative solutions. Whereas the traditional classroom situates learning as a linear path to mastering already established facts, the civic-centered design classroom situates learning as a messy journey to discovering knowledge and the capacity for change.

The civic-centered design classroom also establishes the conditions for the formation *and* recognition of student voice. The very design of the traditional classroom—teacher-driven, top-down, and memorization of facts—closes down the opportunities for most students to cultivate a distinct voice or point of view. Indeed, there can be no voice if students are not able to engage in inquiry, discovery, and knowledge production. In the case of our project, student voice emerges in the form of giving a unique account of food and social justice issues in their community through the medium of game design.

Predictably, we found ourselves bumping up against the tensions between these competing notions of schooling. At Freeway, like most schools, the civic-centered design model opposed virtually every definition of schooling and learning familiar to students and teachers alike. As a result, the integration of civic-centered design techniques was not easy.

The Design Challenge

One way of addressing the civic opportunity gap is to create environments that elicit civic behavior (Hart & Kirshner, 2009; Levinson, 2010). What kinds of community institutions promote youth civic knowledge, mindedness, and voice? We experimented with a studio space that provided students access to computers, cameras, tablets, and various software. In addition, the space offered access to learning and media production activities that were social, collaborative, and intentionally designed to engage the local community. We aspired to help students develop the skills and disposition to see themselves much like designers see themselves: as agents capable of imagining and creating change. From a research perspective we wanted to explore how civic-centered design helps catalyze new ways of recognizing youth voice and doing community engagement.

In the game design class students were expected to create simple games with the classroom software. The instructor gave students the option to work with our project or pursue their own individual game design project in the class. Among the 21 students, roughly half, 10, chose to work on our project. Our design challenge required students to build a game that addressed the issue of childhood obesity. We chose this topic for three reasons. First, Freeway was located among a list of zip codes populated by youth from lower-income Hispanic, African American, and immigrant households. Children and teens from these areas were disproportionately more likely than teens from white, Asian, and affluent zip codes to be obese for a variety of reasons, including geography, income inequality, and food desert conditions (Centers for Disease Control and Prevention, 2013). Second, because childhood obesity intersects with a mix of academic subject areas including science (e.g., biology), health (e.g., nutrition), and social studies (e.g., social inequality), we concluded that the project could support the development of academic skills such as inquiry, writing, and analysis. A series of prior discussions with the teacher and the district officials led us to select a project that could model how game creation could intersect with more traditional academic courses and learning activities.

Finally, we wanted to select a topic that facilitated an opportunity for students to experience real-world engagement with their community in the design of their game. The very neighborhood that students lived in could serve as an effective setting for catalyzing youth civic engagement, media making, and voice. As Hart and Kirshner (2009) explain, "clear, present, and compelling issues are more likely to engage adolescents in civic and political activity than are complex concerns" (p. 107). Thus, we hypothesized that students could see how issues of food, social inequality, and childhood obesity converged with social justice issues to affect their community.

While game creation was an aspect of the challenge, the primary aim was to encourage students to see games as a medium for cultivating greater knowledge and a more audible voice in their school and in their community. From our perspective the game design process was as much about developing a disposition for critical thinking, civic media making, and community engagement than it was for creating a playable game. As a result of these expectations our learning outcomes included some nontraditional metrics such as:

- the ability to give a critical account of their food environment and of their place in it
- the ability to translate ideas about their food environment into creative content and civic media
- the ability to integrate aspects of their world into the game and story that they created
- the ability to advocate for a healthier food environment

Next, I discuss two specific civic-centered design techniques that we introduced to the students and how the techniques established opportunities for civic education, creative action, and civic voice. The first example illustrates the possibilities of civic-centered design to tap the creative and critical thinking capacities of students from lower-income schools. The second example illustrates the perils that resource-constrained schools face when educators tinker with nonconventional learning techniques. The implication for developing and recognizing student voice are also considered.

Pathways to Youth Civic Voice:
Leveraging Student Expertise

One of the first civic-centered design exercises that we adopted was affinity mapping, a graphic technique that allows designers to sort seemingly disparate ideas into ordered patterns and categories (Gray, Brown, & Macanufo, 2010, pp. 56–58). We chose this technique because it encouraged students to reflect on their environment and to identify several factors related to childhood obesity, which is a complex social and public health problem. Further, affinity mapping allowed students to organize a lot of information and ideas quickly and into categories that could facilitate understanding and making. The maps identified emergent patterns and themes that could become the building blocks of their game. The exercise was also an opportunity for students to, quite literally, form a decidedly civic voice.

We divided the students into two teams and prompted them with this question: what factors contribute to the childhood obesity epidemic? Each student received several post-it notes to write or draw their ideas. It took them a few minutes to get started, but once they gained momentum the students generated several ideas. Group One had a fast food motif. Several team members drew McDonald's arches or identified the fast food giant as a major factor in childhood obesity trends. Some of the students referenced how pervasive fast food is in their neighborhood and around the school. "They are everywhere," one student quipped.

The group made a number of thoughtful connections. For instance, one student noted that "video games are a reason for obesity." Another student responded, "but wait there's a difference between button-mashers and Wii Fit, so that might not be exactly true." During the exercise students became quite vocal as they proceeded to identify many factors related to childhood obesity.

Group Two also generated several responses to the prompt. They drew pictures of food and restaurant chain logos. McDonald's was also a prominent topic of conversation in Group Two. One student remarked, "Not lovin' it!" which was a play on the hip-hop-inspired jingle "Lovin' It" that was widely used in McDonald's global marketing and branding campaigns.

After ten minutes we asked each team to post all of their notes on a large board that was visible to both groups. The students produced a long list of factors, generating enough sticky notes to fill four large poster sheets. Next, we asked them to find patterns and to discuss the relationships among the ideas that they captured. Then we asked them to sort the notes into clusters.

TABLE 5.1.
Results from Affinity Mapping Exercise

Group 1	Group 2
Fast food	Family
Society	Media
Family	Lifestyle
Lifestyle	Food
Technology / Video games	Psychological
Bullying	
Conspiracy	

The idea was to begin mapping patterns that could be organized into distinct themes and related groupings.

What patterns emerged from the students, and what did these patterns suggest about their understanding of childhood obesity? Moreover, how did this exercise create a different kind of landscape for valuing and recognizing student voice? After some additional sorting and negotiating with their fellow team members, the teams generated two clusters.

The affinity mapping exercise accomplished three things. First, the clusters provoked conversation and recognition of some of the factors that impact childhood obesity trends. Students were encouraged to begin making connections to their own lives, homes, and community. In other words, the exercise was an opportunity for students to articulate their understanding of the world. Second, the exercise reaffirmed our belief that the civic-centered design classroom can provoke a questioning disposition among students. The exercise sparked several questions: Should this be a game about fast food? Is this a game about the home food environment? Should the story encourage players to think about family, behavioral, and lifestyle issues? This was precisely what we wanted to achieve, that is, for students to use civic-centered design to interrogate the possible causes of childhood obesity and build a game-based story that expresses a point of view regarding the health of their community.

Finally, the affinity mapping exercise offered powerful insight into the mindset of the students and their thoughts about childhood obesity. We discovered that these were issues that some of them had thought about previously. Many of the students demonstrated a critical disposition in their consideration of childhood obesity. Some of them mentioned films like *Fast Food Nation* and *Food, Inc.* Health researchers in the United States consistently connect childhood obesity trends to class, education, geography, and race and ethnicity. When prompted to identify factors associated with the health epidemic, our students identified many of the same factors and made specific connections to their neighborhood.

The affinity mapping technique underscores an important element in initiatives designed to spark youth civic voice and engagement: the need to move from a "deficit model" to an "asset model." In the former, youth community engagement programs are designed to address certain problems associated with "at-risk" youth, whereas programs in the latter, asset model, are designed to build on young people's strengths and capabilities (Eccles & Gootman, 2002). The asset model invites young people to share their skills and expertise to benefit the learning environment. In addition, the asset model leverages the unique perspectives and insights that students develop and highlights their capacity for making unique and substantive community contributions.

Barriers to Youth Civic Voice: Navigating Complex Social Lives

A key element in the civic-centered design classroom is the idea that learning can and should happen in the community. It is critical, then, to create environments that empower students to engage academic content in nonacademic settings including the home, neighborhood, and peer ecology. Because we wanted students to incorporate aspects of their world into the game that they created, we decided that it would be important for them to document their world. To execute this aspect of the project we asked students to use Google Docs, a free collaborative software tool, to share any ideas, reflections, or media that commented on their wider food environment. In addition, we wanted to establish an environment in which student learning, voice, and game creation was social, networked, and community-based.

From our perspective, this element of the project would create an opportunity for students to share ideas, collaborate away from school, and incorporate aspects of their world into the design of their game. For example, we believed that students could capture photos of their home and local food environment or interview peers and family members to inform their understanding of childhood obesity. However, we quickly discovered that the idea of working with collaborative online documents outside of class was essentially off-limits for many Freeway students.

The task wrongly assumed that all students have reliable broadband home Internet access and upgraded computers to participate in this form of networked learning and academic engagement. Despite the broader adoption of Internet-based technologies, especially via mobile devices, youth from lower-income homes are much more likely than their counterparts in higher-income homes to live in households that do not offer access to broadband Internet (Horrigan, 2015). If only a few students live in homes that are equipped to support networked learning, then the opportunities to grow their knowledge through out-of-class engagement are severely weakened. Some researchers refer to this as the "homework gap" (Horrigan, 2015). Many of the students, we discovered, did not have experience with online and collaborative software applications.

Second, the assignment assumed that all students lived in a home environment that supported out-of-school engagement with school assignments. In several cases familial and financial reasons thwarted students' ability to expand formal learning beyond the classroom. Some students, for example, were expected to watch over younger siblings after school, while others took on jobs that provided their families much-needed financial assistance. The home lives of children vary across race, ethnicity, and class. These differences have serious implications for student lives and the opportunities available to them (Lareau, 2003). Children from lower-income or immigrant households may take on the role of brokers or adult-like responsibilities that help maintain familial stability (Katz, 2014). Consequently, their capacity for participating in out-of-school or extracurricular activities may be limited.

In order for community-engaged forms of learning to thrive, the conditions must be established across multiple settings, including, for instance, school, home, and the local community. When one or more of these nodes fails to effectively provide the resources and the opportunities for academic engagement, the prospects for cultivating more dynamic forms of learning, civic engagement, and civic voice are undermined.

The effort to link the students' learning and game creation practices to activities outside of the classroom via more informal modes of information gathering and knowledge production is, in theory, a good idea. However, for many of the students that we worked with, engagement with academic learning was primarily a school-based activity. Hence, the idea that they would work on the game project at home, on the weekend, or via online networks was largely outside the scope of the learning norms and habits that had been established at school or at home. It is crucial to note that learning norms and habits are social, not inevitable. It is not that Freeway students were incapable of more distributed forms of academic engagement; they simply had never been expected to do so. Additionally, financial and familial circumstances made this form of academic and civic engagement difficult to achieve.

This particular obstacle underscores the challenges that schools in resource-constrained communities face when they adopt civic-centered design techniques. In addition to grappling with internal challenges such as inadequate instructional and curriculum materials, schools are challenged by external factors such as home environments that struggle to sustain the resources that support academic engagement outside the classroom. Economic disparities are consistently identified as a major influence on academic outcomes (Duncan & Murnane, 2011). As we learned, economic disparities also influence the academic opportunities available to students, including the opportunities for civic-related educational experiences and the making and recognition of student voice.

Conclusion

In the example discussed above, Freeway students embraced the opportunity to pursue more creative and academically oriented pathways to civic education. They identified a number of factors related to childhood obesity, including many that are frequently cited by research and medical professionals. Their openness to civic-centered design suggests that students who are labeled as "disadvantaged" or "at-risk," for example, are capable of more rigorous creative and cognitive tasks when provided the opportunity. This was one of the few opportunities in the context of formal schooling in which students were encouraged to express their voice *and* be recognized for doing so. Schools, generally speaking, are not designed to recognize, empower, and validate student efforts to "give an account of themselves and of their place in the world." This is especially true when the voice is from bodies that, historically, have been marginalized and seldom valued by educational institutions.

These same students struggled to engage the design challenge outside of the classroom. This was evident in the inability of students to use collaborative software to generate and share ideas related to their project when they were away from the classroom. The constraints that we encountered underscore the challenges that resource-constrained schools face in their adoption of new learning futures and their ability to close the civic opportunity gap.

As technologies like games are established as a part of the schooling environment, educators must think carefully about how learning can be transformed and student voice amplified. When media technologies like games are adopted primarily to teach students technical skills or as preparation for entry into the paid labor force, the prospects for expanding learning to other domains of competency—civic learning, critical thinking—are overlooked. Along with the adoption of technologies in the classroom, teachers and administrators must be more creative and purposeful in the design of the curriculum and the learning outcomes that they establish for students.

One of the conclusions from our yearlong ethnography is that schools tend to invest in a limited vision of digital media and learning. The very adoption of new technologies—games, the Internet, mobile devices—is often viewed as a sign of progress and new learning futures. This, in our view, is a mistake. In other words, progress should not be measured in terms of how much technology schools acquire but rather how technology is used as a platform for critical thinking, media making, and civic voice.

Based on our work with Freeway students, we strongly believe that civic-centered design can inspire learning that is experiential, production-oriented, and connected to the everyday lives of students. Civic-centered design requires students to exhibit greater agency in their own academic development and opens up the classroom to richer and more meaningful opportunities to do community engagement. Students are encouraged to ask questions and to speak. The creation of civic media, for example, reflects the innovative use of technology to mobilize and validate youth civic voices.

Typically, the incorporation of technologies like games or disciplines like design into the K–12 curriculum reflects the broad push to develop the STEM literacies of students. The emphasis on STEM is a response to several factors, including a changing occupational landscape (Levy & Murnane, 2004), skill bias technical changes in the labor market (Goldin & Katz, 2008), and concerns about America losing ground in the global race for supremacy in education, technology, and innovation. However, the focus on STEM comes at the risk of eclipsing the consideration of other kinds of skills, including, for example, the development of civic knowledge and civic behaviors. In addition to leveraging digital media and learning to expand the economic opportunities available to young people, schools must address how digital media and learning can expand the opportunities for students to participate in the civic life of their communities and be heard.

NOTES

1. Freeway High School is a pseudonym for the school where we conducted our ethnographic study.
2. All school demographics were collected from the school district and the Texas Education Agency and are based on the year that we conducted our study.
3. Two members of our research team attended the game design classes weekly for an entire year and kept meticulous fieldnotes. In addition to the in-depth interviews, the duration of the fieldwork established the opportunity to conduct participant observations and analyze the artifacts that students produced.

REFERENCES

Bogost, I. (2011). *How to do things with video games.* Minneapolis: University of Minnesota Press.
Butler, J. (1990). *Gender trouble.* New York, NY: Routledge.
Centers for Disease Control and Prevention. (2013). Obesity—United States, 1999–2010. *MMWR, 3*(62), 12–128.
Cohen, C., & Kahne, J. (2012). *Participatory politics: New media and youth political action.* Oakland, CA: Mills College School of Education, MacArthur Network on Youth Participatory Politics.
Corporation for National and Community Service. (2005). *Building active citizens: The role of social institutions in teen volunteering.* Washington, DC: Youth Helping America Series.
Couldry, N. (2010). *Why voice matters: Culture and politics after neo-liberalism.* London, UK: Sage Publications.
Duncan, G. J., & Murnane, R. J. (Eds.). (2011). *Whither opportunity? Rising inequality, schools, and children's life chances.* New York, NY: Russell Sage Foundation.
Eccles, J., & Gootman, J. A. (2002). *Community programs to promote youth development.* Washington, DC: National Academy Press.
Facer, K. (2011). *Learning futures. education, technology and social change.* London, UK: Routledge.
Flanagan, C., & Levine, P. (2010). Civic engagement and the transition to adulthood. *Future of Children, 1*(20), 159–179.
Gee, J. P. (2004). *Situated language and learning: A critique of traditional schooling.* London, UK: Routledge.
———. (2007). *What video games have to teach us about learning and literacy* (2nd ed.). New York, NY: St. Martin's Griffin.
Gibson, M., & Levine, P. (2003). *The civic mission of schools.* New York, NY, and Washington, DC: Carnegie Corporation of New York.
Goldin, C., & Katz, L. F. (2008). *The race between education and technology.* Cambridge, MA: The Belknap Press of Harvard University Press.
Gordon, E., & Mihailidis, P. (2016). *Civic media: Technology, design, practice.* Cambridge, MA: MIT Press.
Gray, D., Brown, S., & Macanufo, J. (2010). *Gamestorming: A playbook for innovators, rulebreakers, and changemakers.* Sebastopol, CA: O'Reilly Media.
Hart, D., & Kirshner, B. (2009). Civic participation and development among urban adolescents. In J. Youniss and P. Levine (Eds.), *Engaging young people in civic life* (pp. 102–120). Nashville, TN: Vanderbilt University Press.
Hatch, J. A. (2002). *Doing qualitative research in education settings.* Albany: State University of New York Press.

Horrigan, J. B. (2015). The numbers behind the broadband homework gap. *Pew Research Center.* Retrieved from http://www.pewresearch.org/fact-tank/2015/04/20/the-numbers -behind-the-broadband-homework-gap/.

IDEO. (2012). *Design thinking for educators* (2nd ed.). Palo Alto, CA: IDEO.

Institute of Play. (2014). *Glossary.* Retrieved from http://www.instituteofplay.org/about /context/glossary/.

Jenkins, H. (2009). *Confronting the challenges of participatory culture: Media education for the 21st century.* Cambridge, MA: MIT Press.

Kahne, J., & Middaugh, E. (2009). Democracy for some: The civic opportunity gap in high school. In J. Youniss and P. Levine (Eds.), *Engaging young people in civic life* (pp. 29–58). Nashville, TN: Vanderbilt University Press.

Kang, J. C. (2015, May 4). Our demand is simple: Stop killing us. *New York Times Magazine.* Retrieved from http://www.nytimes.com/2015/05/10/magazine/our-demand-is-simple -stop-killing-us.html?_r=0.

Katz, V. S. (2014). *Kids in the middle: How children of immigrants negotiate community interactions for their families.* New Brunswick, NJ: Rutgers University Press.

Langdon, D. (2011). STEM: Good jobs now and for the future. *Economics and statistics administration issue brief #03-11.* Washington, DC: US Department of Commerce: Economics and Statistics Administration. Retrieved from http://www.esa.doc.gov/sites /default/files/stemfinaljuly14_1.pdf.

Lareau, A. (2003). *Unequal childhoods: Class, race, and family life.* Berkeley: University of California Press.

Lenhart, A. (2015). Teens, social media & technology overview 2015. *Pew Research Center.* Retrieved from http://www.pewinternet.org/2015/04/09/teens-social-media-technology -2015/.

Levine, P. (2007). *The future of democracy: Developing the next generation of American citizens.* Medford, MA: Tufts University Press.

Levinson, M. (2010). The civic empowerment gap: Defining the problem and locating solutions. In L. R. Sherrod, J. Torney-Purta, and C. Flanagan (Eds.), *Handbook of research on civic engagement in youth* (pp. 331–361). Hoboken, NJ: John Wiley & Sons, Inc.

Levy, F., & Murnane, R. J. (2004). *The new division of labor: How computers are creating the next job market.* Princeton, NJ: Princeton University Press.

LUMA Institute. (2012). *Innovating for people: Handbook of human-centered design methods.* Pittsburgh, PA: LUMA Institute.

Margolis, J., Estrella, R., Goode, J., Holme, J., & Nao, K. (2008). *Stuck in the shallow end: Education, race, and computing.* Cambridge, MA: MIT Press.

McLeod, J., Sha, D., Hess, D., & Lee, N. (2010). Communication and education: Creating competence for socialization into public life. In L. R. Sherrod, J. Torney-Purta, and C. Flanagan (Eds.), *Handbook of research on civic engagement in youth* (pp.363–391). Hoboken, NJ: John Wiley & Sons, Inc.

National Commission on Excellence in Education. (1983). *A nation at risk: The imperative for educational reform.* Washington, DC: US Government Printing Office.

Oakes, J. (2005). *Keeping track: How schools structure inequality.* New Haven, CT: Yale University Press.

Pacione, C. (2010). Evolution of the mind: A case for design literacy. *Interactions, 17*(2), 6–11.

Partnership for 21st Century Skills. (2008). *21st century skills, education & competitiveness: A resource and policy guide.* Retrieved from http://www.p21.org/storage/documents/21st _century_skills_education_and_competitiveness_guide.pdf.

Rideout, V. J., Foehr, U. G., & Roberts, D. F. (2010). *Generation M2: Media in the lives of 8- to 18-year-olds.* Menlo Park, CA: The Kaiser Family Foundation.

Squire, K. R., & Jenkins, H. (2004). Harnessing the power of video games in education. *Insight, 3*, 5–33.

Straubhaar, J. (Ed.). (2012). *Inequity in the technopolis: Race, class, gender, and the digital divide in Austin.* Austin: University of Texas Press.

US Department of Education. (2002). *Meeting the highly qualified teachers challenge: The secretary's annual report on teacher quality.* Washington, DC: US Department of Education, Office of Postsecondary Education, Office of Policy Planning and Innovation.

Watkins, S. C., Cho, A., Lombana-Bermudez, A., Shaw, V., Vickery, J., & Weinzimmer, L. (forthcoming). *The digital edge: The evolving world of social, educational and digital inequality.* New York: New York University Press.

Wells, J., & Lewis, L. (2006). *Internet access in US public schools and classrooms: 1994–2005.* Washington, DC: US Department of Education, National Center for Education Statistics.

Youniss, J., & Levine, P. (Eds.). (2009). *Engaging young people in civic life.* Nashville, TN: Vanderbilt University Press.

Zimmerman, A. M. (2012). *Documenting DREAMs: New media, undocumented youth and the migrant rights movement.* MacArthur Youth Participatory Politics Research Network. Retrieved from https://ypp.dmlcentral.net/sites/default/files/publications /Documenting_DREAMs.pdf.

CHAPTER SIX

Diversifying Digital Clubhouses

Creating Pathways of Opportunity for Girls in Games and Technology

AMANDA OCHSNER

Digital devices and media are deeply integrated into how individuals connect with others in both work and play. As social media, video games, mobile devices, and wearable technologies become increasingly ubiquitous, people with the skills to program and design for digital tools and interactions will remain in high demand (Grover & Pea, 2013; US Department of Labor, 2013). An upcoming challenge for both institutions of higher education and technology-based industries is meeting that demand with a workforce of designers and digital problem solvers who are as varied and diverse as the populations using them. This chapter contributes to these contemporary conversations on increasing diversity and inclusivity in technology fields by reporting on research that examines the experiences of women who work in video games, an industry that has been known for being unsupportive of—and even hostile to—women. The goal of the chapter is to point to ways that educators, researchers, and industry leaders may be able to engage and support women in game development and design.

I begin by examining discrepancies between the populations who use digital technologies and the populations who have the skills to design for them. The next section outlines research that points to the underlying causes of this design gap. Finally, the main research portion of this chapter reports on findings from interviews with women who work in the game industry. The interviews focus on participants' learning trajectories and professional pathways, revealing the issues and challenges they identify as core influences on their professional pathways. Identifying themes across participants' experiences, I argue that supporting young women in identifying games and technology as a part of their possibility spaces earlier, and emphasizing the diverse range of potential pathways to games and technology, may be productive for increasing women's engagement and expertise with digital tools and technologies. While a study centered on 21 women's experiences is not necessarily generalizable to other underrepresented populations in game and technology careers, it can begin to point researchers and educators toward practices that they can utilize in their efforts to create more equitable outcomes for girls and women pursuing careers in games and technology.

Reviewing the Research on Women in Games and Technology

Recent statistics show promise in the areas of gender and racial diversity when looking specifically at access and use of digital tools and games. Access to computers and high-speed Internet has leveled out across genders in recent years (Ono & Zavodny, 2003; Wasserman & Richmond-Abbott, 2005). Similarly, Pew surveys show that girls and women use digital tools and media as much as, or even more than, their male counterparts (Lenhart, 2015). Among adults, women are somewhat more likely to use social networking sites than men, with 72% of women claiming to access at least one social networking site on a regular basis compared to 66% of men (Pew Research Center, 2016). Among youth, girls outrank boys in use of visually oriented social media platforms, reporting higher rates of use of websites and apps like Instagram, Snapchat, Pinterest, and Tumblr (Lenhart, 2015). While less likely to report having access to a tablet, desktop, or laptop computer, Black teens are more likely to report having access to a smartphone (83%) compared to their White and Hispanic peers (71%). A study by the Pew Research Center (Lenhart, 2015) reports that 100% of Black teens use the Internet on a mobile device at least occasionally.

Just as women now use the Internet as frequently as men, women have also become increasingly active as game players. Recent surveys from the Entertainment Software Association (ESA) show that 45% of game players are female; women 18 and older represent a larger portion of the game-playing population than boys under 18 (Entertainment Software Association, 2013). However, data on youth and games suggest that there are some discrepancies in access to game consoles. Teen girls lag boys in video game play, with 70% of girls reporting having access to a game console, as opposed to 91% of boys (Lenhart, 2015). More research is needed to determine exactly why girls report access to game consoles in smaller numbers than their male counterparts, though as I will extrapolate below, this could have to do with trends in how parents make decisions about the location of devices like computers and game consoles in the home. It is worth noting that Black teens are more likely to report playing video games than their White or Hispanic peers, with 83% of Black teens reporting playing games, compared to 71% of White and 69% of Hispanic teens. Data suggests that gameplay among teens is distributed relatively evenly across the socioeconomic spectrum (Lenhart, 2015).

As use of technologies has trended toward leveling out across race and gender, several inequities remain in the gaps between the people who use these everyday technologies and those who are equipped with the education and skills to design and create them. The rates of women enrolling in computer science and coding classes, working in the digital game industry, and working in leadership and executive roles in technology companies lag far behind the numbers for men. In 2013, girls were more likely than male students to take an AP exam (Kurtzleben, 2014), but they accounted for only 19% of those who took the AP computer science test (Ericson, 2014). The rates of Hispanic and Black students taking the AP computer science exam also lag behind in recent years (Ericson, 2014). Recent statistics on computer and information science degrees suggest similar numbers—women obtained just 18% of the degrees in these fields in 2012 (National Center for Women & Information Technology, 2012).

Statistics on the game industry workforce show a similar gender breakdown. The latest International Game Developers Association (IGDA) developer survey indicates that women make up about 22% of the digital game industry, with another 2% identifying as transgender or androgynous (Edwards et al., 2014). While that shows a significant rise compared to the 2009 survey, where women composed less than 12% of the game industry workforce, recent demographic surveys by the ESA suggest that women are overrepresented in departments like public relations and marketing, compared to game development roles such as programming, design, or art and animation (Entertainment Software Association, 2013).

Women of color are particularly underrepresented in game industry careers, in part because the industry itself is predominantly White. Among respondents of the most recent IGDA Developer Satisfaction Survey (Weststar & Legault, 2015), 76% of respondents identified as White/Caucasian/European. Nine percent of survey takers identified as East Asian, 7.3% as Hispanic or Latino, and just 3% identified as Black / African / African American. Overall, women—and especially women of color—are not learning how to design and develop for digital media and platforms in equal numbers compared to men. This poses some critical challenges for researchers and educators interested in increasing participation from underrepresented groups, whose potential contributions in development and design are currently undervalued.

The first step to implementing solutions for these inequities is to identify the contributing causes. Research suggests that many of the exclusionary practices that deter women from learning about computers and technology begin in early childhood and are the result of attitudes and actions not by those who would intentionally exclude girls but by well-intentioned parents and teachers. While some of this research is from a few decades ago, the numbers of women graduating with degrees in computer science has not risen significantly in recent years (National Center for Women & Information Technology, 2012), suggesting that social and cultural forces that have been found to deter girls and women in the past are still likely relevant.

Margolis and Fisher (2002) discovered that women majoring in computer science at Carnegie Mellon University report that their fathers spent more time teaching their male children about computers compared to their daughters. In classrooms, female teachers are less likely to be perceived as expert users of technology regardless of their actual level of expertise (Jenson & Brushwood Rose, 2003). The authors of this study believe this issue most negatively affects female students, whose female teachers are likely to serve as their primary examples and role models for interacting with computers and technology. By middle school, boys are more likely to use a computer at home and to participate in computer-related afterschool clubs or summer camps (Barker & Aspray, 2008). In homes where the family shares a single computer, it is much more likely to be located in a boy's bedroom than his sister's (Margolis & Fisher, 2002).

In addition to differences in time spent on computers, other broad trends emerge with regard to use of computers. For youth with computers in the home, boys are more likely to play games and program, viewing the computer as a recreational toy. Girls, on the other hand, tend to view computers more as a tool and use them to accomplish specific tasks, such as homework and email (Kafai & Sutton, 1999; Cassell & Jenkins, 1998; Barker & Aspray, 2008). An informal study of a computer-based afterschool program showed that girls were motivated to learn about computers to "get ahead in the world," whereas boys enjoyed playing and messing around with technology (Cassell & Jenkins, 1998). Ito and colleagues (2010) argue that there are significant benefits of becoming a tinkerer and explorer of technology, particularly for those who engage in increasingly more complex tasks over time. It is concerning that only some populations of students benefit from these practices while others lack encouragement and mentoring from experienced parents, teachers, and role models.

Just as computers are often culturally tagged as more appropriate for boys, so too are video games. Many girls and women encounter skepticism over whether they should play games, and condescension over what and how they choose to play. This is an issue I examined in a recent qualitative research study focused on the #1ReasonWhy Twitter hashtag, in which game players and developers engaged in a widespread online conversation about the roles of women in games. The thematic threads of the conversation coalesced around the myriad ways women are made to feel that they do not belong in games (Ochsner, forthcoming). Qualitative coding of more than 2,000 tweets in this conversation revealed that as consumers, girls and women frequently faced skepticism that they were purchasing games for themselves and were frequently assumed to be buying gifts for brothers, boyfriends, or husbands. As players they hear things like "girls just aren't good at video games" and report being accused of cheating or facing uncomfortable amounts of aggression if they happen to display skill at a game in a social context. Some female players report that other players accuse them of not having a genuine interest in games and assume they play just to seek attention from men. Others are told that "proper girls" are not interested in games and that their time would be better spent in search of a boyfriend.

Seeing that it is still common for both gamers and nongamers alike to question whether girls and women belong as game players, it is not a surprise that many young women find that their parents, teachers, and mentors do not encourage them to pursue careers in games. That lack of support and encouragement in game-playing contexts may affect the likelihood that a female student will enroll in a computer science or game design class, or whether she will decide to pursue a career in games or technology.

Reversing these trends and recruiting more women as programmers, game developers, and technology industry leaders is crucial not just because these jobs tend to come with competitive benefits and relatively high salaries (Gamasutra Salary Survey, 2014; Siwek, 2014) but also because the industry is missing out on a significant pool of creative talent. This has implications for the ways we interact with digital tools (Hayes, 2010). Research shows there are far-reaching consequences when design landscapes do not consist of a diverse pool of problem solvers and designers. *Science* (Woolley et al., 2010) found that the proportion of women in a group was positively and significantly correlated with the group's collective intelligence. In their opening pages of *Unlocking the Clubhouse,* Margolis and Fisher (2002) cite examples that demonstrate how lack of diversity on design teams can result in product design that does not serve the needs of a diverse user base. If we want to recruit more women to technology fields like game design, or make the game industry a better place for the women who work in technology, it is imperative that their contributions be recognized and valued.

Much research explores the gender divide in technology fields broadly (Cohoon & Aspray, 2008). Related fields like computer science have benefited from in-depth ethnographic accounts of the education trajectories of young women, such as Margolis and Fisher's (2002) *Unlocking the Clubhouse.* To date, there is less research on the trajectories of women who design games. Past studies focus on one-time game design efforts with younger girls (Denner, 2007; Denner & Campe, 2008; Kafai, 1996, 1998) or specific industry issues like crunch time (Consalvo, 2008).[1] Many educators and industry leaders lack understanding of the learning pathways, experiences, and expectations of women who have made careers in game design. The result is these educators and leaders are left underinformed about the resources and supports women need to persist in the face of career challenges they are likely to face in the game industry. This study seeks to examine how participants describe their educational and professional pathways to games and to understand their experiences as women working in the industry.

Methods and Analysis
Participants

Twenty-one people participated in this study—20 women and one participant who identifies as gender queer. To recruit participants, I reached out to game developers and members of the games press. Having worked as an editor in the games press prior to beginning graduate school, I had a relatively robust network of game industry professionals who were willing to support this research study. These individuals aided with participant recruitment by sending emails to their professional networks or posting about the study on their Facebook pages and Twitter feeds. I also utilized snowball sampling in cases where participants offered to put me in touch with other women in their networks who they thought would be willing to share their experiences with a researcher.

In designing this study, I sought to explore the different educational and professional pathways that lead women to careers in games. The criteria for participating were not overly specific or prescriptive. To participate, individuals had to self-identify as game industry professionals and have worked in games as their primary professional affiliation for at least two years. These criteria were designed to be inclusive of not just women who hold a specific title, like game designer or game programmer, but also of women who work in a variety of professional capacities within the game industry. I talked to designers, programmers, and producers but also spoke with women in localization, quality assurance, and game journalism. I interviewed two executive directors at nonprofit organizations focused on games, and also I talked to two CEOs working to raise venture capital funds for their growing companies. Finally, some of the women among the research participants had recently left their formal jobs in games, opting to change directions to pursue personal indie design projects or become public speakers and game advocates.[2] See table 6.1 for a more in-depth overview of participants' roles and workplaces.

The majority of participants attended traditional four-year public and private universities, with a total of 21 earned degrees from these types of schools. Four had degrees from a college of art and design and three attended a technical research institution. Additionally, one participant had a community college degree, and one earned a degree from an online university. In selecting participants, the goal was not to meet specific quotas for degrees earned, job titles, age, or race but rather to select participants for diversity in their educational pathways and professional experiences. While this particular study does not explore issues of race and intersectionality, these are important topics for future research.

Interviews

This study utilized an interviewing strategy inspired by the open interview used in person-centered ethnographic research (Hollan & Wellenkamp,

TABLE 6.1.
Research Participants

Participant Name	Primary Industry Job	Primary Workplace
Andrea	Director of Programming	Mid-size game studio
Annabelle	Quality Assurance Lead	Large commercial studio
Bethany	Chief Executive Officer	Independent game studio
Casey	Programmer	Educational game studio
Cassie	Game Designer	Educational game studio
Debbie	Artist	Educational game studio
Erin	Executive Director	Non-profit education org
Eva	Game Designer	Educational game studio
Grace	Game Designer	Mid-size game studio
Josephine	Indie Game Designer	Independent game studio
Kate	Game Journalist	Game-based press outlet
Kim	Executive Director	Non-profit advocacy org
Maggie	Chief Executive Officer	Mid-size game studio
Margaret	Game Developer	Independent game studio
Marie	Industry Recruiter	Commercial game studios
Mia	Chief Executive Officer	Mobile game studio
Naomi	Game Designer	Independent designer
Natalie	Artist	Mid-size game studio
Savannah	Producer & Localization	Large commercial studio
Sera	Quality Assurance	Variety of Game Studios
Teagan	Game Designer	Independent artist & designer

1994; Levy & Wellenkamp, 1989; Stevens et al., 2008) and the three-part interview series outlined by Seidman in his book *Interviewing as Qualitative Research* (2013). The most appealing feature of Seidman's technique is its focus on understanding participants as unique individuals. For this research, it was important that the interviews reveal not the experiences of participants—what they have done—but also what personal meanings they ascribe to their experiences (Seidman, 2013).

I conducted interviews over a period of six months, in four different states, including two game conferences—one academic and one industry-focused. The majority of the interviews were conducted in-person—at coffee shops and cafes, in hotel rooms, and in outdoor spaces near the conference venues. Three of the interviews were conducted over Skype. Interviews ranged from 40 minutes to nearly 4 hours in length. I recorded and transcribed each interview personally, ultimately generating nearly 500 pages of transcripts. As part of the transcription process, I assigned each participant a pseudonym and removed identifying information such as company names and locations. Since women who work in games are frequently targets of harassment, particular care went into obscuring information that could put participants at risk.

Using a semistructured interview protocol, each interview had three major parts: the first focused on each participant's education experiences and trajectory to games, the second focused on their current experiences as a woman or gender queer person in the game industry, and the final section emphasized what it means to participants to be in games and what they expect from the future for diversity and inclusivity in the industry. The interview protocol for each section contained six to eight prepared questions, but depending on the participant's experience and the direction the interview went, I asked each participant slightly different versions of questions and asked them to elaborate on topics unique to their experience.

Procedure for Analysis

The analysis process began with one round of descriptive coding (Saldaña, 2013) on each interview before generating a more focused coding scheme for a second round of coding and memo writing. I completed all coding and memo writing using qualitative research software *MAXQDA*. The final coding scheme consisted of two different types of codes—pathway codes about participants' personal and professional pathways, and value codes, applied to sections where participants talk about things and people they value. By coding for major themes in participants' pathways and by identifying similarities and differences in the values of participants, I was able to identify shared themes and threads in participants' trajectories and experiences in the game industry.

In the following sections, I focus on two themes that apply directly to researchers and educators interested in issues of digital equity and opportunity—introducing games as a possible career path early on in girls' childhoods and making girls aware of the many skills, roles, and pathways that can lead to careers in games. The data contains other avenues worth exploring in future published work, but these two themes are most relevant for this book's readers. I begin by outlining the potential positive impacts of introducing girls to games and game making early.

Introducing Games as a Possible Career Path

Among the women in this study, several of the participants articulated that introducing girls to games as a potential career path early on can have a tremendous impact on how they interact with technology throughout their youth. Eva, a game designer for a company that makes games for learning, called this phenomenon making games a part of girls' "possibility space." In this section, I highlight four interviews where the participants were especially articulate about the importance of introducing games as a part of girls' possibility spaces. One is a conversation with Savannah, where she described a persistent love of games in her childhood but lack of guidance from adults in her life on games as a possible career pathway. The second interview in this section was with Josephine, who came to game design later than most of the participants, in part because of labels assigned to her by teachers and administrators. The two concluding interviews with Eva and Sera discussed their work as mentors and advocates for girls to help them feel comfortable and confident with their skills in technology. In each of these interviews, the participant described how her experience led her to believe in the importance of supporting girls in identifying games as a possible trajectory.

At the time of her interview, Savannah worked as an English localization editor for a major game publisher in the Pacific Northwest. She entered the game industry midway through her career after completing her undergraduate degree in English and a graduate degree in creative writing. Savannah has been an avid gamer since early childhood. This love of games did not immediately translate into a natural pathway to games for Savannah, however. She explained, "Nobody ever mentioned [games] as a possible career choice for me. Nobody ever asked me, 'What are your interests? You like video games? Well why don't we look at a career path that way?' And I think that's a big lost opportunity."

At several points in her interview, Savannah expressed feeling frustrated by the fact that her teachers, counselors, and family members projected a narrow vision for what they told her she could do, encouraging her to become a teacher because it was a traditionally acceptable path for young women. "Being a teacher is great," she says. "We definitely need teachers. But why are we only encouraging little girls to be teachers?"

Savannah eventually found her way to games, starting out in the industry as an English localization editor. Realizing that there were career paths in the game industry that aligned with her background in English and creative writing was powerful for Savannah. Once she identified a career in games as a possibility, she moved forward by attending conferences and pursuing networking opportunities. She even made a long-distance move to be better positioned to work in games. When we spoke, Savannah was pursuing a more recent career aspiration—becoming a narrative designer. Savannah is confident in her ability to learn new skills, but she expressed that she sometimes feels a bit behind—that she is lacking skills that she may have pursued earlier on if games had been a part of her trajectory.

Like Savannah, indie game developer Josephine also described not realizing that games were a possible career path in her childhood. Josephine's story differs a bit from Savannah's, however, in that she did not play many video games in her childhood. Overall, she had very little exposure to technology in her youth. Josephine's family did not own any game consoles, and she did not have access to a home computer until she was 17. In high school Josephine learned only basic word processing skills and was not encouraged to delve deeper into technology. If anything, she was discouraged from technology, as a result of an early diagnosis with a learning disability. Because her school only encouraged students who were classified as "gifted" to pursue technology, Josephine felt alienated throughout her K–12 education. She explained, "The tech stuff was for the gifted kids. I was shut out of a lot of that. It was obvious to me growing up in school that I can't do that because they have the gifted kids doing that."

In college, Josephine became deeply enamored with the game *Myst* and realized she was interested in making her own games and began experimenting with computer programming in her free time. She explained her realization: "I was just playing around with Flash and realized that I could re-create *Myst*. I don't think I was thinking about it like, 'Oh, I can make games.' It was just I want to make this thing and see what I can do with it. And then it morphed into, 'Oh, I can make games.'" Josephine said that this realization led to her to become "slightly obsessed" with the idea of making games, so she began to teach herself ActionScript, an object-oriented programming language for the Adobe Flash Player platform. Not having access to mentors to scaffold her progress with learning to program and design games, she initially made games by experimenting and setting personally meaningful goals.

Eva's interview highlighted the impacts she has seen when girls are introduced to game-making early on. She says that girls who know how to make games will often choose to make a game instead of taking a more traditional approach to school projects, such as writing a report or making a poster. By going through that process of choosing to make a game and then making it, girls acquire experience and confidence with the game-making process. She notes that a key moment is when girls see themselves as game designers. "It just changes their thinking. And when that's a part of their possibility space," she says, "the change is big."

Another interviewee, Sera, emphasized the importance of creating safe, inclusive, and supportive environments for girls to explore games as a possibility. She believes it is critical that these opportunities span from middle school up through a young woman's first years in the game industry. Having always valued volunteer work, Sera is involved with a number of education initiatives with groups like the Girl Scouts and youth groups. She said, "The key is reaching the girls when they're in middle school and junior high to combat the culture that says the engineering and math stuff is for boys." Sera has found that just showing girls that game design is fun and that it is an option for them can be really powerful. "Women are not this mythical thing in games, even if it looks like it sometimes," she added. She recently co-managed a project where girls attended a workshop for game design and STEM (science, technology, engineering, and math) skills. In addition to making and playtesting games, they also had the opportunity to talk to female developers. "We saw a lot of girls coming out and saying, maybe I can be an engineer or maybe I can be a game developer," she explained. Identifying these types of careers as possible pathways early on can have a major impact on what kinds of opportunities girls are likely to seek out and pursue.

The importance of supporting girls in identifying games as a potential career path came up frequently in many of the interviews. Interview participants expressed wishing that their parents, teachers, and other role models had suggested or supported games as a possible career path earlier in their educational trajectories. Savannah and Josephine's career outcomes would suggest that they are success stories in their current situations, but both women expressed feeling let down by their experiences with formal school institutions. Eva and Sera's experiences working with youth show that early exposure to game design can be empowering.

Several of the study participants, like Savannah, described having a persistent passion for games throughout their childhoods but noted that no one ever encouraged them to consider games as a possible professional pathway. Savannah expressed feeling like the adults in her life encouraged her to pursue traditionally feminine careers such as teaching. She believes she would have benefited from having someone encourage her at a younger age to consider how her lifelong passion for video games might lead to a career.

Stories like Josephine's suggest that some young women lack access to mentors and experiences that introduce game design as a possibility. Josephine lacked exposure to technology early on because of the early diagnosis of her learning disability and her lack of resources both at home and in school. Education researchers Ray McDermott, Shelley Goldman, and Hervé Varenne (2006) documented how the diagnosis of learning abilities sometimes results in gatekeeping procedures in schools, where students who have been diagnosed with a learning disability are unable to access the same opportunities and resources as students who are seen as gifted or advanced. Josephine's description of her experience in school suggests that having the label of a learning disability may have led her to be excluded from opportunities for advanced engagement with technology, a skill set she was already at risk of being excluded from based on her gender and family income. Instead of helping her to find this passion for games and programming, Josephine's experience with school was the exact opposite. Her formal schooling left her believing that tinkering and creating with technologies was only for a small segment of gifted students. Lack of access to technology and tech-savvy mentors at home exacerbated this assumption.

It may be that earlier access to these types of resources could help young women like Savannah and Josephine get an earlier start with learning skills and building networks in areas like games, technology, and coding. Transforming educational spaces into places that challenge gender and racial stereotypes rather than perpetuate them is critical. One positive experience early on has the potential to empower girls not just with the skills and knowledge of basic game design but also to pave the way for the girls to develop identities as technologically competent young women who can imagine themselves as professional game designers and leaders in technology fields (Denner, 2007; Denner, Bean, & Martinez, 2009).

Being able to develop an identity as a tech-savvy person or as a game designer early on may have the effect of helping students in underrepresented groups seek out resources to help them understand how to pursue careers in games or technology (Goode, 2010). In the next section, I highlight how the interviews revealed that there are diverse pathways for getting into the game industry but that many young people operate under the misconception that there are certain skills or credentials, such as computer programming, that are required. Combating these misconceptions by emphasizing that there are many ways to pursue game careers may encourage students who would otherwise believe that working in games is beyond their capability.

Showcasing the Many Skills, Roles, and Pathways That Lead to Games

A second theme that came up frequently when I asked women about their trajectories to game careers centered on their beliefs about what skills or experiences are required to work in games. Several of the participants described a disconnect between a specific pathway that they *thought* was required to get into games and a reality in which a diverse array of skills, roles, and trajectories might lead to a career in games. This section highlights the reflections of four participants who talked about their experience of discovering and communicating that people with a diverse array of skills contribute to making games.

Cassie described that she did not believe she had an appropriate skill set to work in games because she majored in English during college. Erin, who leads a student group at a large university, says she sees many women who share Cassie's thought process—that their chosen major does not align closely enough with the game industry for them to feel comfortable pursuing a career in the field.

Others have majors that are a natural match for careers in games but face other roadblocks. For example, Andrea chose to major in computer science at her university but midway through her studies encountered a teacher who questioned whether women have the ability to do the advanced math required for completing a degree in computer science. Finally, I write about Teagan as an advocate for marginalized game players and designers. Teagan's work aims to empower diverse voices in game design, including underrepresented groups who often do not feel confident that they belong in the game industry.

People often believe that a degree in computer science is required to work in games, but the diverse backgrounds of participants in this study suggest that this might be more misconception than reality. More participants in this study have degrees in English (four participants) than in computer science (three participants). Others majored in geography, philosophy, and printmaking—all majors that one would not typically associate with a career in games. Many of the women reported that before they had their first job in games, they thought it would be impossible for someone with their skill set and experience to get into the industry. Similarly, several of the women expressed feeling like they were behind because they did not earn college degrees that had more obvious and direct pathways to games.

One of these participants is Cassie, an English major. At the time of her interview, Cassie was working as a game developer at a prominent educational game studio in the Midwest. During college at a large state university, Cassie became convinced that games have the potential to be powerful teaching tools for students. However, even as her interest in making educational games grew, she doubted that she had the skills to contribute to creating the changes she wanted to see. As an English major, Cassie did not believe she had the skills required to work in game design. She described thinking, "I probably can't do that [design games] because I have an English degree. And I don't know anything about making games." She was ready to opt out of game design as a possible trajectory on the grounds that she did not feel she had the right credentials to be a successful game designer.

One issue that came up frequently in the interviews was that some women rule out career paths in games as a possibility because they are not proficient in computer programming. Erin was particularly articulate about this issue. Erin is the executive director of a student-centered nonprofit organization at a large university in the Upper Midwest. Her organization aims to support students who are interested in pursuing careers in games. Since the geographic area where this university is located is not a major hub for the game industry, Erin and her partners work to help students find internships and build networks in games. She reported that many of the students they serve stopped attending the organization's meetings and events because they did not think they had the right skill set for pursuing games. She explained: "There was a big discussion where a lot of students were saying, 'Oh, I want to work in games, but I'm not a developer. I'm not computer science. What can I do? I don't think I can do anything.' And then they shut down. And they left." Erin said the misconception that only people who are proficient programmers can work in the game industry holds many students back from taking advantage of opportunities. She believes this is particularly true for students who do not see themselves as fitting the stereotypical game developer profile, which particularly affects women and students of color. These students are at risk for ruling themselves out for professional pathways in games before they really get started.

Other participants had an interest in games or computer science but were identified by others as not fitting the right profile. One of these stories is from Andrea. Andrea earned a computer science degree from a large university in the Midwest. Having had exposure to computer science as early as elementary school, Andrea was more confident in her ability to learn computer science than many of the participants in the study. This confidence, however, did not make her immune to other people trying to deter her. She shared her experience with a math class in college: "To get your Comp Sci degree at my school you take three semesters of Calculus. It's not light on the math. I had a math TA tell me flat out that women were no good at math. I had to come to his office hours to ask about something and he was like, 'You didn't do very well on the test because women are no good at math. You guys should just go somewhere else.' I dropped that class section. I did not want to deal with that guy." Fortunately, Andrea joined a different section, passed the calculus class, and completed her computer science degree even when her boyfriend at the time dropped out of the program. Someone telling her she did not fit the right profile for her interests did not deter her.

Gender queer indie game developer, artist, and programmer Teagan is an advocate for marginalized game players and developers. Like Erin, Teagan is concerned about what happens to people who do not fit the game developer profile or stereotype. Observing that gaming communities often marginalize games that cover serious topics like gender, identity, and diversity, Teagan observed firsthand the "death of a thousand paper cuts and micro-aggressions" that has become a part of the rhetoric around women in technology. Early experiences in games made Teagan realize "there was a general culture that is not overtly, but covertly, hostile to people like me. And women also. And anybody who isn't of the traditional player demographic."

Rather than becoming demoralized, Teagan was inspired to become an advocate for marginalized gamers who are underrepresented in the current game market. "I'm an artist first," Teagan says. "But I empower other artists too because I want a community of people." Teagan's approach is to empower people to tell their own stories through interactive narrative. Teagan explained: "Part of building a community is to empower, to create the community that you want to see. So if I empower the voices I want to see more of in my community, then educating them and giving them the tools to learn this stuff is really important."

This same sentiment of supporting communities of diverse voices in game design came up in Erin's interview: "We need to find the communities of designers. We need to find the communities of artists. We need to find sound designers. We need to find all of these people and tap into those communities and bring them all together." By bringing different types of people with different backgrounds in to make games together, Erin's organization is able to foster diversity and help students gain confidence, believing that they have something of value to contribute. She said, "For students, and for female students especially, finding a space where they feel like they have a support system and a safe space is tough."

The threads from the interviews described above suggest that young people develop misconceptions about the requirements of working in the game industry or other technology-based fields. Sometimes these misconceptions come from other people and work to deter young people who do not fit a specific profile or stereotype from pursuing opportunities in games and technology. Andrea made it through the math courses required for her computer science degree, but other students might have been more adversely affected or discouraged by similar experiences and risked dropping out along the way.

Another misconception is the belief that computer programming is the singular pathway to a career in games. Cassie is not alone in thinking that her degree does not align closely enough with the game industry for her to be a good candidate for jobs in games. There is a widespread perception that game designers are either lifelong programmers or graduates with highly technical degrees like computer science. Of course, this is often the case, but it is not the *only* pathway to a career in game development.

Learning to program is an increasingly important skill in the contemporary world—one that has been getting well-deserved national attention from major political leaders like President Obama with his Computer Science for All initiative (The White House, 2015). However, emphasizing the role of programming too much may inadvertently give some students the impression that there is one single path to a career in games or other technology fields. Since women are heavily underrepresented in computer science classes, this misconception is likely to disproportionately affect young women.

Accounts from the participants in this study suggest that overemphasizing programming is intimidating to some young women and can act as a deterrent. These types of misconceptions prevent some students from pursuing classes and opportunities that could position them as strong candidates for top-tier jobs in technology industries. When these students are deterred from taking the first steps into those careers because they discount their value before entering the industry, we lose perspectives, ideas, and skills that could otherwise do a lot to diversify games and technology industries more broadly.

Conclusion: Opening the Doors to Digital Clubhouses

In this chapter, I outlined some of the ways in which well-intentioned parents and educators become accidental participants in practices that discourage and deter girls and women from engaging in game design, computer programming, and other technology-related skills. I discussed why increasing the number of girls and women in computer science, games, and technology matters and what is at risk if young women continue to feel excluded from digital clubhouses—spaces like home, afterschool game design programs, computer science classes, and professional workplaces in the game and technology industries. Using data from interviews with women who work in the game industry, I outlined two recommendations for educators to keep in mind as they work to design experiences that are inclusive to women and other underrepresented groups. These include introducing games to girls' possibility spaces earlier on and showcasing the diversity of skills, roles, and pathways that young women can take to pursue games and technology professionally.

Granted, interviewing 21 women in the game industry is just a small step on a much larger trajectory of research exploring avenues for increased diversity and equity in games and technology. While this research is able to hint at possible directions that educators, mentors, and other stakeholders might take, additional research is necessary to determine what specific actions hold the most promise for creating empowering experiences for girls in technology. Future studies could investigate the utility of existing resources and evaluate new curricula and programs designed to promote increased diversity and equity.

Finally, this chapter retains a focus specifically on girls and women, but there are other marginalized and excluded groups whose participation is just as critical. Women of color face additional barriers that may require other types of interventions, resources, and programs to boost their participation as game designers and digital content creators. Research focusing specifically on intersectionality and the experiences of women of color is needed to reach the most underrepresented populations in the digital game industry, such as Black and Hispanic women.

In the current climate of the game and technology industries, many people struggle to feel a sense of belonging, and they doubt that their contributions will be valued. But there are also increasing numbers of parents and teachers, industry leaders, and scholars—like those who have contributed their voices to this volume—who are eager to throw open the doors to inclusivity. There is no single solution, nor is this a task that can be accomplished overnight. Changing culture is complicated. But by making conscious efforts to diversify digital clubhouses, educators, mentors, and industry leaders can contribute to a more connected and creative digital landscape for all.

NOTES

1. Crunch time is a common practice in the gaming industry when the development team is perceived as being behind on the development timeline and the developers are encouraged or required to work overtime hours. Some development studios are notorious for planning crunch into the development cycle, essentially expecting that all projects will reach a point where the team is required to put in crunch hours.

2. Indie, or independent games, are games made by individuals or small teams without financial backing from a game publisher. Many game developers opt to make independent games to have greater freedom to pursue their own ideas or to focus on innovation.

REFERENCES

Barker, L. J., & Aspray, W. (2008). The state of research on girls and IT. In J. M. Cohoon & W. Aspray (Eds.), *Women and information technology* (pp. 3–53). Cambridge, MA: MIT Press.

Cassell, J., & Jenkins, H. (1998). Chess for girls? Feminism and computer games. In J. Cassell & H. Jenkins (Eds.), *From Barbie to Mortal Kombat: Gender and computer games* (pp. 2–45). Cambridge, MA: MIT Press.

Cohoon, J. M., & Aspray, W. (2008). A critical review of the research on women's participation in postsecondary computing education. In J. M. Cohoon & W. Aspray (Eds.), *Women and information technology* (pp. 137–180). Cambridge, MA: MIT Press.

Consalvo, M. (2008). Crunched by passion: Women game developers and workplace challenges. In Y. Kafai, C. Heeter, J. Denner, & J. Y. Sun (Eds.), *Beyond Barbie and Mortal Kombat: New perspectives on gender and gaming* (pp. 177–191). Cambridge, MA: MIT Press.

Denner, J. (2007). The Girls Creating Games Program: An innovative approach to integrating technology into middle school. *Meridian: A Middle School Computer Technologies Journal, 1*(10).

Denner, J., Bean, S., & Martinez, J. (2009). The girl game company: Engaging Latina girls in information technology. *Afterschool Matters, 8*, 26–35.

Denner, J., & Campe, S. (2008). What games made by girls can tell us. In Y. Kafai, C. Heeter, J. Denner, & J. Y. Sun (Eds.), *Beyond Barbie and Mortal Kombat: New perspectives on gender and gaming* (pp. 129–145). Cambridge, MA: MIT Press.

Edwards, K., Weststar, J., Meloni, W., Pearce, C., & Legault, M.-J. (2014). Developer satisfaction survey 2014: Summary report. *International Games Developer Association*. Retrieved from https://c.ymcdn.com/sites/www.igda.org/resource/collection/9215B88F-2AA3-4471-B44D -B5D58FF25DC7/IGDA_DSS_2014-Summary_Report.pdf.

Entertainment Software Association. (2013). *Essential facts about the computer and video game industry*. Retrieved from http://www.isfe.eu/sites/isfe.eu/files/attachments/esa_ef _2013.pdf.

Ericson, B. (2014). *Detailed data on pass rates, race, and gender for 2013*. Retrieved from http://home.cc.gatech.edu/ice-gt/556.

Gamasutra. (2014). *Gamasutra salary survey 2014*. Retrieved from http://www.gamasutra.com /salarysurvey2014.pdf.

Goode, J. (2010). The digital identity divide: How technology knowledge impacts college students. *New Media & Society, 12*(3), 497–513.

Grover, S., & Pea, R. (2013). Computational thinking in K–12: A review of the state of the field. *Educational Researcher, 42*(1), 38–43.

Hayes, C. C. (2010). Computer science: The incredible shrinking woman. In T. J. Misa (Ed.), *Gender codes: Why women are leaving computing* (pp. 25–39). Hoboken, NJ: Wiley & Sons.

Hollan, D. W., & Wellenkamp, J. C. (1994). *Contentment and suffering: Culture and experience in Toraja.* New York, NY: Columbia University Press.

Ito, M., Baumer, S., Bittanti, M., boyd, d., Cody, R., Herr-Stephenson, B., . . . Tripp, L. (2010). *Hanging out, messing around, and geeking out: Kids living and learning with new media.* Cambridge, MA: MIT Press.

Jenson, J., & Brushwood Rose, C. (2003). Women@work: Listening to gendered relations of power in teachers' talk about new technologies. *Gender & Education, 15*(2), 169–181.

Kafai, Y. B. (1996). Gender differences in children's constructions of video games. In P. Greenfield & R. Cocking (Eds.), *Interacting with video* (pp. 39–66). Norwood, NJ: Ablex Publishing.

———. (1998). Video game designs by girls and boys: Variability and consistency of gender differences. In J. Cassell & H. Jenkins (Eds.), *From Barbie to Mortal Kombat: Gender and computer games* (pp. 90–117). Cambridge, MA: MIT Press.

Kafai, Y. B., & Sutton, S. (1999). Elementary school students' computer and Internet use at home: Current trends and issues. *Journal of Educational Computing Research, 21*(3), 345–362.

Kurtzleben, D. (2014, January 14). AP test shows wide gender gap in computer science. *US News and World Report.* Retrieved from http://www.usnews.com/news/blogs/data-mine/2014/01/14/ap-test-shows-wide-gender-gap-in-computer-science-physics.

Lenhart, A. (2015). Teen, social media and technology overview 2015. *Pew Research Center.* Retrieved from http://www.pewinternet.org/files/2015/04/PI_TeensandTech_Update2015_0409151.pdf.

Levy, R. I., & Wellenkamp, J. C. (1989). Methodology in the anthropological study of emotion. In R. Plutchik and H. Kellerman (Eds.), *Emotion: Theory, research, and experience* (vol. 4, pp. 205–232). New York, NY: Academic Press.

Margolis, J., & Fisher, A. (2002). *Unlocking the clubhouse: Women in computing.* Cambridge, MA: MIT Press.

McDermott, R., Goldman, S., & Varenne, H. (2006). The cultural work of learning disabilities. *Educational Researcher, 35*(6), 12–17.

National Center for Women & Information Technology. (2012). *By the numbers.* Retrieved from http://www.ncwit.org/sites/default/files/legacy/pdf/ByTheNumbers09.pdf.

Ochsner, A. (forthcoming). Reasons why: Examining the experience of women in games 140 characters at a time. *Games and Culture.*

Ono, H., & Zavodny, M. (2003). Gender and the Internet. *Social Science Quarterly, 84*(1), 111–121.

Pew Research Center. (2016). *Social media fact sheet.* Retrieved from http://www.pewinternet.org/fact-sheet/social-media/.

Saldaña, J. (2013). *The coding manual for qualitative researchers* (2nd ed.). Thousand Oaks, CA: Sage.

Seidman, I. (2013). *Interviewing as qualitative research: A guide for researchers in education and the social sciences* (4th ed.). New York, NY: Teachers College Press.

Siwek, S. E. (2014). Video games in the 21st century. *Entertainment Software Association.* Retrieved from http://www.theesa.com/wp-content/uploads/2014/11/VideoGames21stCentury_2014.pdf.

Stevens, R., O'Connor, K., Garrison, L., Jocuns, A., & Daniel M. A. (2008). Becoming an engineer: Toward a three dimensional view of engineering learning. *Journal of Engineering Education, 97*(3), 355–368.

US Department of Labor. (2013). *Bureau of Labor Statistics: Occupational outlook handbook.* Retrieved from http://www.bls.gov/ooh/.

Wasserman, I. M., & Richmond-Abbott, M. (2005). Gender and the Internet: Causes of variation in access, level, and scope of use. *Social Science Quarterly, 86*(1), 252–270.

Weststar, J., & Legault, M. J. (2015, September 2). *International Game Developers Association developer satisfaction survey 2015—summary report.* Retrieved from https://www.igda.org/?page=dss2015.

The White House. (2015). *Fact sheet: President Obama announces Computer Science for All initiative.* Retrieved from https://www.whitehouse.gov/the-press-office/2016/01/30/fact-sheet-president-obama-announces-computer-science-all-initiative-0.

Woolley, A. W., Chabris, C. F., Pentland, A., Hashmi, N., & Malone, T. W. (2010). Evidence for a collective intelligence factor in the performance of human groups. *Science, 330*(6004), 686–688.

CHAPTER SEVEN

Supporting Youth to Envision Careers in Computer Science

CRYSTLE MARTIN

Coding creates opportunities for youth to develop interests and to envision potential avenues for those interests. There remains a persistent gap in the participation of African American and Hispanic workers in computer science fields (NCWIT, 2015; NCSES, 2015), particularly with coding. A starting point to address this gap would be to facilitate early opportunities for underrepresented youth to explore coding and envision future coding careers. The intent of the chapter is to illustrate ways in which youth who are underrepresented in computer science are exposed to coding as an interest and how this exposure, when supported by peers and adults, impacts their process for envisioning future computer science careers.

I begin by examining research on early exposure to out-of-school interests and the impact that can have for girls and youth of color in future aspirations. I then present empirical findings from interviews with youth who participate in the online coding community *Scratch*. The interviews focus on participants' entry into coding through *Scratch*, and how using the tool prompted participants to envision careers in coding. I contend that entry into coding, with support from peers and caring adults, can create sustained participation, deepened interest, and envisioned future careers in computer science. As I elaborate below, coding is using a specified set of characters that is translated by the computer into an output like software or a video game. The importance of coding pertains to the growing gap between the number of computer science positions and the number of qualified applicants for those positions (Kalil & Jahanian, 2013). This study offers a starting point to examine opportunities to support underrepresented youth by introducing coding, cultivating interests, and channeling those interests into coding-related careers.

Impact of Extracurricular Activities on Youth Interest and Aspiration

Starting in early adolescence, youth begin to think concretely about their futures, and these early thoughts impact how youth develop interest in a career (Auger, Blackhurst, & Wahl, 2005; Bandura, Barbaranelli, Caprara, & Pastorelli, 2001; Riegle-Crumb, Moore, & Ramos-Wada, 2011). For many youth of color and girls, early exposure begins in school settings. However, research highlights that, despite attempts to address inequality through formal education, gender and racial/ethnic disparities have become more stratified (Riegle-Crumb & King, 2010). Women and girls from low-income families face more obstacles, such as lack of access to academic classes and out-of-school activities, which in turn reduce their career aspirations and expectations (Domenico & Jones, 2007; Khallad, 2000; Toglia, 2013; Watson, Quatman, & Edler, 2002).

A report from the National Women's Law Center offers several suggestions to help eliminate educational disparity in STEM (science, technology, engineering, and math) for diverse youth. The report suggests "increasing access to educational opportunities that promote diversity and reduce racial isolation" and "ensuring access to curricula that will help students build strong academic foundations . . . such as STEM courses and courses . . . that develop critical-thinking, reading, and math skills" (NAACP, 2014, p. 38). It also encourages schools to "improve extracurricular opportunities and participation among African American girls" and to "improve STEM opportunities and achievement for African American girls" (NAACP, 2014, p. 43) but does not offer specific recommendations to carry out these charges.

Analysis of extracurricular activities by Covay and Carbonaro (2010) suggests that higher levels of participation by upper-income families contribute to advantages in noncognitive and cognitive skills. This is not an irreconcilable equity gap, but it is important to understand that the gap between what upper-income and lower-income families spend on enrichment activities has been consistently widening. Expenditure on these activities for the bottom income quintile has stagnated since the early 1970s (Duncan & Murnane, 2011). However, for those in the top income quintile it has grown by more than two-and-a-half times in the same time period, widening existing inequalities.

Research on interest and exposure as a way to impact youth career paths does offer some hope to impact the existing inequality; even brief exposure to a topic can spark a lasting interest or highlight a potential career that the youth may want to pursue (Modi, Schoenberg, & Salmond, 2012; National Research Council, 2011). Youth of color and white youth report almost equal rates of initial interest in STEM as a college major despite dramatic differences in the rates at which they pursue STEM majors (Anderson & Kim, 2006; Hanson, 2006). This can be caused by many factors, including lack of support from caring adults and mentors, lack of understanding of career options, and structural and institutional barriers. It is necessary for learners to have access to continual opportunities for positive experiences that offer up future trajectories (Ahn et al., 2014).

The equity gap begins to break along gender, race/ethnic, and socioeconomic lines, and it ripples from K–12 education to career choices. Of the 25% of women in computing jobs, women of color make up the smallest percent (NCWIT, 2015). Of this 25%, 3% are African American women and 1% are Latinas. This is compared to white women (16%) and Asian women (5%). Only 5% of scientists and engineers working in science and engineering occupations are African American, and 6% are Hispanic, compared to 71% white and 17% Asian (NCSES, 2015).

Based on previous work suggesting that improvement in STEM opportunities could be obtained through interest-driven and informal learning spaces, this study focuses on coding in online communities. Interest-driven spaces offer youth the opportunity to explore identity and agency (Martin, 2012, 2014), trying on different roles that they could transfer outside of that setting. Transfers can include connecting to related career paths. Ochsner (2012) found that people used their video game and fan fiction online communities as places to try out and visualize different career paths.

What Is Coding and Why Is It Important?

Coding is what makes it possible to create software, apps, and websites. It involves using a language made of letters and numbers that a computer can read to create a program or output. Learning to code develops problem solving, creativity, digital literacy, and computational thinking skills (Brennan & Resnick, 2012; Togyer-Sun, 2011). The popular press has extolled the virtues of coding and has supported shifts to integrate it into youth education (Crow, 2014; Dishman, 2016; Kohli, 2015; Mims, 2015; Missio, 2015). In 2015, President Obama (2016) launched the Computer Science for All initiative, which made coding a national education priority. Coding is not only relevant to computer science; it can be useful across virtually all fields of expertise. Computational thinking, the framework often used in computer science to create code, involves problem solving, design thinking, and understanding human behavior and is used as a way to interact with and overcome issues in the world, whether virtual or physical (Brennan & Resnick, 2012; Wing, 2006). Computing is involved in all aspects of life, whether it is shopping online, filing taxes, checking out a book at the library, or registering to vote. Jobs in software development are projected to grow 17% between 2014 and 2024 (Bureau of Labor Statistics, 2016). But coding is used by more than just those in software development; it is used in many professions such as research, web design, and art.

Computing jobs are among the fastest-growing and highest-paying, yet few women and minorities are benefiting from these occupations (Bureau of Labor Statistics, 2016; US Department of Labor, 2010). Only 26% of women were in the computing workforce in 2013; of those, 3% were African American women, 5% were Asian women, and 2% were Hispanic women (NCWIT, 2012). The gap in gender and race starts before people reach a career in computer science. In 2012, 57% of undergraduate degree recipients were women, but only 18% of computer and information science undergraduate degree recipients were women (NCWIT, 2012). Girls comprise 56% of all Advanced Placement test-takers but only 19% of AP computer science test-takers (College Board, 2015). People of color represent 13% of Advanced Placement computer science exam-takers (9% Hispanic, 4% Black), 17% of computer science bachelor's degrees (9% Hispanic, 8% Black), and 14% of people employed in computing occupations (8% Black, 6% Hispanic) (College Board, 2015).

Increasing diversity in participation in computer science is important to the improvement of computer science. Studies have shown that increased diversity improves problem solving (Ashcraft & Blithe, 2010; Barker & Aspray, 2006; Papastergiou, 2008; Wulf, 1999). Many barriers remain for reaching equity in coding: unequal opportunities, lack of role models, computing curricula disconnected from interest and environment, and computing portrayed in popular media as masculine and geeky (NCWIT, 2012). These barriers linger for girls and youth of color because of the lack of access to role models and opportunities to expose them to computer science.

Connected Learning

The connected learning framework (Ito et al., 2013) provides mechanisms to trace connections from an interest to career. The framework will be used as an analytical lens through which to examine the data presented in this chapter. Connected learning examines the connections between different aspects of a youth's learning ecology, particularly in three spheres: peer culture, interest, and opportunity (which can include academic, future, and civic; figure 7.1). It focuses on translating and linking informal learning to academic success and eventually career success. Connected learning examines the connections made by youth between their peer, interest, and academic/future opportunity spheres. It also seeks to make those potential connections more equitably available to underserved youth who do not always have access to a robust range of informal learning opportunities because of limited resources (Duncan & Murnane, 2011; Ito et al., 2013).

Research on connected learning has demonstrated that youth in interest-driven communities, like video games and knitting, can connect skills they develop in their interest spaces to economic, civic, and academic opportunities

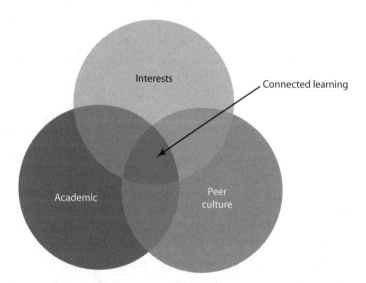

Figure 7.1. Connecting Spheres of Learning. *Source:* Ito et al., 2013; Connected Learning: An Agenda for Research and Design. Image used under Creative Commons Attribution-Noncommercial-No Derivative Works 3.0 United States License.

(Kow, Young, & Salen Tekinbaş, 2014; Pfister, 2014; Rafalow & Salen Tekinbaş, 2014). Rafalow and Salen Tekinbaş (2014) in a study of *LittleBigPlanet 2* players found that because of their involvement in an online community, a few participants were able to connect their interest to economic outcomes, like securing jobs related to their interest. One participant who made economic connections parlayed their participation from *LittleBigPlanet 2* into a position working for Media Molecule, the developer who created the game. In a study of Hogwarts at Ravelry, an online knitting community, Pfister (2014) describes the connections that participants made between their fibercrafting and economic gain. Several participants started selling knitting and crocheting patterns as well as fibercrafts, turning their interest into an entrepreneurial venture. In this chapter, I use the connected learning framework as a lens to explore the intersection of interest and opportunity. I use this intersection to understand the role that exposure to an interest can play in terms of youth envisioning future careers.

Methods

This study focuses on data collected from the online coding program *Scratch,* which will be described below. The *Scratch* community was chosen for this study for its direct connection to informal STEM learning, its large user base, and the diversity of spaces where *Scratch* is used. This section will start with a description of the research context of *Scratch* to help orient the reader.

Research Context

Scratch is a free online visual coding language used for authoring multimedia projects. A visual coding language uses snap-together block-based elements that interlock like Legos instead of written text (figure 7.2). Users program in *Scratch* by dragging blocks from a palette and attaching them in a jigsaw-like fashion. *Scratch* is designed this way to remove barriers to entry into coding, by allowing people to code without having to know how to write the syntax themselves. While it is designed primarily for ages 8 to 16 (https://scratch.mit.edu/parents/), the online community hosts participants younger than 8 through retirement age. The community, as of June 2016, has more than 12 million registered users, more than 15 million projects shared, and nearly 80 million comments posted. Those who participate in the *Scratch* community are called Scratchers.

The online community is made up of two main areas: content creation and the forums. Content creation is where Scratchers make projects. A project can encompass anything, but most fall into six genres: animations, games,

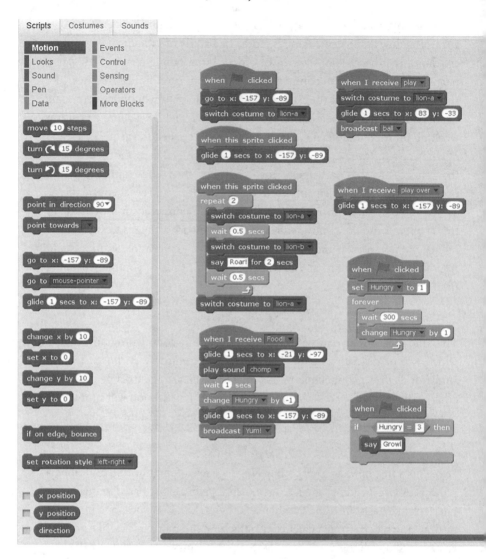

Figure 7.2. Screenshot of the *Scratch* Scripting Interface by the Author. *Source: Scratch. Scratch* is a project of the Lifelong Kindergarten group at the MIT Media Lab. Used under Creative Commons Attribution Share-Alike License 2.0.

simulations, music, art, and stories. Projects can be interactive or passive. The interface borrows elements from popular social media platforms, allowing Scratchers to "love" or "favorite" projects by clicking on the heart or star at the bottom of the project (figure 7.3). Projects can also be remixed and shared again.

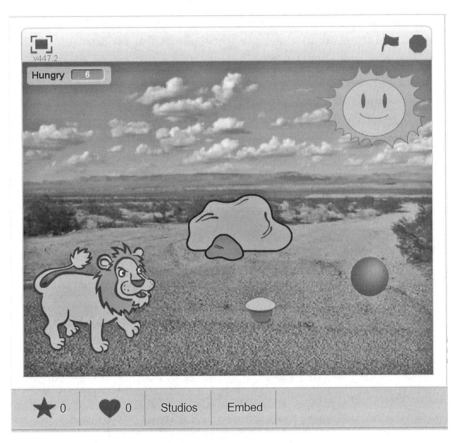

Figure 7.3. Screenshot of Virtual Pet Project by the Author. *Source: Scratch.*
Image used under Creative Commons Attribution Share-Alike License 2.0.

The second area is the forums. Here, members of the *Scratch* community ask and answer longer-form and more technical questions as well as discuss changes to *Scratch* as a coding program and as a community. Many members who participate here are advanced Scratchers and help others solve coding issues.

Participants

Twenty-one females and 19 males participated in this study, for a total of 40 interviews. The participants were youths ranging in age from 8 to 21 years old. All participants were attending school, and most were in high school. A majority of the study participants are considered underrepresented in the computer science field.

I recruited Scratchers from three different spaces: the online *Scratch* community, existing out-of-school/afterschool groups that use *Scratch* to teach coding, and workshops facilitated in conjunction with librarians at two public library systems. Recruitment locations were diversified to capture the breadth of entry points for youth into *Scratch*. I used direct outreach as well as snowball sampling. Those participants recruited from the online community were selected based on their activity level. Other participants were selected based on their participation in *Scratch*-related out-of-school activities.

Through this study, I sought to understand the entry points to *Scratch* for youth, especially for those who came from backgrounds underrepresented in coding. The criteria for participation were not prescriptive, but I actively sought girls and youth of color for interviews. The participants needed to self-identify as being Scratchers or being engaged with *Scratch*. Because *Scratch* offers many different avenues of participation, I did not impose specific limitations, which could privilege certain types of participation over others. I interviewed expert and novice Scratchers who used *Scratch* in a variety of ways. These different use scenarios created opportunities for youth to envision themselves as different types of Scratchers: coders, animators, game designers, and artists. A few of the Scratchers interviewed were expanding their coding practice to other programming languages beyond *Scratch* but still considered *Scratch* important to their practice.

Observations and Interviews

The data presented in this chapter derive from a study investigating opportunities and barriers to equity in coding. Using a sociocultural approach (Vygotsky, 1978), I utilized ethnographic methods (Hammersley & Atkinson, 2007) as a basis for the study. I conducted interviews over an 18-month period with youth who live in the United States and Western Europe. I interviewed each participant once, with follow-up questions conducted through email. Some interviews were conducted in-person, and others by phone or video conferencing. I recorded all the interviews and sent them to a professional transcriptionist for transcribing. Once the interviews were transcribed, I assigned all participants a pseudonym and assigned pseudonyms to all identifying names mentioned by the participants.[1]

The interviews were conducted using a protocol that I developed based on computational thinking and the connected learning framework, which focuses on equity in learning to code. Based on observations from fieldnotes,

I also developed additional questions about community practices. Since this was a semistructured interview protocol, questions and order were flexible based on context and the unique experiences of the respondent.

I conducted 500 hours of observations of the community over 13 months from October 2014 to October 2015 to develop a deeper understanding of the inner workings of *Scratch* community structures. Collecting fieldnotes from the online community required many hours of reading through conversations on the forums and collection of two types of information: descriptive—data taken directly from the forums—and reflective—data that included insights from my observations. A thorough and in-depth understanding of the community was necessary to identify the community's social norms and priorities, including how people generally interact and what quality participation looks like. I used the observational data to supplement my understanding of the *Scratch* community for this analysis.

Analysis

Analysis entailed qualitative coding (Saldaña, 2016) with a priori and emergent codes. The a priori coding drew codes from computational thinking (Brennan & Resnick, 2012) and connected learning (Ito et al., 2013). I completed all coding using the online qualitative research software *Dedoose*. In this chapter I share findings related to the themes of: (1) entering into coding as an interest and (2) envisioning connections from an interest to a career. The two themes are derived from the codes of interest and opportunity from the connected learning portion of the coding scheme. Table 7.1 shows the demographic information of participants from the study who are included in this chapter, as well as the theme they relate to which necessitated their inclusion. Given the large size of the interview sample for an ethnographic study, only participants included in the chapter are included in the table. Analysis specifically looks at the intersection of the interest and opportunity sphere (see figure 7.1), and what these connections and misconnections can tell us about supporting equity in technology fields for diverse youth.

Entering into Coding through Scratch

I asked each participant to describe his or her entry into coding through *Scratch*. Many had been exposed to *Scratch* in school as a one-off use for an assignment. Some had their initial interaction with *Scratch* through an after-school/out-of-school program that was designed to teach coding. A couple

TABLE 7.1.
Research Participants

Participant Name	Age	Gender	Race	Theme
Adelina	16	Female	Mexican	Envisioning Connections
Antonio	14	Male	African American	Entry into Coding
Damian	17	Male	Unknown	Envisioning Connections
Jessica	14	Female	White	Envisioning Connections
Jia	14	Female	Chinese	Entry into Coding
Laretha	16	Female	African American	Envisioning Connections
Pedro	13	Male	Latino	Entry into Coding
Uphoma	13	Female	African American	Entry into Coding

participants were exposed to *Scratch* and coding through family members. For many, the initial experience was enough to pique their interest, which led them to pursue *Scratch* and coding more deeply.

This section will describe the early experiences of four youths as they began to use *Scratch*. Early exposure to an interest like coding can lead to envisioned career paths, which is significant because youth begin to develop career aspirations early in life. To broaden early exposure to activities broadens what careers the youth can envision. The introduction to coding for participants happened through three entry points: out-of-school activities, school and teachers, and family and friends. Early exposure only introduces the potential interest; it is the support of caring adults and peers that facilitates the youth transitioning to sustained engagement. Uphoma and Pedro were first introduced to *Scratch* in school but continued to pursue it outside of a formal learning context with the support of peers and mentors. Antonio was introduced to *Scratch* and coding in an out-of-school activity but continued to explore *Scratch* on his own with the support of friends and teachers. Jia was introduced to *Scratch* through her brother. She experienced barriers to improvement and participation because of lack of support, especially at the beginning of her use of *Scratch* and learning to code. Each interviewee expresses the importance of learning to code and the importance of *Scratch* in their learning.

School as an Entry Point for Coding

Exposure to coding often comes in the form of one-off exposure in school. Uphoma is an African American 13-year-old from a borough of New York who grew up in a single-parent household. She had originally heard about *Scratch* in 6th grade but started using *Scratch* regularly as part of an afterschool program. When asked about using *Scratch* Uphoma says, "Oh, I love *Scratch* because . . . it's very good for a person that's, like me, that's in the sixth grade that doesn't know anything about *Scratch* and to learn how to code. I feel as if it has helped me use other coding resources so I am now better at using coding in other parts of school, like computer class. I'm able to code more because of *Scratch.*" She elaborated about the connections she saw between coding and school. "Sometimes I get ideas from things that go on in my favorite ELA [English language arts] class, like maybe a book we're reading. Sometimes I get inspiration from that kind of standpoint and that makes me want to make a game." Her mother actively supported her participation in the *Scratch* club. "Yes, my mom sometimes she inspires me to make games. She looks over my games and she tells me what she thinks I should add and she tells me whether or not my ideas are good or not good and she gives me good feedback." Uphoma's introduction to *Scratch* and coding in a supportive afterschool setting, where she had peers and a caring adult mentor to help her learn, facilitated her exploration of coding. Her mother's support was also essential in helping her to build confidence in her abilities and value what she was doing.

Pedro's initial interaction with coding also came through school. A 13-year-old Latino student from South Los Angeles, Pedro describes his initial exposure to coding: "It was during, well, last year during my sixth grade electives. It was a math class where we started to do coding. It wasn't *Scratch,* but after that, I was really interested in coding. So I decided to do my own research and found *Scratch.*" He liked *Scratch* because "you don't have any limits, like you can get really creative. You can upload like any image you want, the endless creativity. It's really fun." Pedro is supported in this interest by peers at school "who know how to code" and the youth education organizer of a local community center that he frequents after school. Pedro, like many of the youth interviewed, was willing to do research to find ways to continue to explore his new interest in coding. Pedro was introduced to coding through school, but when his formal learning context did not continue to support his new interest, he found his own way of pursuing it. Access to peers who knew how to code, as well as a mentor in an informal learning setting who fully supported his participation, allowed Pedro to continue to pursue coding on his own.

Out-of-School Activities as Entry Point for Coding

Antonio is a 14-year-old African American high school student who was first introduced to coding and *Scratch* through an out-of-school program. "Well, when I was younger, maybe four years ago, I'm not sure, I went to [a local college],[2] their [summer enrichment][3] program. And I've always had like an interest in computers, so I took a few computer classes and one of the classes involved *Scratch.* And I said, hey, why not? And I wanted to try it." Antonio continued to pursue *Scratch* on his own. Four years after he started his interest in *Scratch,* which had been completely in an informal learning context, he connected coding back to the formal learning context of school. "Yeah. I'm in a computer science class and we're doing *Scratch* now and I help the class." He sees *Scratch* as an expansive learning context. "I mean, there's endless possibilities of what you can do with *Scratch.* The only limit you have is your mind. Actually, and your skill, like your understanding of *Scratch,* but . . . I like it. I mean, because even if I'm helping, like teaching and stuff, I'll still learn new things. There's so many different ways to do one thing, so it's kind of cool." He has started to expand his coding, learning to code in Java. Antonio's introduction to coding in an out-of-school setting led him to an interest in coding, which he pursued on his own, supported by friends and teachers. He is able to tie his interest back to a formal context because his expertise in *Scratch* and the encouragement of his teacher allowed him to help other students in class learn *Scratch,* which he feels further facilitates his own development with coding.

Family/Friends as Entry Point for Coding

Jia, a 14-year-old Chinese American high school student living in the Greater Los Angeles area, entered into *Scratch* entirely outside of any kind of educational structure. She started using *Scratch* at the age of 9. Her brother introduced her to it when she was looking for a way to remake a game she liked because she wanted to make changes to it. She spent a good part of her early time in the *Scratch* community creating a platformer.[4] "My early experiences in the community were okay, but I got to a really slow start. I put a lot of effort into my projects (considered a lot of effort at that age) but barely anyone saw it. I became friends with [two well-known Scratchers][5] and they really motivated me but I still had moments when I felt like I wanted to give up because it seemed that my efforts weren't bringing me anywhere." She feels that this lack of exposure is partly due to her novice understanding at the time of *Scratch,* as she did not know how "featuring or curating worked." The lack of notoriety and visibility on the website creates a barrier for her, making her interactions less fulfilling.

She also feels that gender issues, which inhibit her projects from being seen, are at work in the community. She particularly sees a problem with a group of boys who were a bit younger than she, but who she feels were taking advantage of the system to gain popularity and accolades for their work.[6] "One thing that really bothers me is this group: 11 to 13-year-old males with design accounts who gain popularity very fast by making connections with well-known Scratchers. This isn't necessarily bad, but really bothers me. They switch accounts a lot too which lets them constantly qualify the requirements for being curated when they actually would have surpassed them." Jia sees these practices as unfair to those who are novices, noting that it makes it difficult for those just developing their skills to be recognized for their accomplishments.

The slow start in the community has led Jia to be somewhat apprehensive about sharing her participation with those outside the community. She notes that she has felt "a little embarrassed," so she does not usually share her involvement with *Scratch* and coding with other people, including teachers. She also rarely shares what she does on *Scratch* with her friends, because it is "more part of my internet life than my real life." Her parents are not supportive, viewing her work on *Scratch* "as just games, playing, and wasting my time." However, her brother, who originally introduced her to *Scratch*, plays her games and other projects, giving her support as well as keeping an eye on the comments to make sure she is being treated well. Over time she has become gradually more open "as *Scratch* and programming is starting to become . . . part of me." Despite the adversity she faces using *Scratch,* she enjoys it enough to take computer science classes in school and wants to pursue computer science as a career. Jia's experience is indicative of being introduced in an isolated setting and having little support from peers, family, or caring adults to support her interest in coding. However, her perseverance and continued support from her brother helped her to overcome barriers.

The participants' exposure to coding derived from three sources: out-of-school activities, family and friends, and school and teachers. More than by other means, 18 out of 40 participants reported being introduced to *Scratch* in out-of-school settings. Those who were introduced through out-of-school activities all continued to pursue coding through informal learning contexts. A small group was able to make connections back to formal learning settings. Jia connects her coding experience to her English language arts course and Antonio is able to help fellow students learn to code because of the expertise he developed out of school.

Participants' introduction to coding and *Scratch* in school was the second most common source (16 out of 40). However, none of the participants actually used *Scratch* long term through school. Those who were introduced through school participated in *Scratch* through the online community and out-of-school activities. Although formal learning contexts can create an opportunity for exposure, they do not seem to create an environment that facilitates long-term exploration of the interest. This appears to be from lack of a sustained social environment; the participants who were most successful were able to access sustained social environments with others who supported their interest.

Support from peers and caring adults is key to the successful exploration and development of coding no matter the point of entry. The selection of participants who are actively using *Scratch* definitely weighted this data in favor of those who had supporters who encouraged their interest in coding, but for those who did not have the support the impact was obvious. Pedro's experience shows that even passing exposure can be empowering and can create opportunities for strong interest development. The more consistent the support, the more likely the youth was to continue and excel in coding.

Several study participants describe a passion for coding but note that they lack support and even endure active dissuasion by adults in their life. Those who experience this lack of support often ignore the lack of support, not understanding the impact it could have on them. For example, Jia says that her parents are "pretty old" and do not play games, which is why she thinks they do not support her interest in coding.

A report released by the Girl Scouts of America indicates that girls who have participated in "hands-on science activities, gone to science/tech museums, and engaged in an extracurricular STEM activity" are more likely to be interested in STEM and the potential of STEM careers (Modi, Schoenberg, & Salmond, 2012, p. 13). Basic exposure for underrepresented youth, like Uphoma, Pedro, Jia, or Antonio, can help youth realize entirely new interests.

Exposure and supportive mentors can help youth who are normally underrepresented in coding to find a passion for these fields. A positive early exposure to an interest, one that has low barriers to entry and opportunities, can motivate youth to pursue a sustained interest in coding. Positive initial experiences can allow for strong motivation to pursue an activity like coding pushing past obstacles (Zhu et al., 2013). What I have found in this research is that youth who have strong support in pursuing their interest in coding are able to envision the connection between coding as an interest and computer science as a career. This is expounded on in the second theme.

Envisioning Connections from Scratch *to Envisioned Future Opportunities*

The second theme that surfaced from the interviews is youth seeing connections from *Scratch* to computer science futures. For youth to successfully envision connections seems to require outside support from afterschool organizations, caring adults, and knowledgeable peers. This section illustrates envisioned connections and misconnections that four youths make between their *Scratch* experience and other opportunities, highlighting the potential connections that youth make to envisioned future careers. Adelina makes strong connections between her introduction to *Scratch* and her envisioned future career. Laretha and Damian describe the potential future career opportunities that they see from their participation in *Scratch.* Jessica describes the barriers she faces in pursuing coding.

Coding to Envisioned Computer Science Futures

Adelina is a 16-year-old high school student from Los Angeles who immigrated to the United States from Mexico when she was young. Adelina is passionate about coding and STEM access for girls and has taken on a strong advocacy role for this cause. She was originally introduced to coding through *Scratch* at a summer immersion program hosted by a local university designed to introduce girls to coding. From this initial exposure to *Scratch,* Adelina has been an avid coder. She explains, "I loved [*Scratch*] . . . because it's very fun because . . . [t]here were virtual codes for Legos. Compared to Python and all those it's much, much easier to use it. Of course you're only limited to what *Scratch* can do . . . but you can make your own games, you own personalized games, and I love that. I love that you could precise it in a way that seemed really, really easy." The immersion program had a profound effect on Adelina. It not only introduced her to coding but also to the presence of a gender gap and digital equity issues in STEM and STEM-related fields.

> I think that was an amazing way to start, because [the summer immersion program],[7] they are fighting the gender gap in STEM field. One of the factors that society, they think that coding is only for men since it's hard, and that we are not strong enough or smart enough to learn how to code, and it really helped us

break that wall that coding is one of the easier things to do and might be easier than calculus. It was really a breakthrough. A lot of us was like, hey, we can do the things as guys can do. *Scratch* was really a big eye opener, and it was the door to many opportunities awaiting other languages. I guess it has a really . . . it's a deep and really lovely memory of my first time using code.

She treated the information she received from the summer program like a call to action, which energized her passion for coding.

Adelina started coding with *Scratch* in the summer of 2015, and in the space of less than a year she had learned Python and Java. She was also building an app with an application builder for Apple smartphones to help people use resources in their local community to "transition from their ordinary lives into zero waste lifestyle."[8] Along with these informal learning experiences, she is taking computer science classes now (her school offers both honors and AP versions of the curriculum) and continues to pursue coding with a passion. She plans to apply to Stanford for computer science and make a change to the culture of computer science to close the gender gap.

Adelina was introduced to coding through an out-of-school activity, which became a more sustained interest for her. She explores this interest passionately outside of school but also takes AP and honors coding classes. Her class choices are strategic because of her envisioned future of pursuing computer science at an Ivy League school. She is doing everything she thinks appropriate to make this envisioned future a reality. Adelina is successful in coding because she had the support of the friends she made in the summer intensive group and because of encouraging parents.

Damian is a 17-year-old high school senior from New England. He is very active on *Scratch,* very personable to talk to, but only has two friends on *Scratch* and just as few in-person. When he first started using *Scratch,* Damian did not communicate much with other Scratchers, but he says, "Somewhere along there I became more active in the other areas of the *Scratch* website, like commenting on projects and leaving detailed reviews of what I thought the Scratcher could improve on their *Scratch* project." During this phase of his participation in the community, he created a thread on the *Scratch* forum where he would workshop ideas with other Scratchers, helping them refine their concepts or offering project ideas if they were stuck. He explains, "I guess eventually the *Scratch* team noticed my activity on *Scratch* and they offered me to become a *Scratch* mentor, which I accepted."

From his position as a *Scratch* mentor, Damian was later elected to be an administrator for the *Scratch* wiki, which is a resource that is completely community created and maintained. He sees *Scratch* as having a marked impact on his identity and his interest in coding. "*Scratch* put me into a situation where I really liked coding. And combined with the computer science classes I've taken at my high school I've just grown a really deep interest in computer science—what I can do with it, how I can explore my interests, my ideas that way, and so on. So without *Scratch* I would imagine I wouldn't be so interested. I also would imagine I wouldn't be as good at coding, or art, or creativity." The recognition and valuation he received from members of the *Scratch* team, the *Scratch* wiki administrators (which are a separate entity from *Scratch*), and his teachers, facilitate his ability to envision coding and mathematics as a future academic major and possible career. "Currently I'm thinking in college I want to major in programming and mathematics because those are two of my strong suits. I do a lot of programming in my free time, and I'm pretty nifty with math, if I say so myself," he said. He is applying to MIT, with an interest in studying mathematics and computer programming. Damian is able to envision a career in computer programming and math because of support from the *Scratch* team, the support of the *Scratch* community, and his teachers. Their combined support helped this previously isolated teen find a strong interest, which led to a well-defined, envisioned future.

Laretha, a 17-year-old African American high school junior, was a teen instructor for *Scratch* workshops in South Los Angeles. She leverages her interest in coding to envision what she views as an unexpected career. She had responded to an ad sent to her school by the local library looking for a teen intern. The librarian who hired her offered her agency, giving her the responsibility of facilitating the workshops in a style that she saw as best. This gave Laretha the experience of being in a position of responsibility for a group of youths and made her the go-to person when participants in the workshops had questions. Laretha took the position as a teen instructor because of her interest in coding, but she did not actually have much interest in being a teacher. "It's really interesting and kind of ironic because I always told my mom, 'I'm never going to be a teacher, or this or that,' or 'I don't work well with kids.' But after I came here I realized that I do actually have a little interest in that because I find a way to guide them through, and they acknowledge that." She was able to connect her interest in coding to a possible career in teaching.

Misconnections between Coding and Future Activities

Jessica, a white 14-year-old and very active Scratcher, was unable to make connections between her interest in coding and envisioned careers. She encountered *Scratch* through her brothers, who were all using it to learn basic coding. She started using it herself but found coding difficult to the point where she gave up trying. She says, "If I get totally stuck then I kind of just stop working on it. I kind of just go away from it." Instead of coding, she started using *Scratch* "to make art projects," she says. "I think most of my projects were about art because I'm not very good at coding. So generally art-based projects." Now, her brothers have lost interest but she is still very active on *Scratch*, even though she has not learned to code yet. She sees the value in learning to code but cannot get past the barriers of feeling frustrated while learning. She wants to be an illustrator, but she does not see a strong connection between the art skills she was developing in *Scratch* and those that will support her in being an illustrator. Lack of support, even though she has three people in her household who can code, inhibits her from using *Scratch* to its fullest potential.

Her school also provides a barrier, as it is gender segregated and only the boys have a coding club. Despite what seems like a well-supported entry into coding, with three people in her household who can code, a gender barrier remains. Her brothers and her father did not value her interest in coding or *Scratch*, but she participates in the community to the best of her ability on her own. However, without the help and support of others she is both unable to learn to code and unable to see the full potential of *Scratch* to help her prepare for her envisioned career.

These four participants' stories illustrate how tools like *Scratch* can prompt students to explore envisioned futures in STEM careers. Eighteen of the 40 youths interviewed envision careers and future plans in coding-related fields, which originate from their use of *Scratch* and interest in coding. The participants could envision careers, but only some could make what seem like concrete envisioned career plans. What can be gleaned from these examples is that outside support seems to be essential for youth to take an interest and recognize the opportunities that they access from that interest.

Support from caring peers and adults from the online community may create an environment where they can envision taking their interest beyond an informal or afterschool learning space. Adelina and Damian are not unique in setting large goals for themselves based on their interest in coding and participation in the *Scratch* community. Several other underrepresented participants also shared "dream" goals, like working at Google or going to Ivy League schools for computer science.

There is a persistent feeling among youth that coding is important to their future, but they are not always sure what that means or how to access it. The importance of learning to code has become a refrain in the culture at large with the new White House initiative Computer Science for All (The White House, 2016) and the American Library Association's initiative Libraries Ready to Code (ALA, 2016). These recent calls for coding education and increased access demonstrate a broader understanding that coding is important for a wide variety of careers. A barrier for many youths is that the people who support them do not understand the connections between coding and career options. Parents also need to understand the value of coding and actively support their children's interests.

Without this support, the connections between interest and future opportunity are often unreachable for the youth. Jessica has a parent and two brothers who could code, and yet she has not learned how to herself, despite being the only one of her siblings still using *Scratch*. She is also unable to see the connection between her interest in illustration and coding. To be a contemporary illustrator takes more than just skill with paper and pencil. Illustrators must use digital tools, and they often use coding to create illustrations and animations. It is not enough to introduce youth to an interest—it requires support from peers and adults, valuation by adults in the lives of youth, and a social environment for learning.

Since youth from diverse backgrounds are still heavily underrepresented in computer science fields, it is important to look for ways to connect youth with computer science so they can explore it as a possible career path. What the participants in this study have relayed through their interviews is that exposure to and support for interests is paramount for envisioning future coding careers. Coding as a field gains a "two-dimensional perspective and unique life experiences" (Farinde & Lewis, 2012) each time youth normally underrepresented in coding take on that career path, which strengthens the field as a whole. These examples reiterate the importance of exposure for youth in selecting career trajectories (National Research Council, 2011; Modi, Schoenberg, & Salmond, 2012) and the role interest can play in creating opportunities for youth to envision career and academic opportunities.

Conclusions: Connecting to the Future

I have described different entry points and envisioned futures from an interest-based online coding program, and the supports, which can help youth make strong connections to future options. The youth in this study had three sources of entry. They were exposed to coding through out-of-school activities, through school, and through family and friends. The youth who were able to envision a future career needed peers, caring adults, and a social environment to explore. Those who are able to combine strong entry points with enduring support were the most successful in envisioning strong plans for envisioned future careers. The support of others for their interest in coding has a noticeable impact on how much they participated in coding and whether they are able to make connections to coding beyond coding on *Scratch* as something they did for "fun."

Lack of support, as is seen in the case of Jessica, prevents youth from fully engaging in their interest and making connections from the interest to other related opportunities and envisioned careers in computer science. Lack of support can create barriers to entry into coding, but it is much more likely to create a barrier to connecting to coding opportunities and careers.

This study begins to map how underserved youth envision coding careers from participation in coding as an interest, and the types of supports that are needed. Determining what type of support is most effective to help youth connect between coding and an envisioned future or career will require more research. Enumeration of specific barriers youth face in entering into or connection beyond an interest, and designing solutions to overcome these barriers, will also require more exploration. Tracking youth with an envisioned career in coding and computer science to learn the barriers they face while pursuing this future would also be useful in determining the longer-term barriers that youth face moving from coding as an interest to coding as a career.

What is needed for youth to be able to make the connections out of their coding interest is for peer and adult mentors to offer exposure to computer science and other careers that utilize coding; create and support opportunities for youth to have their coding valued outside informal settings; and encouragement to think creatively about their coding, what they learn from it, and how it can be applied in other contexts. This research demonstrates that by understanding essential practices for supporting underrepresented youth, educators and parents can make targeted efforts to support sustained interest and engagement in coding.

ACKNOWLEDGMENT

This work was funded by a National Science Foundation Cyberlearning grant, undertaken by the Digital Media and Learning hub at the University of California, Irvine; the *Scratch* Team at the Massachusetts Institute of Technology; and the Berkman Center for Internet and Society at Harvard University.

NOTES

1. In this chapter, I include race, age, and location whenever it is known.
2. Changed for anonymity.
3. Changed for anonymity.
4. A platformer is a video game that involves guiding an avatar through a series of puzzles where the player must jump between suspended platforms, over obstacles, or both to advance the game, oftentimes while avoiding or defeating enemies.
5. Names removed for anonymity.
6. Jia feels that new Scratchers get an inherent benefit because other Scratchers help them to promote their work.
7. Changed for anonymity.
8. Zero Waste is a philosophy that encourages the redesign of resource life cycles so that all products are reused. No trash is sent to landfills or incinerators.

REFERENCES

Ahn, J., Subramaniam, M., Bonsignore, E., Pellicone, A., Waugh, A., & Yip, J. (2014). "I want to be a game designer or scientist": Connected learning and developing identities with urban, African-American youth. *Proceedings of the Eleventh International Conference of the Learning Sciences (ICLS 2014).* Boulder, CO: International Society of the Learning Sciences. Retrieved from http://ahnjune.com/wp-content/uploads/2014/04/ICLS2014-Sci-Dentity -camera-ready.pdf.

American Library Association (ALA). (2016). *ALA, Google launch "Libraries ready to code."* Retrieved from http://www.ala.org/news/press-releases/2016/04/ala-google-launch-libraries -ready-code-0.

Anderson, E., & Kim, D. (2006). *Increasing the success of minority students in science and technology.* Washington, DC: American Council of Education.

Ashcraft, C., & Blithe, S. (2010). *Women in IT: The facts.* Boulder, CO: National Center for Women & Information Technology.

Auger, R. W., Blackhurst, A. E., & Wahl, K. H. (2005). The development of elementary-aged children's career aspirations and expectations. *Professional School Counseling, 8*(4), 322–329.

Bandura, A., Barbaranelli, C., Caprara, G. V., & Pastorelli, C. (2001). Self-efficacy beliefs as shapers of children's aspirations and career trajectories. *Child Development, 72*(1), 187–206.

Barker, L. J., & Aspray, W. (2006). The state of research on girls and IT. In J. M. Cohoon & W. Aspray (Eds.), *Women and information technology: Research on underrepresentation* (pp. 3–54). Cambridge, MA: MIT Press.

Brennan, K., & Resnick, M. (2012). New frameworks for studying and assessing the development of computational thinking. *Proceedings of the American Educational Research Association (AERA) annual conference*. Retrieved from http://scratched.gse.harvard.edu/ct /files/AERA2012.pdf.

Bureau of Labor Statistics. (2016). *Occupational outlook handbook 2016–17 edition*. Washington, DC: US Department of Labor. Retrieved from http://www.bls.gov/ooh/computer-and -information-technology/software-developers.htm.

College Board. (2015). *AP program participation and performance data 2015*. Retrieved from https://research.collegeboard.org/programs/ap/data/participation/ap-2015.

Covay, E., & Carbonaro, W. (2010). After the bell: Participation in extracurricular activities, classroom behavior, and academic achievement. *Sociology of Education, 83*(1), 20–45.

Crow, D. (2014). *Why every child should learn to code*. Retrieved from https://www .theguardian.com/technology/2014/feb/07/year-of-code-dan-crow-songkick.

Dishman, L. (2016). *Why coding is the job skill of the future for everyone*. Retrieved from http://www.fastcompany.com/3060883/the-future-of-work/why-coding-is-the-job-skill-of -the-future-for-everyone.

Domenico, D. M., & Jones, K. H. (2007). Career aspirations of women in the 20th century. *Journal of Career and Technical Education, 22*(2). Retrieved from https://ejournals.lib.vt .edu/index.php/JCTE/article/view/452/394.

Duncan, G. J., & Murnane, R. J. (2011). *Whither opportunity? Rising inequality, schools, and children's life chances*. New York, NY: Russell Sage Foundation. Retrieved from https:// www.russellsage.org/publications/whither-opportunity.

Farinde, A. A., & Lewis, C. W. (2012). *The underrepresentation of African American female students in STEM fields: Implications for classroom teachers*. Online Submission. Retrieved from http://www.davidpublishing.com/davidpublishing/Upfile/7/17/2012 /2012071766162033.pdf.

Hammersley, M., & Atkinson, P. (2007). *Ethnography: Principles in practice*. London, UK: Routledge.

Hanson, S. L. (2006). African American women in science: Experiences from high school through the post-secondary years and beyond. In J. Bystydzienski & S. Bird (Eds.), *Removing barriers: Women in academic science, technology, engineering, and mathematics* (pp. 123–141). Bloomington: Indiana University Press.

Ito, M., Gutiérrez, K., Livingstone, S., Penuel, B., Rhodes, J., Salen, K., . . . & Watkins, S. C. (2013). *Connected learning: An agenda for research and design*. Irvine, CA: Digital Media and Learning Research Hub. Retrieved from http://dmlhub.net/publications/connected -learning-agenda-for-research-and-design/.

Kalil, T., & Jahanian, F. (2013). *Computer science is for everyone!* Retrieved from https://www .whitehouse.gov/blog/2013/12/11/computer-science-everyone.

Khallad, Y. (2000). Education and career aspirations of Palestinian and US youth. *Journal of Social Psychology, 140*(6), 789–791.

Kohli, S. (2015). The economic importance of teaching coding to teens. *The Atlantic*. Retrieved from http://www.theatlantic.com/education/archive/2015/05/the-economic-importance-of -teaching-coding-to-teens/393263/.

Kow, Y. M., Young, T., & Salen Tekinbaş, K. (2014). *Crafting the metagame: Connected learning in the StarCraft II community*. Irvine, CA: Digital Media and Learning Research Hub.

Margolis, J., Estrella, R., Goode, J., Holme, J., & Nao, K. (2008). *Stuck in the shallow end: Education, race and computing*. Cambridge, MA: MIT Press.

Margolis, J., Goode, J., & Bernier, D. (2011). The need for computer science. *Educational Leadership, 68*(5), 68–72.

Martin, C. (2012). Video games, identity, and the constellation of information. *Bulletin of Science, Technology, and Society, special issue: Game On: The Challenges and Benefits of Video Games, Part I, 32*(5), 384–392.

———. (2014). *Voyage across a constellation of information: Information literacy in interest-driven learning communities.* New York, NY: Peter Lang.

Mims, C. (2015). Why coding is your child's key to unlocking the future. *The Wall Street Journal.* Retrieved from http://www.wsj.com/articles/why-coding-is-your-childs-key-to-unlocking-the-future-1430080118.

Missio, L. (2015). Why kids should learn to code (and how to get them started). *CBC/Radio-Canada.* Retrieved from http://www.cbc.ca/parents/learning/view/why-kids-should-learn-to-code-and-how-to-get-them-started.

Modi, K., Schoenberg, J., & Salmond, K. (2012). Generation STEM: What girls say about science, technology, engineering, and math. *Girl Scouts of the USA.* Retrieved from http://www.girlscouts.org/content/dam/girlscouts-gsusa/forms-and-documents/about-girl-scouts/research/generation_stem_full_report.pdf.

NAACP Legal Defense and Education Fund (LDF) and National Women's Law Center (NWLC). (2014). *Unlocking opportunity for African American girls: A call to action for educational equity.* New York, NY: LDF Communications Department. Retrieved from http://www.nwlc.org/sites/default/files/pdfs/unlocking_opportunity_for_african_american_girls_final.pdf.

National Center for Science and Engineering Statistics (NCSES). (2015). *Women, minorities, and people with disabilities in science and engineering.* Bethesda, MD: National Science Foundation. Retrieved from http://www.nsf.gov/statistics/2015/nsf15311/digest/nsf15311-digest.pdf.

National Center for Women and Information Technology (NCWIT). (2012). *Girls in IT: The facts.* Retrieved from https://www.ncwit.org/sites/default/files/resources/girlsinit_thefacts_fullreport2012.pdf.

National Center for Women and Information Technology (NCWIT). (2015). *Women in IT: The facts.* Retrieved from https://www.ncwit.org/resources/women-tech-facts-2015-16-update.

National Research Council. (2011). *Successful K–12 STEM education: Identifying effective approaches in science, technology, engineering, and mathematics.* Washington DC: The National Academies Press. Retrieved from http://www.nap.edu/catalog/13158/successful-k-12-stem-education-identifying-effective-approaches-in-science.

Ochsner, A. (2012). *Typically untypical affinity practices making a Mass Effect.* Unpublished thesis, Department of Curriculum and Instruction, University of Wisconsin–Madison.

Papastergiou, M. (2008). Are computer science and information technology still masculine fields? High school students' perceptions and career choices. *Computers & Education, 51*(2), 594–608.

Pfister, R. C. (2014). *Hats for house elves: Connected learning and civic engagement in Hogwarts at Ravelry.* Irvine, CA: Digital Media and Learning Hub. Retrieved from https://dmlhub.net/wp-content/uploads/files/hatsforhouseelves.pdf.

Rafalow, M., & Salen Tekinbaş, K. (2014). *Welcome to Sackboy Planet: Connected learning among LittleBigPlanet 2 players.* Irvine, CA: Digital Media and Learning Hub. Retrieved from https://dmlhub.net/wp-content/uploads/files/welcometosackboyplanet.pdf.

Riegle-Crumb, C., & King, B. (2010). Question a white male advantage in STEM: Examining disparities in college major by gender and race/ethnicity. *Educational Researcher, 39*(9), 656–664.

Riegle-Crumb, C., Moore, C., & Ramos-Wada, A. (2011). Who wants to have a career in science or math? Exploring adolescents' future aspirations by gender and race/ethnicity. *Science Education, 95*(3), 458–476.

Saldaña, J. (2016). *The coding manual for qualitative researchers.* Thousand Oaks, CA: Sage.

Toglia, T. V. (2013). Gender equity issues in CTE and STEM education. *Tech Directions, 72*(7), 14–17.

Togyer-Sun, J. (2011, March 3). Research notebook: Computational thinking—What and why? *The Link.* Retrieved from http://www.cs.cmu.edu/link/research-notebook-computational -thinking-what-and-why.

US Department of Labor (2010). *Current population survey, detailed occupations by sex and race.* Washington, DC: Bureau of Labor Statistics.

Vygotsky, L. S. (1978). *Mind in society: The development of higher psychological processes.* Cambridge, MA: Harvard University Press.

Watson, C. M., Quatman, T., & Edler, E. (2002). Career aspirations of adolescent girls: Effects of achievement level, grade, and single-sex school environment. *Sex Roles, 46*(9–10), 323–335.

The White House. (2015). *Fact sheet: President Obama announces Computer Science for All initiative.* Retrieved from https://www.whitehouse.gov/the-press-office/2016/01/30/fact -sheet-president-obama-announces-computer-science-all-initiative-0.

Wing, J. M. (2006). Computational thinking. *Communications of the ACM, 49*(3), 33–35.

Wulf, W. (1999). Testimony to the Commission on the Advancement of Women and Minorities in Science, Engineering, and Technology Development. *Committee on the Diversity of the Engineering Workforce.* Retrieved from https://www.nae.edu/Testimonytot heCommissionontheAdvancementofWomenandMinoritiesinScienceEngineeringand TechnologyDevelopment.aspx.

Zhu, H., Zhang, A., He, J., Kraut, R. E., & Kittur, A. (2013). Effects of peer feedback on contribution: A field experiment in Wikipedia. In *CHI 2013 Proceedings of the SIGCHI Conference on Human Factors in Computing Systems* (pp. 2253–2262). New York: Association for Computing Machinery. Retrieved from http://dl.acm.org/citation.cfm?id=2481311.

CHAPTER EIGHT

African American Youth Tumbling Toward Mental Health Support-Seeking and Positive Academic Outcomes

LYNETTE KVASNY AND FAY COBB PAYTON

The persistent underrepresentation and relative underperformance of African American collegians are matters of ongoing concern to campus leaders and policymakers. A growing body of scholarship points to social, financial, and academic factors that serve as barriers to African Americans' ability to access, afford, and succeed in college. These barriers include poor academic preparation that undermines students' performance in college; lack of guidance, information, and social support in helping students navigate the college experience; and the financial burden arising from the increasing cost of college and the decline in financial aid (Nagaoka, Roderick, & Coca, 2009). However, to date, less research addresses how African American college students seek support from socially similar peers.

In this chapter, we focus on the use of social media to facilitate the support-seeking practices of African American college students dealing with the psychosocial adjustments associated with being a minority at a Predominantly White Institution (PWI). Allen (1992) and Fischer (2007) note that the transition to college sets the stage for student success. However, African American students at PWIs do not tend to perform as well academically as their White and Asian peers. This outcome is partially explained by problems adjusting to cultural differences. Most African American students enter college as first-generation students, come from low-income families, and experience a predominantly White campus as racial ethnic minorities (Allen, 1992; Fischer, 2007; Steele, 1997). These differences may lead to several challenges, including establishing relations with White students and faculty, coping with academic requirements, and feeling included in the broader college community. This psychosocial adjustment is also shaped by a national trend of declining support among Whites for race-based affirmative action programs and policies, the minuscule number of tenured African American faculty and administrators who might serve as role models and mentors to African American students, and the negative racialized experiences reported by many African American students attending PWIs (Allen, 1992). The *Journal of Blacks in Higher Education* (2015), for instance, tracks campus racial incidents ranging from racially themed parties, name calling, racial slurs on social media, and physical attacks. These incidents take an emotional toll and contribute to feelings of social isolation and emotional pain, which are evidenced in mental health challenges such as anxiety, depression, and suicidal thoughts. Smith (2008) coined the term "racial battle fatigue" to describe the physical and psychological toll taken due to perceptions of unceasing discrimination, microaggressions, and stereotype threat.

With all of these stressors, mental health promotion is particularly important for African American collegians. According to the US Department of Health and Human Services' Office of Minority Health (2014), African Americans of all ages suffer from disproportionately high rates of mental illness. For instance, adult African Americans are 20% more likely to report serious psychological distress and are more likely to have feelings of sadness, hopelessness, and worthlessness than are adult Whites. However, African American adults are half as likely (8.7% Black versus 16.0% White) to have sought or received mental health counseling or treatment in the past year.

To improve mental health and educational outcomes for all students, college campuses across the United States are working to improve their outreach as the number of students seeking aid increases. According to an annual study by the University of California at Los Angeles Cooperative Institutional Research Program (Rios-Aguilar, Eagan, & Stolzenberg, 2015), incoming college students in 2014 reported the lowest level of emotional health since the survey's inception 49 years ago. These first-year students reported that they were most concerned about finances, feelings of depression, and being overwhelmed. In fact, 22% of respondents reported utilizing campus mental health services.

While the authors of the UCLA study report an association between depression and time spent online, the direction of causality is not clear. However, what is clear is that online social media communities like Tumblr offer collective spaces in which geographically dispersed African American students can seek social support from peers as they make their psychosocial adjustment to college. In the following section, we review literature on African Americans and mental health, and support seeking online. We then empirically examine how three African American communities on Tumblr (*Black Women Confessions, Black Girl + Mental Health,* and *Black Mental Health*) use this social media platform to provide informational and expressive aid to enable community members to persist at PWIs. We conclude with a summary of our research findings, which demonstrate how students appropriate the technological features that Tumblr affords to offer instrumental (information resources and tangible advice) and expressive (empathy, affection, and encouragement) social support. These technological features facilitate the creation of blogs that use a variety of media formats, including text, video, images, and GIFs. The blog content that is created is expressed from the standpoint of uniquely African American cultural experiences. Reblogging and asks, additional technological features, are used creatively not only to share content but to engage in threaded discussions. Students also create their own Tumblr features such as "masterposts" to collaboratively create ongoing lists of references and resources.

African Americans and Mental Health Help-Seeking Practices

African American college students' perceptions of racial discrimination and locus of control are particularly important when addressing mental health concerns. Seaton, Upton, Gilbert, and Volpe (2014) conducted surveys with 314 African American high school students and found that participants with racial discrimination experiences were more likely to display depression symptoms, such as difficulty concentrating and remembering details, difficulty making decisions, and feelings of hopelessness and helplessness. However, those who actively sought social support had lower depression symptoms than those who used distraction and avoidance coping strategies. In fact, avoidant coping strategies significantly increase the relationship between perceived discrimination and depression symptoms when youth feel that perceived racially discriminatory treatment is being systematically imposed on them and relief from this oppressive system is beyond their control. These findings are further supported by a study by Scott and House (2005) and Bogart and colleagues (2013) that also examine the linkage between perceived racial discrimination and depression symptoms in African American youth. They report that higher levels of racial discrimination distress were related to greater use of avoidant coping strategies and that teens who felt that they had more personal control over perceptions of racial discrimination were more likely to use help-seeking coping strategies.

African Americans in general and college students in particular have cultural beliefs, attitudes, and customs that may be at odds with conventional mental health treatment. For instance, research by McGee and Stovall (2015) has shown that African American collegians studying at PWIs can have a heightened sense of urgency, given the pressures associated with fitting in, career competition, postgraduation planning, academic performance, increasing financial debt, and feelings of both social and professional isolation. African American college students studying at PWIs are often at higher risk for depression because of the added pressure of dealing with microaggressions and implicit biases and feelings of racial isolation as well as poor academic and social support on college campuses. These risks can be compounded by certain courses of study, particularly in science, technology, engineering, and mathematics (STEM) fields, where African American students and faculty are woefully underrepresented.

While African American teens and adults are at greater risk for psychological distress, they face significant attitudinal barriers and cultural beliefs that lead them to be less likely to seek treatment and to access services (US Department of Health and Human Services, 2014). These attitudinal barriers to help-seeking include denial, embarrassment, refusal of help, lack of insurance, lack of knowledge about treatment, stigma, fear, and feelings of hopelessness. Nationally, only 16% of African Americans, in comparison with 24% of White Americans, will receive mental health treatment. In Sayles, Ryan, Silver, Sarkisian, and Cunningham's study (2007), over 10% of African American college students who reported a diagnosis of depression did not seek treatment at available facilities. Although mental health treatment today is better than it ever has been, stigma is still severe enough that people avoid seeking care or treatment, or they do not continue with treatment once started (Corrigan, 2004).

Together, African American college students' racial identity and youth status suggest that they are less likely to seek help, especially for highly stigmatized diseases such as mental illness. According to Corrigan (2004), stigma demoralizes individuals and decreases their potential to participate in social activities, including seeking care and treatment. People may recognize that they have a problem but want to avoid being labeled as having a certain disease, thereby avoiding any clinical assistance, diagnosis, or social support. While many diseases have stigma associated with them, for many people—especially African American youth—two of the most significant are mental health disorders and HIV/AIDS.

These avoidance behaviors are not unfounded. The impacts of morally corrupt medical doctors and unethical research studies continue to influence cultural barriers associated with seeking healthcare. For example, the Tuskegee Study of Syphilis in the Negro Male, which examined the effects of untreated syphilis among African American men, persisted from 1932 to 1973 and has left African Americans distrustful of healthcare workers and institutions. This mistrust was considered not only understandable but necessary for self-preservation and family protection (Scott, McCoy, Munson, Snowden, & McMillen, 2011; Washington, 2006). Consequently, African Americans often look to family, friends, and the church for information and support before trying to navigate the professional healthcare system.

To make sense of attitudinal barriers, the mental health of African Americans must be understood within the wider historical and cultural context of slavery followed by the race-based denial of access to health, housing, employment, and educational resources, which has resulted in longstanding socioeconomic disparities (US Department of Health and Human Services, 2010). African American adults living in poverty, for example, are two to three times more likely to report serious psychological distress, including suicide, than those living above poverty. Suicide also affects African American teens at a much higher rate than African American adults. African American teenagers (8.2%) are more likely to attempt suicide than are White teenagers (6.3%) but are less likely than Whites to die from suicide (US Department of Health and Human Services, 2014). Even so, suicide was the 16th leading cause of death for African Americans of all ages and is the third leading cause of death for African American males ages 15 to 24 (Suicide Prevention Resource Center, 2015). African Americans, on average, die by suicide at the age of 32, which is a full decade earlier than the White Americans' average of 44 years of age (Garlow, Purselle, & Heninger, 2005).

According to the US Department of Health and Human Services (2001), only one out of three African Americans who needs mental healthcare receives it. Moreover, once they find treatment, African Americans are more likely to stop treatment early and are less likely to receive follow-up care (American Psychiatric Association, 2014). African Americans are also misdiagnosed and underdiagnosed because, in part, mental health research has historically focused on White populations. The help-seeking efforts of African Americans have also been stymied because of limits in culturally and linguistically competent care, few racial/ethnic minority mental health providers, and a lack of consumer knowledge of available resources (Kleinman, 2004; Snowden & Pingitore, 2002). As a result, African Americans often receive a lower level of care. Individuals may shy away from hospitals and doctors for fear of discrimination, unequal treatment, poor information sharing by practitioners, and the inability of providers to address particular issues with cultural competence.

Culture bears on whether people seek help, what types of help they do seek, what types of coping styles and social supports they have, and how much stigma they attach to mental illness (Office of the Surgeon General, 2001). Culturally, African Americans display lower levels of trust of medical institutions but a high degree of trust in the church. The church has historically played a central role in supporting the general health of African Americans, but some congregations are not as aware that mental disorders deserve the same kind of medical support and attention as other clinical conditions. Among some in the African American community, mental illness is instead seen as an outcome of spiritual weakness that can be solved entirely through spirituality (American Psychiatric Association, 2014; National Alliance on Mental Illness, n.d.).

Importantly, research has shown that as some younger African Americans have gotten older, their own experiences, coupled with those shared by older members of their families, have carried on the feelings of mistrust (Lindsey, Chambers, Pohle, Beall, & Lucksted, 2013). Mistrust also occurs because there are few racial/ethnic minority mental health providers. Consequently, African American youth mention that they are concerned about mental health practitioners, two-thirds of whom are White (Tylee, Haller, Graham, Churchill, & Sanci, 2007), not understanding their culture, or stereotyping them, or misdiagnosing them (Lindsey et al., 2013).

Scott and colleagues (2011) outline the more specific challenges of young African American men. Often they describe negative social interactions with Whites, such as clerks following them in stores, people putting up car windows as they pass, or women clutching their bags as if scared that they might be robbed. Such interactions engender feelings of shame, isolation, and devaluation. When these young men attempt to seek help in a mental health-care setting with practitioners who do not look like them and often have not had the same experiences, they are unsure of whether the practitioner, the mental health system, or both are really there to help them or can even begin to understand their frustrations. In fact, Scott and colleagues (2011) report that when introduced to the system, these young men are often categorized as simply aggressive and hostile but not necessarily depressed or anxious. As a result, more complex and deeper mental health issues are never diagnosed or treated. Tylee and colleagues (2007) note that, when seeking treatment for mental health via counseling sessions, African American males are more likely to engage when the healthcare professional is interested and addresses negative feelings they may have toward White people and the specific experiences related to being a young African American male. This is a compelling example of how healthcare and health information must be culturally appropriate to be most useful.

Support through social media websites such as blogs, Facebook groups, health forums, and online support groups offers a means of tailoring health information to diverse populations in ways that are culturally appropriate and emotionally supportive. For example, researchers report that sharing experiences with same-race colleagues or friends plays a significant role in protecting African Americans from the harmful psychological effects of the racial trauma experienced while navigating in predominantly White settings (McGee and Stovall, 2015). With social media websites, African American users can form communities that offer a sense of social belonging, trust, acceptance, and encouragement as well as useful information about mental health services. Used in conjunction with the valuable and vital counseling provided by mental health professionals who understand the role that race plays in producing psychological distress, support through social media can help to reduce the perceived racial trauma experienced by African Americans and increase their ability to cope with depression, isolation, anxiety, and other mental health issues.

Online Social Support for Mental Health

While social media is not the magic bullet to curb longstanding health disparities, it is a promising tool in the field of health promotion (Payton, 2009).

For instance, Ziv (2014) highlighted the research of both social and medical scientists to track mental health using Twitter, facial recognition, and linguistics. Johns Hopkins University researchers have parsed people's Twitter feeds and identified whether a person displays symptoms associated with depression, bipolar disorder, posttraumatic stress disorder, or seasonal affective disorder. This research suggests that people experiencing depression symptoms use social media to share information and discuss issues associated with their illness.

Our research finds that African American millennials are significant users of social media tools, such as YouTube and Twitter (Payton & Galloway, 2014; Payton, Kvasny, & Kiwanuka-Tondo, 2014). In fact, African American teens and young adults use mobile devices and text messaging more often than their peers in other racial and ethnic groups (Montague & Perchonok, 2012). Moreover, Montague and Perchonok (2012) report that social media, video, and cell phone technologies can be used to positively affect the health and wellness of historically underserved populations, if they are tailored toward the intended population. Since African Americans are less likely to seek treatment for mental health illnesses from professionals and are proficient users of mobile technology and social media, we posit that online communities like those found on Tumblr may offer information resources and social support from empathetic and knowledgeable peers.

The Internet holds much promise as a communication channel for providing timely, accurate, and culturally relevant information in a way that reduces stigma. While one in three American adults are using the Internet to seek health information (Fox & Duggan, 2013), college students use the Internet more often than the wider population (Ivanitskaya, O'Boyle, & Casey, 2006). Further, there is widespread use of mobile devices, computers, and social media apps for accessing and disseminating information among African American youth and young adults (Smith, 2014). The Pew Internet and American Life Project (Fox & Duggan, 2013) reports that 65% of women and 47% of African Americans go online for health information, own smart and mobile devices to access, and share and even curate online information. The Internet is expected to reduce longstanding health inequalities and reach those with stigmatized illnesses or those interested in learning more about stigmatized medical conditions (Berger, Wagner, & Baker, 2005).

While the Internet can be a great equalizer in terms of accessing health information, there is also a dark side. Selwyn (2004), Kvasny (2005), Brock

(2007), and Kvasny and Payton (2008) alert us to the fact that when terms like the "digital divide" are used to characterize African Americans' experience with the Internet, it can have negative consequences. This deficit framing places more focus on presumed shortcomings of users' technical abilities and access to the Internet, while ignoring other significant factors like disparities in the availability of relevant content and the capability to create and utilize content effectively. As Hargittai (2002) notes, "People may have technical access, but they may still continue to lack effective access in that they may not know how to extract information for their needs from the Web."

However, before individuals can find content to meet their perceived information needs, that content must exist online. The availability of culturally relevant content is crucially important in the context of mental health. For instance, and as mentioned earlier, deaths from suicide among African American youth are lower than for Whites. However, the gap is starting to narrow as suicide attempts among African American youth increase. One of the early flags for a potential suicide is suicidal ideation, or thinking about and having a specific plan for carrying out suicide. This ideation is often expressed online (Ziv, 2014). What some counselors have found is that suicide ideation plays out very differently among African American youth than it does among White youth. Without noting these differences and creating content that health professionals can use to accurately evaluate and respond to African American youth, this group of patients will remain undertreated (American Association of Suicidology, 2015).

There are also disparities in the ability to create and curate content. In a study of African American women's attitudes toward the Internet as a health information resource, for instance, Warren, Allen, Okuyemi, Kvasny, and Hecht (2010) found that participants differentiate between consuming and creating Internet content. While consuming content was perceived to be within the women's realm of control, content creation was perceived as a control element of the Internet that was mostly reflective of White culture.

Similarly, software developers reproduce inequality through the design of the human-computer interface and the production of content that fails to accommodate the cultural perspectives of ethnic minorities (Nakumara, 2002). The lack of diversity in the technology workforce is one telling indicator that helps to explain implicit biases in software design. For example, Google released its workforce diversity data in 2015, and the numbers showed that its workforce is notably and disproportionately "white and male" (Associated

Press, 2014). Google, along with the heads of several leading technology and Internet firms with similar workforce statistics, confirmed that they must diversify their workforce to facilitate growth and content availability that suits the needs of their customers.

Despite these disparities in Internet skills, use, and content, online resources are an important vehicle that youth use to locate and consume health information. While Internet access is readily available to and used by college students, Ivanitskaya, O'Boyle, and Casey (2006) showed that online health literacy is still lower than expected among this group. Higher health literacy leads to improved self-care and healthcare utilization (Stansbury, Wimsatt, Simpson, Martin, & Nelson, 2011). The first step in improving mental health literacy for youth is having a better understanding of their perspectives on mental health as well as how they seek out, interpret, and utilize health information. Yet, very little information has been collected about what experiences and factors may influence how, why, and when they seek out mental health support. To inform this knowledge gap, we analyze how African American college students use Tumblr to seek and offer social support to one another. By understanding the types of social support that are sought and offered, and how the group leverages software features to meet their information and communication goals, healthcare providers can more effectively work with technologists to design and develop software and content to meet the cultural and informational needs of African American youth and young adults.

Methodology

We adopt the framework used by Lee and Kvasny (2014) in their study of social media and social support for parents who have children diagnosed with rare chronic diseases. Social support is based on empathy, and is found to be most effective when it comes from socially similar others who are facing the same or similar circumstances (Cobb 1976; Thoits, 1995). Our analysis focuses on how content and the technological features of Tumblr are leveraged to provide instrumental and expressive social support to a psychologically distressed person by similar others (table 8.1).

To locate appropriate blogs, the authors entered the term "#black #mental health" into the Tumblr search engine. We then sorted the resulting posts by "most popular" and scrolled through the results to find those related to college students. In this process, we identified three blogs (*Black Women Confessions, Black Girl+Mental Health,* and *Black Mental Health*) that had the largest number of posts. In each blog, we selected the first 10 posts with pertinent mes-

TABLE 8.1
Forms of Social Support

Function	Definition	Supportive Action
Instrumental Aid	Material aid or behavioral assistance provided by others that enables the fulfillment of ordinary role/responsibilities.	Providing financial support, information or advice related to the health concern that makes it easier for the affected party to cope with her stressful circumstance.
Expressive Aid	Assertions or demonstrations of love, caring, esteem, sympathy, and group belonging.	Compassion, sympathy, spiritual advice, and feelings of group belonging provided to a person by another facing the same or similar circumstance.

sages and content. The entire post (the original post and comments) was extracted from these three Tumblr blogs to be used for subsequent analysis.

While the authors did not plan to focus on African American women, their voices dominated the content on Tumblr. This gender difference, with women being more engaged in using the Internet for health-related information, is consistent with prior literature that reports that women have stronger social motivations for and experience with health information seeking (Warren, Jung, Hecht, Kvasny, & Henderson, 2010). The demographics of Tumblr users also suggest that young, urban, African American, college-educated women would be a well-represented population. A Pew Internet survey of social media use (Desilver, 2013) found that Tumblr is mostly used by young adults. Among young adults who use Tumblr (13% of 18- to 29-year-old Internet users), men and women are equally represented. Tumblr users are also skewed toward urban (7%) and educated (7%) Internet users. In fact, 65% of Tumblr's audience is college educated. Hispanics and African Americans make up 29% of Tumblr's user base, which suggests that Tumblr is an effective social media site for reaching communities of color (Plachecki, 2013).

To analyze the Tumblr posts, a coding scheme was developed based on the following two major categories: instrumental support and expressive support. Instrumental posts were coded as information with advice on the depression symptoms and treatment options. These included expressions of symptoms, treatment options, opinions, and experience. Expressive messages and posts were coded as demonstrations of socioemotional support such as peer support, sympathy, compassion, spiritual advice, and encouragement. The researchers used this coding scheme to determine how the affected communities were using social media for the provision of online social support. In addition to the content of the post, we categorized posts by the Tumblr features that are employed. The results discussed in the next section represent innovative uses of Tumblr features, as well as the more interesting quotes and content that emerged from our analysis.

Results
Instrumental Social Support

There are a number of Tumblr features that are used to request and provide advice on the depression symptoms and treatment options. One common way that students seek support is through "asks," which occur when Tumblr bloggers want to pose a question to their audience ("followers"). The following example from *Black Mental Health* illustrates an ask from an anonymous follower seeking social support: "Anonymous asked: I start school very soon. Last year was my freshman year of college and I feel like it fucked me up mentally. I'm more anxious and uncomfortable around people, even more than I used to. There's so much stuff going on campus that I get overwhelmed and just want to lock myself in, which just makes socializing HARDER on me. I feel immature and dont know how I'll manage this year . . . sorry just wanted to vent."

The blogger, who is also a student, responds by empathizing with the anonymous follower:

> Uuuggh☻. Im so sorry youre going through all of this, Love. (And im really sorry it took me a while to answer this. With school beginning and all . . .) TRUST me when i say i feel you. Weeks before school began, i just remember cryyying and crying and crying because not only did i feel exhauated that i would have to socialize even more pretty soon, but i felt so damn WEAK for not being able to just take a stand and get through this. I know how sometimes anxiety is like your worst enemy; you try to just bust through it but it just. Wont. Let. You. Be. Stronger. Its tiring, i know.

The blogger goes on to provide actionable advice to help the follower manage her mental distress. "You must must MUST practice self care and love right now. Do every fucking thing that helps you relax and makes you feel at home with yourself. Watch Jam's [YouTube] video where she talks on self care . . ."

Reblogging is another Tumblr feature commonly used to share culturally relevant mental health resources. In the following post, "If you're a college student suffering from anxiety and depression," the blogger shares her own story and practical advice to similarly situated college students. This post uses storytelling to encourage others to reach out to professors for emotional support:

> Idk if this is relevant for anyone who's following me, but I just wanted to share a little advice/experience of mine that might help if you're suffering from anxiety or depression or any type of illness, especially mental, that's affecting your schoolwork. If you're torn between telling your professors about a mental illness you have (if you haven't already gone through the Student of Disabilities Office) so that they won't just think you're a lazy, incompetent student and not telling them because you think they'll judge you or because you don't want to rely on anyone for help, I think you should tell them.
>
> There will always be professors who are complete assholes of course, and generally you can tell who those professors will be, but I finally decided to let my professors know what was going on with me and how hard things have been, and they were completely supportive. I was so nervous because I go to a PWI (Johns Hopkins University of all places, where it's practically filled to the brim with rich, elitist people who are unbelievably smart but also obnoxious and overly competitive, especially if you're pre-med), so I thought professors here would either be similar to the students or would be tired of excuses from students, but that definitely wasn't the case. Two of my professors were extremely supportive, and told me that they themselves had suffered from depression and anxiety at earlier times in their life. One of them even offered to hold a semi-regular meeting with me if I had a bad depressive episode and just couldn't find the energy to come to class; another said that I could stop by her office or her house (which is close to campus) at anytime if I just needed to get away from it all. Turns out she's done that for multiple students, and her son went through a similar experience at a PWI and had to drop out, so she was not judgmental at all.
>
> So obviously, everyone's experience is different and some professors won't be as supportive; but as someone who struggled for close to three years about whether or not to tell my professors the truth, it helped so much when I finally told them. I was able to get an extension on a few assignments and papers and my professors let it slide every now and then if I missed a few classes.

The author of this post discusses the feelings of being an outsider at a PWI and her fear of being misjudged by her professors as lazy and incompetent.

Her desire to achieve academic success motivated her to disclose her mental health status to her professors and this helped her to achieve positive academic outcomes. Others who found this advice useful can "like" or reblog to share this advice with their followers.

Tumblr bloggers also leverage a variety of media genres to provide instrumental aid. For example, bloggers post informative YouTube videos from African American scholars and healthcare professionals, such as author and editor Meri Nana-Ama Danquah's presentation at the 2003 Depression on College Campuses Conference. They host interview series with African American professionals such as Diamond, a published writer and editor for the Black Youth Project. There are also posters from public health campaigns, such as Mental Health Awareness Week, which occurred from October 5 to 11, 2015.

Another common method used by Tumblr bloggers are resource lists, called "masterposts," that are constantly updated and reblogged. The Self-Care Masterpost, for example, lists over 50 online resources for help with a variety of mental health issues including depression, anxiety, suicide, insomnia, eating disorders, bullying, abuse, addiction, loneliness, and self-harm. Over 482,000 Tumblr users have reblogged and/or liked this post.

Expressive Social Support

Expressive posts offer socioemotional support, such as peer encouragement, sympathy, compassion, and spiritual advice. This is perhaps evidenced most powerfully by visual media. One example is a link to a photo series on the Huffington Post that shows that mental illness does not discriminate. The photos in this series are minimalist, showing simply a portrait of a young person of color holding a note that unashamedly states his or her diagnosis. The purpose of the photo project is to challenge mainstream narratives about mental illness that often exclude people of color, and to enable people of color to assert their own narratives to combat stigma.

The stigma associated with mental illness can be so overwhelming that African American women often describe choosing recovery and self-help as acts of resistance. GIFs are frequently used in Tumblr to add emphasis when reblogging or to extract sharable sound bites from video. One of the most emotionally compelling pieces is the GIF set "This is What it Feels Like to be Depressed" reblogged from Siz Videos. The GIF set is presented in the form of a liberating letter in which a young African American woman talks to depression, "her childhood friend," and lets it know that it cannot silence her any longer. The GIF set has over 144,000 likes and/or reblogs.

Black Women Confessions offers a space for African American women to anonymously share poignant, culturally bound stories. The stories are composed entirely as text and many deal with mental health topics. In the following confession, the author discusses her mistrust of her White therapist: "Felt so uncomfortable with my white therapist today was only my second session but idk if I'm going back, she seemed extremely insincere and not very empathetic, it rubbed me the wrong way." Mistrust is a common theme with others offering similar confessions: "My therapist is white and because of this I feel that I cannot be open with her" and "I'm finally getting therapy . . . My only worry is that the therapist might pull the 'black women aren't prone to mental health issues.'" This strong Black woman trope (Collins, 1990) exists both inside and outside of African American communities, and it comes at the expense of the women's proper diagnoses and treatment.

Another post speaks to the cultural belief that mental health challenges are the work of the devil and can be combated through prayer. This reinforces a finding in the literature that, for many African Americans, churches and peer groups are highly used resources for mental healthcare. In the following example, the author is alarmed and fearful that she is hearing voices, and the support that she receives from her grandmother is to drive away an internal demon through prayer: "I see ghosts and hear voices when I'm alone. I told my grandma about the voices when I was little and they rubbed olive oil on my forehead and tried to pray out 'the devil' so I don't tell any one anymore . . . But I think I'm going crazy. I've been having suicidal thoughts sense [*sic*] I was little, but now I have flashbacks too and homicidal thoughts. The voices are on and off. Am I ill?"

Finally, the women on this blog speak specifically to the psychosocial challenges of entering and persisting in college. Financial debt and academic performance loom heavily on the minds of African American collegians. The following student is concerned about how her poor academic performance has caused her to lose her scholarship, and the financial burden that this places on her parents. She also evidences signs of psychological distress as she shares that her life feels meaningless: "I'm in so much debt already and I'm not even a college sophomore yet. My first semester GPA was so shitty I don't even qualify for most scholarships. Now not only is it biting me in the ass but now my parents are being required to pay for my fuck ups

($2000 in 9 days . . .). I'm just ready to off myself and stop dragging my life and them down this hole with me. My life is already over. What's the point."

This confessional space is also powerful for showing the importance of treatment and care in helping students to diagnose and cope with mental illness. The following quote situates a young collegian's story of diagnosis and treatment. While this is genuinely good news, the young lady is concerned about sharing her diagnosis with her family because they see mental illness as a personal weakness rather than a medical condition. "When I was younger, I was so shy that I would cry if I noticed someone looking at me. My cousins always made fun of me for it, so I trained myself to stop crying, but people staring still terrified me. I got to college and went to see the school psychologist, turns out I suffer from severe anxiety. I hadn't even considered that because my family always used to say mental illness was a white people thing. Now idk how I'm gonna tell them when I get home from school."

For the next post, we see the same delight in finding a diagnosis, along with a fear that treatment will come with an economic cost that will bar a college student from obtaining ongoing care: "This is the girl from before that talked about her OCD [obsessive-compulsive disorder] struggle. I just looked up the prices for Cognitive Behavioral Therapy for OCD patients seeking treatment and I wanna cry. It's $300 for the first session and $175 for each individual session after that. And insurance may not cover it. I don't wanna give up hope but it looks like it's impossible to get help at these prices. I'm still in college."

This quote demonstrates how followers may come back repeatedly to update others on their progress, and in doing so create a feeling of community. Sometimes the women's plea for help is as simple as a sentence. "I want to get through college without a suicide attempt." Or "I can't even get out of bed to go to class today." Or, as one premed student laments, "I wish that I had a support system apart from myself." Without safe spaces that these blogs provide, African American women collegians may lack a supportive peer network that can offer words of encouragement and empathy.

Conclusion

The purpose of our research is to explore how African American college students use Tumblr to provide support to and seek social support from their peers. We used an analytical framework to explore instrumental and expressive aid sought and provided by people experiencing psychological distress and their socially similar others. Our findings suggest that social media plays an integral role in facilitating support-seeking practices that are consistent with African Americans' cultural beliefs. Specifically, the Tumblr blogging community provides a safe space that offers healing to those African American women who have experienced psychological trauma. Women confess their experiences with racism, concerns about their finances, and fears of seeking professional mental health counseling. However, women also communicate resilience as they discuss racial pride and sisterly solidarity. They offer information resources, as well as strategies for self-care. It is in these self-affirming discussions that the mental strengths and coping strategies that African Americans develop to protect themselves from negative campus experiences are evidenced.

One unintended finding was that most blogs relevant to our study were authored by African American women. Researchers report that prevalence rates of depression, anxiety disorder, and phobia are higher among African American women than African American men (National Alliance on Mental Health, n.d.). We argue that this may help to explain the overrepresentation of blogs authored by African American women.

The practical implications of our study suggest the need for additional support systems for African American college students. Universities should provide protected spaces, both online and in person, where African American students can engage in collective and individual healing. Universities should also support intercultural groups to improve African American students' connections to the larger university community. A stronger sense of belonging can give students a greater sense of purpose and agency and provide them with opportunities to forge important relationships. These are essential traits required for protecting mental health.

Finally, universities should offer affordable counseling services and increase the supply of African American clinicians on campuses. These two factors are critically important for making treatment more accessible to African American students. Studies of medical care reveal that African American physicians are five times more likely than White physicians to treat African American patients and that African American patients rate their physicians' styles of interaction as more participatory when they see African American physicians (Keith, 2000). However, African Americans seeking help from a mental health provider of the same race will have difficulty finding such a provider, because there are relatively few African American psychiatrists (Keith, 2000). Social media helps to fill this void by enabling the creation of communities where African American collegians can seek support from socially similar peers.

REFERENCES

Allen, W. (1992). The color of success: African American college student outcomes at predominantly white and historically black public colleges and universities. *Harvard Educational Review, 62*(1), 1–26.

American Association of Suicidology. (2015, October 28). *African American suicide fact sheet.* Retrieved from http://www.suicidology.org/Portals/14/docs/Resources/FactSheets /AfricanAmerican2012.pdf.

American Psychiatric Association. (2014, May 29). *Cultural competence.* Retrieved from http://www.psychiatry.org/psychiatrists/cultural-competency.

Associated Press. (2014, May 28). White and male: Google releases diversity data. *The Washington Post.* Retrieved from https://www.washingtonpost.com/business/economy /white-and-male-google-releases-diversity-data/2014/05/28/1658541c-e6d2-11e3-afc6 -a1dd9407abcf_story.html.

Berger, M., Wagner, T., & Baker, L. C. (2005). Internet use and stigmatized illness. *Social Science and Medicine, 61*(8), 1821–1827.

Bogart, L., Elliott, M., Kanouse, D., Klein, D., Davies, S., Cuccaro, P., . . . Schuster, M. (2013). Association between perceived discrimination and racial/ethnic disparities in problem behaviors among preadolescent youths. *American Journal of Public Health, 103*(6), 1074–1081.

Brock, A. (2007). "A belief in humanity is a belief in colored men": Using culture to span the digital divide. *Journal of Computer Mediated Communication, 11*(1), 357–374.

Cobb, S. (1976). Social support as a moderator of life stress. *Psychosomatic Medicine, 38*(5), 300–314.

Collins, P. H. (1990). *Black feminist thought: Knowledge, consciousness and the politics of empowerment.* New York, NY: Routledge.

Corrigan, P. (2004). How stigma interferes with mental healthcare. *American Psychologist, 59*(7), 614–625.

Desilver, D. (2013, May 20). 5 facts about Tumblr. *Pew Internet Report.* Retrieved from http://www.pewresearch.org/fact-tank/2013/05/20/5-facts-about-tumblr/.

Fischer, M. (2007). Settling into campus life: Differences by race/ethnicity in college involvement and outcomes. *eJournal of Higher Education, 78*(2), 126–161.

Fox, S., & Duggan, M. (2013, January 15). Health online 2013. *Pew Internet Report.* Retrieved from http://www.pewinternet.org/files/old-media//Files/Reports/PIP_HealthOnline.pdf.

Garlow, S., Purselle, D., & Heninger, M. (2005). Ethnic differences in patterns of suicide across the life cycle. *American Journal of Psychiatry, 162*(2), 319–323.

Hargittai, E. (2002). Second-level digital divide: Differences in people's online skills. *First Monday, 7*(4). Retrieved from http://firstmonday.org/issues/issue7_4/hargittai/index.html.

Ivanitskaya, L., O'Boyle, I., & Casey, A. (2006). Health information literacy and competencies of information age students: Results from the interactive online research readiness self-assessment. *Journal of Medical Internet Research, 8*(2), e6.

Journal of Blacks in Higher Education. (2015, October 28). *Campus racial incidents.* Retrieved from https://www.jbhe.com/incidents/.

Keith, V. M. (2000). A profile of African Americans' health care: Subgroup differences in need and access. In C. Hogue, M. A. Hargreaves, & K. S. Collins (Eds.), *Minority health in America* (pp. 47–76). Baltimore, MD: Johns Hopkins University Press.

Kleinman, A. (2004). Culture and depression. *New England Journal of Medicine, 351*(10), 951–953.

Kvasny, L. (2005). The role of the habitus in shaping discourses about the digital divide. *Journal of Computer Mediated Communication, 10*(2). Retrieved from http://onlinelibrary .wiley.com/doi/10.1111/j.1083-6101.2005.tb00242.x/full.

Kvasny, L., & Payton, F. C. (2008). African Americans and the digital divide. In M. Khosrow-Pour (Ed.), *Encyclopedia of information science and technology* (pp. 78–82). Hershey, PA: Idea Group Publishing.

Lee, R., & Kvasny, L. (2014). Understanding the role of social media in online health: A global perspective on online social support. *First Monday, 19*(1–6). Retrieved from http:// firstmonday.org/ojs/index.php/fm/article/view/4048/3805.

Lindsey, M., Chambers, K., Pohle, C., Beall, P., & Lucksted, A. (2013). Understanding the behavioral determinants of mental health service use by urban, under-resourced Black youth: Adolescent and caregiver perspectives. *Journal of Child and Family Studies, 22*(1), 107–121.

McGee, E. O., and Stovall, D. (2015). Reimagining critical race theory in education: Mental health, healing, and the pathway to liberatory praxis. *Educational Theory, 65,* 491–511.

Montague, E., & Perchonok, J. (2012). Health and wellness technology use by historically underserved health consumers: A systematic review. *Journal of Medical Internet Research, 14*(3), e78.

Nagaoka, J., Roderick, M., & Coca, V. (2009). Barriers to college attainment: Lessons from Chicago. *The Consortium on Chicago School Research at the University of Chicago, Center for American Progress.* Retrieved from https://www.americanprogress.org/issues/higher -education/report/2009/01/27/5432/barriers-to-college-attainment-lessons-from -chicago/.

Nakumara, L. (2002). *Cybertypes: Race, ethnicity, and identity on the Internet.* New York, NY: Routledge.

National Alliance on Mental Health. (n.d.). *African Americans.* Retrieved from https://www .nami.org/Find-Support/Diverse-Communities/African-Americans.

O'Boyle, C. (2006). *History of psychology: A cultural perspective.* Mahwah, NJ: Lawrence Erlbaum.

Office of the Surgeon General. (2001). *Mental health: Culture, race and ethnicity.* US Department of Health and Human Services, US Public Health Services. Retrieved from http://www.ct.gov/dmhas/lib/dmhas/publications/mhethnicity.pdf.

Payton, F. C. (2009). Beyond the IT magic bullet: HIV prevention education and public policy. *Journal of Health Disparities Research and Practice, 3*(2), 13–33.

———. (2015). Cultures of participation—For students, by students. *Information Systems Journal, 26*(4), 319–338.

Payton, F. C., & Galloway, K. (2014). Here comes the #Engagement: A serious health initiative made trendy. *XRDS ACM Magazine, 21*(2), 28–31.

Payton, F. C., Kvasny, L., & Kiwanuka-Tondo, J. (2014). Seeking and perceiving online HIV prevention information: Black female college students' perspectives. *Internet Research, 24*(4), 520–543.

Plachecki, L. (2013, July 23). How to make social media demographics work for you. *2060 Digital.* Retrieved from http://2060digital.com/how-to-make-social-media-demographics -work-for-you/.

Rios-Aguilar, C., Eagan, K., & Stolzenberg, E. (2015, October 28). Findings from the 2015 administration of the your first college year survey. *University of California–Los Angeles, Cooperative Institutional Research Program.* Retrieved from http://www.heri.ucla.edu /briefs/YFCY/YFCY-2015-Brief.pdf.

Sayles, J., Ryan, G., Silver, J., Sarkisian, C., & Cunningham, W. (2007). Experiences of social stigma and implications for healthcare among a diverse population of HIV positive adults. *Journal of Urban Health: Bulletin of the New York Academy of Medicine, 84*(6), 814–828.

Scott, L., & House, L. (2005). Relationship of distress and perceived control to coping with perceived racial discrimination among Black youth. *Journal of Black Psychology, 31*(3), 254–272.

Scott, L., McCoy, H., Munson, M., Snowden, L., & McMillen, J. C. (2011). Cultural mistrust of mental health professionals among black males transitioning from foster care. *Journal of Child and Family Studies, 20*(50), 605–613.

Seaton, R., Upton, R., Gilbert, A., & Volpe, V. (2014). A moderated mediation model: Racial discrimination, coping strategies, and racial identity among Black adolescents. *Child Development, 85*(3), 882–890.

Selwyn, N. (2004). Reconsidering political and popular understandings of the digital divide. *New Media and Society, 6*(3), 341–362.

Smith, A. (2014, October 28). African Americans and technology use. *Pew Internet Research Center.* Retrieved from http://www.pewinternet.org/2014/01/06/african-americans-and-technology-use/.

Smith, W. A. (2008). Higher education: Racial battle fatigue. In R. T. Schaefer (Ed.), *Encyclopedia of race, ethnicity, and society* (pp. 615–618). Thousand Oaks, CA: Sage Publications.

Snowden, L. R., & Pingitore, D. (2002). Frequency and scope of mental health service delivery to African Americans in primary care. *Mental Health Services Research, 4*(3), 123–130.

Stansbury, K., Wimsatt, M., Simpson, G., Martin, F., & Nelson, N. (2011). African-American college students: Literacy of depression and help seeking. *Journal of College Student Development, 52*(4), 497–502.

Steele, C. M. (1997). A threat in the air: How stereotypes shape intellectual identity and performance. *American Psychologist, 52*(6), 613–629.

Suicide Prevention Resource Center (SPRC). (2015, October 28). *Suicide among racial/ethnic populations in the US: Blacks.* Waltham, MA: Education Development Center. Retrieved from http://www.sprc.org/sites/sprc.org/files/library/Blacks%20Sheet%20August%2028%202013%20Final.pdf.

Thoits, P. (1995). Stress, coping, and social support processes: Where are we? What next? *Journal of Health and Social Behavior, 35,* 53–79.

Tylee, A., Haller, D., Graham, T., Churchill, R., & Sanci, L. (2007). Youth-friendly primary-care services: How are we doing and what more needs to be done? *Lancet, 369,* 1565–1573.

US Department of Health and Human Services. (2001). *Mental health: Culture, race, and ethnicity—A supplement to Mental Health: A report of the surgeon general.* Rockville, MD: US Department of Health and Human Services, Substance Abuse and Mental Health Services Administration, Center for Mental Health Services.

———. (2010, December 1). *National action plan to improve health literacy.* Washington, DC: Office of Disease Prevention and Health. Retrieved from http://health.gov/communication/hlactionplan/pdf/Health_Literacy_Action_Plan.pdf.

———. (2014, December 12). *Mental health and African Americans.* Washington, DC: Office of Minority Health. Retrieved from http://minorityhealth.hhs.gov/omh/browse.aspx?lvl=4&lvlID=24.

Warren, J., Allen, M., Okuyemi, K., Kvasny, L., & Hecht, M. (2010). Targeting single parents in preadolescent substance use prevention: Internet characteristics and information relevance. *Drugs: Education, Prevention and Policy, 17*(4), 400–412.

Warren, J., Jung, E., Hecht, M., Kvasny, L., & Henderson, M. (2010). Ethnic and class-based identities on the World Wide Web: Moderating the effects of information seeking/finding and Internet self efficacy. *Communication Research, 7*(5), 674–702.

Washington, H. (2006). *Medical Apartheid.* New York, NY: Knopf Doubleday Publishing Group.

Ziv, S. (2014, November 12). Technology's latest quest: Tracking mental health. *Newsweek.* Retrieved from http://www.newsweek.com/2014/11/21/technologys-latest-quest-tracking -mental-health-283944.html.

CHAPTER NINE

Black Student Lives Matter

Online Technologies and the Struggle for Educational Justice

DAVID J. LEONARD AND SAFIYA UMOJA NOBLE

Black Students across the nation, from Historically Black Colleges and Universities (HBCUs) to Predominantly White Institutions (PWIs), are ushering in a new movement for racial justice. Despite narratives lamenting student apathy, the negative influences of hip-hop, and generational divides, Black students have emerged as the nation's conscience, as reminders that indeed, "Black Lives Matter." Social media has been central to these challenges to racism, as it privileges their voices, allowing Black students to circulate and make visible their experiences in the face of widespread discourses that imagine colleges and universities as progressive and postracial.

Digital media scholars continue to investigate narratives of race and gender on the Internet and the ways that both are fundamentally embedded in the social media experience (Brock, 2012; Chun, 2006; Daniels, 2013; Florini, 2013; Senft & Noble, 2013). Working to show the costs and consequences of a racially hostile campus climate (Cabera, 2012; Eaton, 2013; Friedrich, 2013; Groves, 2015; Lee, 2012; Martinez, 2013; Rios, 2015; Shire, 2015; Svrluga 2014), Black students have sought to document their experiences with everyday racism through a range of social media platforms and digital technologies. Social media has been instrumental in providing the space to challenge the dehumanization of Black bodies, voices, and experiences that is commonplace to a reactionary public discourse defined by accusations of oversensitivity, "race card" playing, and irrational anger.

This chapter is, thus, concerned with these emergent Black student movements. We argue that the utilization of online technologies is neither insignificant nor random but rather serves as an important site for the circulation of counternarratives, for indexing injustice and resistance, and fostering community with respect to individual and collective identity formation. We will discuss the ways that social media and online spaces are central to these movements of, for, and by Black college youth. We deploy Fairclough's method of critique of discourses essential to the meaning-making process as a form of "critical social science" needed to contextualize their key messages (Chouliaraki & Fairclough, 1999).

Continuing the longstanding tradition of Black college students taking to the streets to demand racial justice and educational equity (Biondi, 2014), Black student activism has reemerged as a focal point for change at PWIs. In the 1950s and 1960s, Black college students throughout the Jim Crow South joined together to bring down the walls of racial injustice. Through the 1990s, Black students continued to serve as a moral compass for a nation with their involvement in the anti-Apartheid movements, concern with preserving affirmative action and ethnic studies, and otherwise increasing diversity on campus. This tradition continues today. Rather than taking to the streets, today's Black students comprehend social media technologies as central to making their voices heard. Given the power of Black Twitter (Watkins, 2010), social media provides a place and vehicle for "cultural conversations" (Brock, 2012), and a means of "signifyin'" (Florini, 2013).

It is important to see the centrality of digital media to Black student movements and their identities. Social media has been an aggressive space for the circulation of racism by students, as the spectacle of racism is profitable for media companies who traffic in viral content (Noble, 2014). As Black students experience racial hostility and harassment online, social media exists as both a site of expanded community and as a space of commodification, and potential harm.

Black student movements are using technology not just to advance an agenda of social awareness but also to amplify a radical ethos of Blackness that is encoded in these digital spaces. "That is, how 'technocultural assemblages'— digital networks, communication platforms, software processes—are constitutive of online racialized subjectivity and activity," writes Sanjay Sharma

(2013, p. 48). "Participatory social media proliferate online identities, interactions and meanings at speeds and magnitudes which appear to defy conventional hermeneutic approaches" (Sharma, 2013, p. 54). In other words, digital media is both a means to communicate, a method to mobilize outrage, and a useful way of communicating injustice; it also exists as a space to affirm Black humanity and to articulate Black voices seemingly erased through widespread dehumanization (Tynes, Schuschke, & Noble, 2016). While utilizing different technology, these forms of protest are part of a long and rich tradition of using communications platforms as part of oppositional and activist stances (Lievrouw, 2011; Srinivasan, 2013).

Digital Dissemination of Black Student Experiences

The daily headlines reveal the fallacy of postracialism and the lie that America's universities are bastions of liberalism. Contemporary universities are unified by the persistence of anti-Black racism: Blackface parties, affirmative action bake sales, racist vandalism, harassment, physical assault, and hate crimes (Cornell Sun, 2012; Huffington Post, 2011, 2012; Murphy, 2011; Patton, 2015; Robers, Zhang, Morgan, & Musu-Gillette, 2015; Ross, 2016). As such, the experience of Black students remains one defined by everyday hostility and systemic violence. According to Howard J. Ehrlich, almost 1 million students (or roughly 25% of all students of color) experience racially and ethnically based violence, which includes verbal aggression, harassing phone calls, and other types of psychological intimidation each year (quoted in Nunn, 2008). Similarly, Leslie Picca and Joe Feagin (2007), in their book *Two-Faced Racism,* document a collegiate culture where White students regularly use the N-word and tell racist jokes, contributing to a campus climate that negatively impacts the social and academic experiences of Black students.

Whether intentional or not, the impact on Black students is profoundly clear. Rodriguez and colleagues (2005) found that the grade point averages of African American students suffer because of campus racial hostility (Perry, 2015; Taylor, 2005). Leah Kendra Cox describes a similar experience wherein she notes, "In unhealthy climates, students—both majority and minority—are less likely to thrive academically or socially" (quoted in Perry, 2015). She found that a supportive racial climate had more impact than any other factor on the strength of diversity on campus (Cox, 2010). Sylvia Hurtado summarized the existing research on campus climate and African American academic success as follows: "Just as a campus that embraces diversity provides substantial positive benefits, a hostile or discriminatory climate has substantial negative consequences" (quoted in Perry, 2015). Black students don't seem to matter beyond brochures and diversity reports. PWIs have fallen short in creating conditions optimal for Black student success. "Students who reported negative or hostile encounters with members of other racial groups scored lower on the majority of outcomes" (quoted in Perry, 2015). From graduation rates to retention rates, campus climate matters: racism, microaggressions, prejudices, and a lack of diversity impinge on the successes of African American students. Yet, so often, incidents of racism on campus are reduced to "teachable moments," while others, such as Blackface parties, are dismissed as "kids being kids." These incidents and the attendant responses to them are expressions of systemic educational inequity founded upon anti-Black violence.

Change Is Coming: Discourses of Student Protest

While universities continue to market themselves as diverse and welcoming to all students, Black students continue to learn in an anti-Black environment where microaggressions and racial hostility are normative. Faced with a disconnect between the university's rhetorical celebration of postracialism via diversity brochures versus their own lived experiences, Black students are taking to the virtual streets to protest the conditions under which they are forced to learn. Noting their tuition dollars, their utility in campus recruitment, their value on athletic fields, and the emptiness of the rhetoric of inclusion, Black student activists have spotlighted the hypocrisy of today's university, demanding to be heard and to see change.

At UCLA, a group known as the Black Bruins released a video in 2013 decrying low graduation rates, the silencing of Black student voices, and the hollowness of diversity rhetoric. The viral video privileged rage and critique, highlighting the illusion of meritocracy (Moore, 2013) while challenging the systemic practice of using Black collegiate bodies in brochures and on the football field, with an expectation that they rarely be heard. Receiving over 2.3 million views on YouTube, the Black Bruin protest video brilliantly focused on the words of Sy Stokes (2013), who shared the experiences of many Black Bruins. In what is a call to action and a challenge to a system that claims fairness and equity yet rewards those "hitting triples when they were already born on third base," the students demanded to be heard and seen rather than used and dismissed:

This school is not diverse just because you put it on a pamphlet . . .

It's all . . . talk

Just to maintain this fraudulent reputation

Of this institutionalized racist corporation . . .

We have voices that speak defiantly

So we IGNITE the flames to help us find the path to our future

Increasing Graduations, Not Incarcerations, Transforming Education because
  our numbers can't be any fewer . . .

We are tryin' to rewind time with role reversal as our revenge

Because we have no other choice when the university refuses to come to our
  defense

But we have come too far to let history repeat itself. (Stokes, 2013)

Pulling back the curtain on the lack of diversity at one of America's flag-ship universities, a place historically celebrated for its progressive forward thinking, the activism of the Black Bruins galvanized a campus community. It led to a petition demanding change in the face of dwindling numbers of African American students on campus. Soon thereafter, Black law students also protested racism at the law school. Marches supporting affirmative ac-tion would follow, along with the reappearance and expansion of a mural documenting "The Black Experience" at UCLA that was hidden behind a wall in the student union for 20 years.

The students' use of social media was especially important because of their ability to merge words and image while reaching students on other campuses who invariably saw their story, and for those who saw the immense potential of online spaces to document their own campus experiences.

The importance of social media as source of community, as tool of documentation, and as method of organizing continued through 2015 at UCLA, where in the aftermath of a planned "Kanye Western–themed party," one where gross stereotypes of Blackness were on full display at a fraternity party, UCLA students again took to both the virtual and lived streets (Tran, 2015). Embracing the hashtag #BlackBruinsMatter, a remix of Stokes's "Black Bruins" and #BlackLivesMatter, Black students at UCLA sought to dispel the lies of a postracial college experience, spotlighting the cost and harm of race-themed parties, a lack of student and faculty diversity, and a community riddled by colorblind racism (BlackBruinsMatter, 2015). Coalescing their experiences around a hashtag not only allowed students and alumni to chronicle a collective experience as one of alienation, prejudice, isolation,

Figure 9.1. Black Bruins Matter Video by Sy Stokes. *Source:* YouTube.

and hostility but also provided a way to index their support for protests at the University of Missouri and Yale University as part of the larger emergent movement.

Similarly, the University of Michigan would be a site of tremendous student activism in 2013. As with many social movements, the #BBUM (Being Black at the University of Michigan Movement) found a spark to give voice to a simmering dissatisfaction and rage that had hovered over the campus for decades. During the fall 2013 semester, the Theta Xi fraternity planned to host a "Hood Ratchet Thursday" party. Mirroring similar parties at Dartmouth, the University of Illinois at Urbana-Champaign, the University of California at San Diego, and countless other campuses, the planned party promoted longstanding anti-Black stereotypes. Guests partook in activities that included wearing costumes of "rappers, twerkers, gangsters (no Bloods allowed), thugs, and basketball players" (Abbey-Lambertz, 2013).

The response was immediate and swift. In a letter to the school's administration, Erica Nagy and Brian Thomas spotlighted the larger systemic issues plaguing the University of Michigan: "This party is one of many incidents that are symptoms of our disheartening lack of diversity and lack of social justice education and awareness that persists at this predominantly white institution" (Abbey-Lambertz, 2013). The source of outrage was bigger than the party, and the emergent protests would focus on the party as a symptom of a culture of inequality and violence. The party was the result of the lack of diversity on campus, the assault on affirmative action, the emptiness of university rhetoric, and the acceptance of overt campus racism as innocuous and harmless. Noting the declining percentages of Black students resulting from an assault on affirmative action and the university's thirst for "wealthy out-of-state students who are overwhelmingly white," Scott Kurashige, then professor in the Department of American Culture at Michigan, described the #BBUM movement as committed to changing the university's failed diversity policies (personal communication, 2013). "The rise in Black student campaigns is a direct response to the hypocrisy of elite universities, which claim to value their presence but don't really respect their voices. As the number of Black students shrinks, there's this pernicious pressure on them to feel grateful they were even admitted and assimilate into the dominant culture" (personal communication, 2013).

Student activists, including members of the Black Student Union at Michigan, encouraged their peers to share their stories on Twitter, to document their everyday struggles, and to highlight the experiences of #BBUM. According to Dr. Kurashige, "Social media has become a way to puncture the silence and hypocrisy of the 'postracial' order." Quickly, the hashtag trended nationally, with over 10,000 tweets that included #BBUM. Each tweet, in its own way, challenged Michigan to look in the mirror to assess whether diversity and equity were a reality. For example, @Dezha_Marshae tweeted: "Assuming that because I'm Black I don't deserve to be here and am a result of affirmative action, which is not even in place right now #BBUM" (quoted in Hing, 2014).

Beyond exposure, students successfully leveraged the social media campaigns and campus organizing into action. While issues surrounding enrollment, housing, and curriculum remained, in the aftermath of the 2013–14 #BBUM movement, the university agreed to increase funding for the Black Student Union, to expand recruitment efforts of students of color, to create a scholarship for undocumented students, and to fund renovation of the

Kinesiology sophomore Capri'Nara Kendall during the Being Black at the University of Michigan protests on January 20, 2014.

Allison Farrand/ Daily

Figure 9.2. Being Black at the University of Michigan: Reflections After Two Years, March 2016. *Source: Michigan Daily.*

campus multicultural center (Woodhouse, 2014). Activism online, alongside organizing on campus, resulted in material changes at the University of Michigan (Brandon, 2015).

Functioning as more than a tool, the #BBUM also indexed the shared experiences of Black students at Michigan, creating bridges, affective spaces of interaction, and a shared commitment to change within and beyond Ann Arbor. Organizers were able to galvanize other students while challenging unchecked racism and pushing the campus to a moral and political crossroads. They also provided a template for an amplified form of activism that has a longstanding tradition at PWIs. According to Nitasha Sharma, associate professor of African American studies at Northwestern University, this wave of activism is part of that tradition, albeit remixed through the use of online technologies (personal communication, 2013): "I see the activism on these public campuses as a continuum of the same crises impacting the same kinds of demographics over time, I suppose, more than a resurgence. The

Figure 9.3. Being Black at Illinois on Twitter, April 2014. *Source:* Twitter.

very use of social media makes other students on other campuses create their own versions" of social action. Almost immediately following the #BBUM social media campaign, Black students at the University of Illinois at Urbana-Champaign launched #BeingBlackatIllinois in 2014.

At Harvard University, African American students took to Tumblr to high-light the limited diversity, obscured by the hegemonic Whiteness of the Ivies. Their "I too am" campaign was not simply an effort to spotlight the stories of African American students excelling at America's elite institution. It also sought to challenge a campus climate that was neither welcoming nor em-powering. Featuring Harvard students holding signs declaring, "You don't sound Black. You sound smart," and "You're lucky to be Black . . . so easy to get into college," this campaign disrupted colorblind fantasies of many university presidents. It shared the daily comments expressed by White students and faculty, all of which undermines the educational experience. It was not enough to simply challenge the racism on campus; documenting and expos-ing the world to their authentic stories was essential.

Paying homage to Langston Hughes, whose poem "I too" elucidates the second-class citizenship experienced by African Americans, "I, Too, Am Harvard" reveals the persistent power of "double consciousness" 50 years after

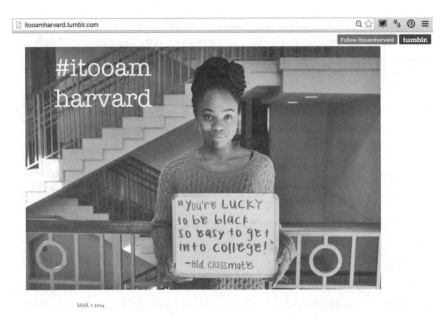

Figure 9.4. "I, Too, Am Harvard" Photo Campaign. *Source:* Tumblr.

the integration of America's colleges and universities. At Harvard and else-where, Black students are "Often . . . questioned, dismissed, brushed off as oversensitive," notes Kimiko Matsuda-Lawrence, a Harvard sophomore who started the campaign after witnessing #BBUM. "To hear our stories echoed in each other's voices, you feel your feelings are valid and legitimate" (Lee, 2014).

Efforts at Harvard sparked students at Ohio State University and Lehigh University, at UC-Berkeley, Northwestern, SUNY at New Paltz, the University of Cape Town, the University of Oxford, the University of Sydney, McGill University, and more than 30 other universities all over the world. Social media enabled Black students to spotlight Black humanity and create spaces where their voices would be heard in spite of efforts to silence their truths. Institutional gatekeepers, who sought to preserve pamphlet diversity that seeks to protect the fun and pleasure of White students, and who also worked to maintain an image based on the illusion of the campus as a postracial playground, were pushed aside with the proliferation of social media. Such campus and social media protests were not simply responding to anti-Black racism on college campuses but to the continued "problem of the color line" (Du Bois, 1900) throughout society.

While Jim Crow is nothing new, the visibility of America's "New Jim Crow" (Alexander, 2012) and the lack of "mercy" (Stevenson, 2014) with the Jena 6, the killing of Trayvon Martin, Mike Brown, Freddie Gray, Eric Garner, and Sandra Bland, to name a very few, inspired Black college students to mobilize their political and social media resources. Today's college students are of Trayvon Martin's generation; they are challenging the message that they have "made it," and they have transcended the racism and violence of white supremacy. Notwithstanding narratives that imagine Black students as "exceptional" (Alexander, 2012), (a)pathetic, and otherwise disengaged from the larger community, Black college students have built bridges directly back to Black neighborhoods. They have protested police shootings by organizing around a #BlackLivesMatter hashtag, coined by Alicia Garza, Patrisse Cullors, and Opal Tometi, to rhetorically combat the dehumanization of Black people by the state.

For example, in an effort to connect to protests in Ferguson following the killing of Mike Brown, students at Harvard and Howard University circulated photos of themselves doing the "HandsUpDontShoot pose" (Stableford, 2014). Other Black college students participated in the #IfTheyGunnedMeDown movement on social media, posting pictures that juxtaposed them in regalia against everyday photos, questioning whether the media would depict them as students or "thugs" if they were gunned down (Vega, 2014). These rhetorical and visual movements, the shared collective outrage, and the efforts to speak politically across class, gender, and geography were evident in these ongoing protests, many of which were staged by college students. Nowhere was this connectivity between #BlackStudentLivesMatter and #BlackLivesMatter more profoundly evident in aligning the struggle against systemic racism on campus and Blue-on-Black violence than at Missouri. One year following international protests demanding justice for Mike Brown, Black Students at the University of Missouri demanded change from their own campus.

Still reeling from the death of Mike Brown and the violence directed at protestors in Ferguson, the University of Missouri would be rocked by a series of racist events on campus that exposed the illusion of racial equity on campus. Organizing around the #ConcernedStudent1950 name, students were not simply demanding accountability from the offending parties but a systemic change to a culture that in their estimation was hostile and destructive to their educational experience. The embrace of #ConcernedStudent1950 was powerful on multiple levels. It allowed for a community to develop around a shared identity, and it challenged the accepted narrative about racial progress. Symbolically named for the first year the University of Missouri was integrated, 1950, students were collectively asking, "What has changed?" Sixty-five years after the integration of the university, Black students were stating that progress had not yet been realized. The hashtag sought to contradict the hypocrisy evident in the university's celebration of diversity while Black students endured everyday racism.

The universalizing hashtag also allowed for Black students and allies to don the identity of a concerned student, that of one no longer accepting narratives of racial progress. According to Bonilla and Rosa, "The hashtag serves as an indexing system in both the clerical sense and the semiotic sense. In the clerical sense, it allows the ordering and quick retrieval of information about a specific topic" (2015, p. 4). In this context, #ConcernedStudent1950 served as an index of false promises and their experiences with racial hostility. It also served as a call to action: concerned and, therefore, ready to demand change.

Black student protests, social media work, and the power in their hashtag didn't result in national mass media attention or compel action from the university president Tim Wolfe. His intransigence and the media silence confirmed their experiences that indeed #BlackStudentLives don't matter. This would change when members of the Missouri (Mizzou) football team joined forces with #ConcernedStudent1950. Their collaboration brought a level of visibility previously unseen. Reflecting on the potential power of students who participate/labor in intercollegiate athletics, Ben Fredrickson notes how the football team's presence on social media turned a local story into an international spectacle. Neither a hunger strike waged by Jonathan Butler, a Black graduate student, nor several racial incidents on campus—racial slurs hurled at the school's Black student body president and at attendants of the Legion of Black Collegians, including a swastika drawn in feces on a dorm room wall— had elicited media attention or action from the university. Even after protesters blocked President Wolfe's car at an October 10 homecoming parade, he refused to address the issues on campus. Wolfe went as far as dismissing their concerns in a pathetic attempt at defining systemic oppression as the belief that they could not succeed (Vandelinder, 2015). Almost all of these events occurred off the national mass media radar until two photos circulated on Twitter: one of Black Mizzou football players and Butler, and another of then head football coach Gary Pinkel, his staff, and the majority of the team (Fredrickson, 2015).

Figure 9.5. University of Missouri Football Team. *Source:* Gary Pinkel, Twitter.

Alongside the threat of boycott, social media allowed members of the Mizzou football team to simultaneously air their grievances, embrace the identity of #ConcernedStudent1950 (and not just student-athletes), and communicate their plans to boycott football activities unless President Wolfe resigned. They were not just standing up against racism on campus, and they were not simply using their voices and platform to join with other students. They were saying that their voices, needs, and lives matter as well. They were making clear that they too were part of an aggrieved Black student community.

Utilizing social media did more than bypass the traditional media; it allowed the players to shape the narrative in their own voices in ways that emphasized their humanity and agency. Given the historic and ongoing dehumanization of Black voices, particularly those of Black youth, and the cultural commodification of Black athletes' bodies at the expense of their voices, the image of them standing together, alongside student protestors, emphasized their collective power, humanity, and identities as students, as Black men, and members of the Missouri community—they were defying the commonplace stereotypes that they were only football players.

At the same time, the decision to tweet a picture of Black "student-athletes" with Jonathan Butler, who at the time was on the fifth day of a hunger strike, disrupted narratives that often position "student-athletes" as existing apart from their nonparticipating peers. This image challenged narratives that both pathologize and celebrate "student-athletes" as either "entitled"/not caring about students or as "heroes living the American dream." The image sought to challenge a narrative that has been central to containing the "revolt of the Black athlete" (Edwards, 1968) for more than 40 years. Dave Zirin notes this as a fundamental lesson resulting from the Missouri protest:

> If there is a lesson here for student activists around the country it should be to try and connect with so called "student-athletes." Don't treat them like they exist in their own space. Don't accede to the way schools already attempt, with separate dorms and cafeterias, to create an environment where they are seg-regated from normal campus life. Fight that. Talk to them, listen to their griev-ances, and make clear to your administration that the athletes, students, and faculty united will never be defeated. The administrators created this world where our universities revolve socially, politically and economically around the exploited labor of big time football. Now let them reap what they sow. (Zirin, 2015)

In the face of media narratives and public discourses that worked to dis-miss the boycott as little more than the actions of a few "ungrateful" and "entitled" (Black) "student-athletes," or as the result of the hypersensitivity of a few race card–playing students, the image of the entire team sitting to-gether, arm in arm, told a different story of community. Given that these "student-athletes" were able to risk so much, and given that Butler was will-ing to risk his life, their collective action illustrated the stakes.

Coach Gary Pinkel also tweeted the following message along with the team photo: "The Mizzou Family stands as one. We are united. We are behind our players. GP." He included the hashtag #ConcernedStudent1950, even though he later deleted his tweet. This is significant because it reveals an initial embrace of the students' narrative of racial tumult. It amplified stu-dent narratives that sought to point out how the racism on campus was more important than a football game. In a moment where fans (and surely donors) were calling on the university to suspend those "student-athletes" by threat-ening to boycott and even take away their scholarships, Pinkel's tweet made it clear he stood with the boycott. His tweet embraced those in the picture and those protesting throughout the campus.[1] In one day, his tweet was retweeted 15,000 times and favorited 13,000 times.

Pinkel, or someone coordinating his Twitter feed, served as an ally, mak-ing clear his and the team's support for the boycott. Social media would be central to these efforts, as his virtual stamp of approval contributed to the photo going viral. At the same time, Pinkel's tweet was able to shape and disrupt an emergent narrative that the players were acting alone or that the community didn't support the protests.

Social Media as Shared Community

Daily posts on Facebook, Instagram, Tumblr, and Twitter documenting student protests importantly highlight youth responses to inequities all while providing the building blocks for a shared community. Just as movement songs brought together local communities working to bring down the walls of Jim Crow, hashtags represent an emergent language that also binds student movements together. It marks who is supportive of the fight, it indexes who is suffering under the conditions of pamphlet diversity, it marks who is an ally and an accomplice, and it makes clear who is committed to fostering change in multiple spaces.

In the days following national mass media attention focused on the University of Missouri, African American students and faculty took to social media to document their experiences at PWIs nationwide. Employing the #BlackOnCampus hashtag, current and former Black students unveiled their campus experiences, again revealing the persistent problem of the color line on America's colleges and universities (Edwards, 2015). It is no wonder that protests emergent across the nation were not only in solidarity with those in Missouri but were also poised to demand racial justice and institutional accountability more broadly (Plaster, Weinberg, & Colville, 2015). Students have not been alone in this fight; Black faculty has been instrumental in saying "Black Lives Matter." They have been participating in actions, offering critical analysis within their classrooms, and offering support to Black students whose voices, experiences, and lives are devalued each and every day. Their involvement also challenges predominant administrative narratives that distance the social experiences of Black students and issues of campus climate from retention, graduation rates, and the classroom.

In fact, following the Ferguson protests, over a thousand Black faculty had signed a letter to their Black students. Expressing their unwavering support and love, the letter prompted thousands of emails and social media shares. The love letter punctuated efforts from Black faculty to help construct a bridge between campus and community, between the classroom and the everyday experiences of Black students:

> We know there is always more that people don't see or hear or want to know, but we see you. We hear you. In our mostly White classrooms we work with

some of you, you who tell us other professors don't see, don't hear you. You, who come to our offices with stories of erasure that make you break down. They don't see me, you say. They don't hear me. We know and don't know how to hold your tears. How do we hold your tears, and your anger? . . . Hold on. We want a future for you, for us right now. We write this in solidarity with the families of Tamir Rice, Mike Brown, Renisha McBride, Trayvon Martin, Rekia Boyd, Aiyana Stanley Jones, and so many others who they are killing, so many others who should have had the chance to be in our classrooms, who should have had the chance to simply be. ("An Open Letter," 2014)

Dr. Rae Paris, the letter's principal author, described the inspiration for the letter as multifaceted, making clear that while the nonindictments of the killers of Mike Brown and Eric Garner, along with the never-ending assault on Black bodies from the state compelled this action, the letter was a response to a culture of academia that consistently devalues Black life. "A Black student came to my office and talked about the experience of being in another class and the condescending ways people talked at the student, and the ways this student felt invisible," notes the professor of creative writing at Michigan State University (personal communication, December 2014). "We might not always be able to be on the ground marching with students, but we are in classrooms. I wanted students to know now in a time when they're hearing story after story of Black murders and death, in a long history of Black murders and death, that we're fighting for us, in our research, our writing, and our teaching, and other places that aren't always visible."

Dr. Django Paris, a professor of education at Michigan State who also worked on the letter, highlighted the bigger issues of equity and justice (personal communication, December 2014): "Having #BlackLivesMatter as part of the title reminds us as Black students and professors that Black lives matter everywhere, including where we teach and learn and work to gain the skills and knowledge to care for our selves and our families." Over and over again, the letter writers deployed the phrase, "We see you, we hear you." This rhetorical device affirmed a principal student grievance: that too often Black lives don't matter within an educational system that disproportionately punishes, pushes-out, fails, and incarcerates Black students from kindergarten through graduate school.

Dr. Jessica Marie Johnson, a faculty member at Michigan State and one of the people instrumental in disseminating the letter, made clear that the organizing of Black faculty is about the anti-Black racism that pervades

campus and community lives; "Students and faculty are encountering police aggression on college campuses and it impacts the way they are able to
function in class, how safe they feel as they move around campus and in
college towns, and their ability to engage with each other and with other
members of the campus community on an equitable basis" (personal communication, December, 2014). Social media was significant in breaking down
walls between faculty and students, allowing for a clear articulation of love
and understanding that was the opposite of the experiences of so many Black
students.

Conclusion

In the midst of the 50th anniversary of Freedom Summer, African American
students and faculty allies continue to remind the nation of the unfinished
struggle for justice. For those on the frontlines demanding that American
colleges and universities fulfill their promises, social media has been fundamental, both in terms of building bridges between faculty, students, and
staff, and between students at public and private institutions. It has been
significant in uniting students at PWIs and HBCUs, and between campuses
and communities by amplifying the voices, visibility, and the availability of
counternarratives. It has been a means of speaking back to institutional narratives of diversity and inclusion. What remains unclear is whether these
concerns will translate into remedies and what the substance of those remedies should be. As Professor Robin D. G. Kelley rightfully argues in his
essay, "Black Study, Black Struggle," there is still much critical work to be
done:

> I think all of us would agree with Ransby's prescient call for "non-reformist"
> reforms, for sustaining the fight to transform universities, not as refuges but as
> social institutions embedded in the broad public life. She correctly cautions
> against romanticizing the search for radical alternatives in disengagement.
> I could not agree more with her call for "a radical recalibration of what uni-
> versities owe" to society as a whole, and that requires rejecting the myth of
> meritocracy, the false division between the university and the world, and the
> idea that intellectuals only reside in the university. (Kelley, 2016)

Though we have argued for the potential of social media to amplify social
protest, we also want to caution over myopic praise that doesn't take account
of limitations and traumas also fostered by social media. Indeed, we have
celebrated social media for its ability to foster an imagined community, to

circulate counternarratives, to index injustice and resistance, and to support individual and collective identity formation. These technologies are clearly powerful tools in the struggle against educational inequality. These are also tools of suppression, violence, and the perpetuation of inequity and injustice. As evidenced by the rhetorical violence and threats directed at activists, and the extensive racism found in social media sites like Yik Yak.

Yet, given the ongoing consolidation of mass media, social media is meaningful in the circulation (and surveillance) of protest messages. Social media is a legible space of protest, and it is pivotal in making visible the crises facing Black college students and their efforts at social change. Social media is not the *substance* of social movements and is not a proxy for organizing structural interventions in the increasingly corporatized university that undermines liberatory possibilities, but it does serve as a means of signaling the potential for deeper critical engagement and action.

NOTES

This chapter includes and builds on an essay written by Leonard, D. J. (Fall 2014) "Tweet This," *The Crisis*. It also builds on King, C. R., and Leonard, D. J. (2007, September) "The Rise of the Ghetto Fabulous Party," *Colorlines*, 27–31.

1. In a later interview, he backtracked from these original statements, noting that his support was for the players but not the movement or the issues they were protesting. He also claimed that he didn't send the tweet and that hashtag should not have been included. He explained the tweet as the result of someone with access to his account sending without authorization.

REFERENCES

Abbey-Lambertz, K. (2013, November 1). "Hood Ratchet Thursday" party at University of Michigan fraternity canceled by school. *The Huffington Post*. Retrieved from http://www.huffingtonpost.com/2013/11/01/hood-ratchet-thursday-party-theta-xi-u-of-m_n_4190523.html.

Alexander, M. (2012). *The New Jim Crow: Mass incarceration in the age of colorblindness.* New York, NY: The New Press.

Biondi, M. (2014). *The black revolution on campus.* Berkeley: University of California Press.

BlackBruinsMatter. (2015). Retrieved from https://twitter.com/hashtag/Blackbruinsmatter.

Bonilla, Y., & Rosa, J. (2015). #Ferguson: Digital protest, hashtag ethnography, and the racial politics of social media in the United States. *American Ethnologist, 42*(1), 4–17.

Brandon, A. (2015, November 18). Reflections on #BBUM two years after launch. *The Michigan Daily*. Retrieved from https://www.michigandaily.com/section/news/bbum-q.

Brock, A. (2012). From the blackhand side: Twitter as a cultural conversation. *Journal of Broadcasting & Electronic Media, 56*(4), 529–549.

Cabera, C. (2012, March 6). NYC college student finds N-word on dorm door. *The Root*. Retrieved from http://www.theroot.com/articles/culture/2012/03/fordham_student_in_nyc _finds_nword_written_on_dorm_door.html.

Chouliaraki, L., & Fairclough, N. (1999). *Discourse in late modernity* (vol. 2). Edinburgh, UK: Edinburgh University Press.

Chun, W. (2006). *Control and freedom: Power and paranoia in the age of fiber optics*. Cambridge, MA: MIT Press.

Cornell Sun. (2012, May 5). Evoking Trayvon Martin, partiers allegedly throw bottles at Black students. *The Huffington Post*. Retrieved from http://www.huffingtonpost.com/the-cornell -sun/citing-trayvon-people-all_b_1496841.html.

Cox, L. K. (2010). *International diversity and the role of a supportive racial climate* (Dissertation). University of Maryland, College Park.

Daniels, J. (2013). Race and racism in Internet studies: A review and critique. *New Media & Society, 15*(5), 695–719.

Du Bois, W. E. B. (1900). The present outlook for the dark races of mankind. *AME Church Review, 17*(2), 95–110.

Eaton, L. (2013, December 11). UNCG library vandalized, racial slurs found. *Fox8*. Retrieved from http://myfox8.com/2013/12/11/uncg-library-vandalized-racial-slurs-found/.

Edward, R. (2015, November 11). #BlackOnCampus hashtag exposes harsh realities of college life. *Chicago Defender*. Retrieved from http://chicagodefender.com/2015/11/11/Blackoncampus -hashtag-exposes-harsh-realities-of-college-life/.

Edwards, H. (1968). *The revolt of the black athlete*. New York, NY: Free Press.

Florini, S. (2013). Tweets, tweeps, and signifyin': Communication and cultural performance on "Black Twitter." *Television and New Media, 15*(3), 223–237.

Fredrickson, B. (2015, November 9). Mizzou football protest proves players have power now. *St. Louis Post-Dispatch*. Retrieved from http://www.stltoday.com/sports/columns/ben -frederickson/benfred-mizzou-football-protest-proves-players-have-power-now/article _cf685318-2122-5fa3-88c4-a77af225de02.html.

Friedrich, A. (2013, December 13). Black U of M students suspect racial profiling by campus police. *Minnesota Public Radio News*. Retrieved from http://blogs.mprnews.org/oncampus /2013/12/Black-u-of-m-students-suspect-racial-profiling-by-campus-police/.

Gray, R., Vitak, J., Eaton, E. W., & Ellison, N. B. (2013). Examining social adjustment to college in the age of social media: Factors influencing successful transitions and persistence. *Computers & Education, 67,* 193–207.

Groves, P. (2015, March 4). Racial slurs at WSU spark protests, discussion. *Moscow-Pullman Daily News*. Retrieved from http://dnews.com/local/racial-slurs-at-wsu-spark-protests -discussion/article_719405b9-719e-5c00-92e1-8a5fd270c1f2.html.

Hing, J. (2014, February 14). When a hashtag sparks more than dialogue. *Colorlines*. Retrieved from http://www.colorlines.com/articles/when-hashtag-sparks-more-dialogue.

Huffington Post. (2011, February 18). *Mark Wattier, Murray State prof, resigns after insulting Black student Arlene Johnson*. Retrieved from http://www.huffingtonpost.com/2011/02/18 /mark-wattier-murray-state_n_825113.html.

Huffington Post. (2012, March 27). *University of Wisconsin–Madison investigating fraternity after racial slur incident*. Retrieved from http://www.huffingtonpost.com/2012/03/27 /university-wisconsin-madison-racial-slur-incident_n_1381165.html.

Jacobs, P. (2013, November 20). Trending #BBUM campaign offers a stark look at being a minority student at a top American university. *Business Insider*. Retrieved from http:// www.businessinsider.com/bbum-offers-a-stark-look-at-being-a-minority-student-at-a-top -american-university-2013-11.

Jennings, A., Blankstein, A., and Xia, R. (2013, May 6). USC students accuse LAPD of bias after party clash. *Los Angeles Times*. Retrieved from http://articles.latimes.com/2013/may /06/local/la-me-usc-lapd-party-20130507.

Kelley, R. D. G. (2016, March 7). Black study, black struggle. *Boston Review*. Retrieved from http://www.bostonreview.net/forum/black-study-black-struggle/robin-d-g-kelley-robin-d -g-kelleys-final-response.

Lee, J. (2014, March 5). "I, Too, Am Harvard" photos tell black students' stories. *USA Today*. Retrieved from http://www.usatoday.com/story/news/nation-now/2014/03/05/black -students-harvard-tumblr/6013023/.

Lee, T. (2012, April 5). George Zimmerman supporter sprays " 'Long Live Zimmerman" on wall at Ohio State University. *The Huffington Post*. Retrieved from http://www .huffingtonpost.com/2012/04/05/george-zimmerman-supporter_n_1406071.html.

Lievrouw, L. A. (2011). *Alternative and activist new media*. Cambridge, UK: Polity.

Martinez, M. (2013, November 22). 3 San Jose State students charged with hate crime against Black roommate. *CNN*. Retrieved from http://www.cnn.com/2013/11/21/justice/san-jose -state-racial-bullying/.

Moore, A. (2013, November 12). UCLA, male Black Bruins and the myth of individual merit. *The Huffington Post*. Retrieved from http://www.huffingtonpost.com/antonio-moore/ucla -male-Black-bruins-an_b_4258192.html.

Murphy, E. (2011, November 15). Williams cancels classes to reflect on hate speech. *Inside Higher Education*. Retrieved from https://www.insidehighered.com/quicktakes/2011/11/15 /williams-cancels-classes-reflect-hate-speech.

Noble, S. U. (2014). Trayvon, race, media and the politics of spectacle. *The Black Scholar*, *44*(1), 12–29.

Nunn, K. B. (2008, April 20). Diversity as a dead-end. *Pepperdine Law Review*, *35*, 3. Retrieved from http://digitalcommons.pepperdine.edu/cgi/viewcontent.cgi?article=1121&context =plr.

———. (2015, December 8). An open letter of love to Black students: #BlackLivesMatter. *Black Space*. Retrieved from http://Blackspaceblog.com/2014/12/08/an-open-letter-of-love-to -Black-students-Blacklivesmatter/.

Patton, S. (2015, September 21). The right wing's war on diversity in higher ed. *Dame*. Retrieved from http://www.damemagazine.com/2015/09/21/right-wings-war-diversity -higher-ed.

Perry, A. (2015, November 11). Campus racism makes minority students likelier to drop out of college. Mizzou students had to act. *The Washington Post*. Retrieved from https://www .washingtonpost.com/posteverything/wp/2015/11/11/campus-racism-makes-minority -students-likelier-to-drop-out-of-college/.

Picca, L. H., & Feagin, J. R. (2007). *Two-faced racism: Whites in the backstage and frontstage*. New York, NY: Routledge.

Plaster, M., Weinberg, T., & Colville, W. (2015, November 12). Interactive map: Schools worldwide support MU. *The Maneater*. Retrieved from http://www.themaneater.com /stories/2015/11/12/interactive-map-schools-nationwide-support-mu/.

Rios, E. (2015, November 9). How campus racism just became the biggest story in America. *Mother Jones*. Retrieved from http://www.motherjones.com/politics/2015/11/university-of -missouri-president-resigns-racism-football-hunger-strike.

Robers, S., Zhang, A., Morgan, R. E., and Musu-Gillette, L. (2015). *Indicators of school crime and safety: 2014* (NCES 2015-072/NCJ 248036). National Center for Education Statistics, US Department of Education, and Bureau of Justice Statistics, Office of Justice Programs, US Department of Justice. Washington, DC.

Rodríguez, M. M. D., Stewart, A., Cauce, A. M., & Antony, J. (2005). Minority academic achievement in a selective public university: The role of the campus environment. *Addressing the achievement gap: Findings and applications* (pp. 3–22). Charlotte, NC: IAP—Information Age.

Ross, L. (2016). *Blackballed: The Black and White politics of race on America's campuses.* New York, NY: St. Martin's Press.

Sen, R. (2012, October 18). The difference between equity and binders full of anybody. *Colorlines.* Retrieved from http://www.colorlines.com/articles/difference-between-equity -and-binders-full-anybody.

Senft, T. M., & Noble, S. U. (2013). Race and social media. In J. Hunsinger & T. M. Senft (Eds.), *The social media handbook* (pp. 107–125). New York, NY: Routledge.

Sharma, S. (2013). Black Twitter? Racial hashtags, networks and contagion. *New Formations: A Journal of Culture/Theory/Politics, 78,* 46–64.

Shire, E. (2015, November 5). Did Yale's "whites only" frat party really happen? *The Daily Beast.* Retrieved from http://www.thedailybeast.com/articles/2015/11/05/did-yale-s-whites -only-party-really-happen.html.

Srinivasan, R. (2013). Bridges between cultural and digital worlds in revolutionary Egypt. *The Information Society, 29*(1), 49–60.

Stableford, D. (2014, August 14). Howard University students pose for group photo with hands in the air. *Yahoo News.* Retrieved from http://news.yahoo.com/howard-university -ferguson-hands-in-the-air-photo-142543122.html;_ylt=A0So8z4_ClJWBbEAYTxXNyoA; _ylu=X3oDMTEydjhqaTFqBGNvbG8DZ3ExBHBvcwMyBHZoaWQDQjA5MzJfMQRzZ WMDc3I-.

Stevenson, B. (2014). *Just mercy: A story of justice and redemption.* New York, NY: Spiegel & Grau.

Stokes, S. (2013, November 4). The Black Bruins. *The University of California Center for New Racial Studies.* Retrieved from http://www.uccnrs.ucsb.edu/news/Black-bruins-spoken -word-sy-stokes.

Svrluga, S. (2014, March 27). OU: Frat members learned racist chant at national SAE leadership event. *The Washington Post.* Retrieved from https://www.washingtonpost.com /news/grade-point/wp/2015/03/27/ou-investigation-sae-members-learned-racist-chant-at -national-leadership-event/.

Taylor, R. (Ed.). (2005). *Addressing the achievement gap: Findings and applications.* Charlotte, NC: IAP—Information Age.

Tran, D. (2015, October 8). #BlackBruinsMatter. *Annenberg Media Center.* Retrieved from http://www.atvn.org/news/2015/10/Blackbruinsmatter.

Tynes, B. M., Schuschke, J., and Noble, S. U. (2016). Digital intersectionality theory and the #BlackLivesMatter movement. In S. U. Noble and B. Tynes (Eds.), *The intersectional Internet: Race, sex, and culture online* (pp. 21–40). New York, NY: Peter Lang.

Vandelinder, E. (2015, November 6). Racial climate at MU: A timeline of incidents this fall. *Missourian.* Retrieved from http://www.columbiamissourian.com/news/higher_education /racial-climate-at-mu-a-timeline-of-incidents-so-far/article_0c96f986-84c6-11e5-a38f -2bd0aabobf74.html.

Vega, T. (2014, August 12). Shooting spurs hashtag effort on stereotypes. *The New York Times.* Retrieved from http://www.nytimes.com/2014/08/13/us/if-they-gunned-me-down-protest -on-twitter.html?_r=0.

Watkins, S. C. (2010). *The young and the digital: What the migration to social network sites, games, and anytime, anywhere media means for our future.* New York, NY: Beacon Press.

Woodhouse, K. (2014, April 21). Black Student Union on talks with University of Michigan administrators: "This is not the end of the road." *MLive.* Retrieved from http://www.mlive.com/news/ann-arbor/index.ssf/2014/04/black_student_union_on_talks_w.html.

Zirin, D. (2015, November 9). 3 lessons from University of Missouri president Tim Wolfe's resignation. *The Nation.* Retrieved from http://www.thenation.com/article/3-lessons-from-university-of-missouri-president-tim-wolfes-resignation/.

Toward Digital Equity

The Role of Context, Quality, and Connections

AMANDA OCHSNER, ZOË B. CORWIN, AND WILLIAM G. TIERNEY

At a time when social media and technology appear more pervasive than ever, we have sought to outline problems that exist with regard to ensuring digital equity, to identify successful strategies for improving current challenges, to suggest opportunities that need to be created, and to consider what different organizations and constituents might do to jump-start the idea of digital equity. In thinking about how the chapters in this book connect with contemporary critical discourses on digital media (boyd, 2014; Freelon, McIlwain, & Clark 2016; Ito et al., 2013; Rideout & Katz, 2016; Snow, 2016), we are particularly compelled by a report that focused on the role of parents as mediators of children's digital media use. In their 2016 report *Families and Screen Time: Current Advice and Emerging Research*, authors Alicia Blum-Ross and Sonia Livingstone contend that organizations advising parents about technology use tend to overemphasize the risks that media might pose and neglect to give equal attention to possible opportunities from use of digital tools and technologies. As a result, many parents believe their role is to set limits, enforce rules, and exercise censorship over their children's media use. By overwhelmingly emphasizing potential for harm, public sentiment toward technology can easily be skewed toward the negative and the potential benefits of digital media overlooked.

Blum-Ross and Livingstone (2016) found that parents who recognize that digital media can create positive outcomes for their children were able to encourage the use of media for creating and learning, connecting with others, and civic action and engagement—all themes that feature in the chapters of this text. However, not all families have equal ability and resources to capitalize on technology. Furthermore, schools are often not prepared to complement and support lower-income parents' efforts to create positive and productive digital media experiences for their children.

Just as the chapters in this volume show, Blum-Ross and Livingstone found that only some children have access to the full range of opportunities presented by digital media and that inequities persist on the basis of gender and socioeconomic status. This reality prevents many youth from using digital media to learn, create, communicate, and participate. For students who are already stigmatized as "at-risk" because of their race, family income, or home zip code—the perception of the potential dangers they might face is often exacerbated. These students are considered the most vulnerable and likely to experience daily struggles with violence, obesity, and mental health—the very issues that many groups warn are risks associated with digital media use (Hopf, Huber, & Weiß, 2008; Livingstone, 2006; Strasburger, Jordan, & Donnerstein, 2010). The tendency to overemphasize potential for risk is likely to be disproportionately targeted to students already considered at-risk, which results in increased efforts to monitor, survey, and restrict their digital media use. The more restricted these students are, the less they are able to access digital media for positive educational outcomes.

In earlier chapters, Kahne, Goode, and their co-authors make arguments similar to Blum-Ross and Livingstone's claim that digital media has potential value as a space for creativity and civic action. In the first and fourth chapters, Tierney, Kolluri, Corwin, and Tichavakunda echo Blum-Ross and Livingstone's assertion that digital tools act as a conduit for relationships and information. Chapters 5 through 9 reflect Blum-Ross and Livingstone's emphasis on the importance of thinking about digital media use, not in terms of *quantity* of use, but in more nuanced terms that address factors such as the context of use, the quality of the content, and the connections that digital media use might support.

Collectively, the chapters in this text move beyond Blum-Ross and Livingstone's focus on parents and provide insight into how other stakeholders and institutions might leverage digital media for positive outcomes for underserved student populations. Our intention throughout the text is not to glorify digital media but rather to expand the way we think about the interaction among digital tools, different social contexts, and diverse populations. Below we offer summative thoughts by building on Blum-Ross and Livingstone's premise that context, quality, and connections matter. These concepts are not only helpful in establishing a conceptual framework for better understanding digital equity, but they also have concrete practical ramifications for putting digital equity into practice.

Context of Digital Media Use

Researchers have long prioritized accounting for the context of education in order to best understand student experiences and learning trajectories. But what does *context* entail when considering digital learning? The chapters in this text suggest that context can be understood by paying attention to physical, temporal, and digital markers. Furthermore, the chapters illustrate how understanding digital context necessitates examining policy and practical environments—and tensions between the two. For example, in chapter 2, Kahne, Evans, Hodgin, and Choi argue that political equity cannot be brought about by simply providing youth access to technology; carelessly inserting digital media into a classroom without acknowledgment of context is not likely to generate learning environments that lead to participatory politics. Rather, youth thrive in practicing participatory politics when they are provided specific kinds of support. Kahne and co-authors suggest that students are best motivated to use technology when they see how it can be used to improve their local communities and that engagement is higher when technology empowers them to share their perspectives on personally relevant social issues. Ideally, digital media illuminates opportunities for students to develop a sense of agency, express their voices, and mobilize for change around social issues they care about.

Establishing contexts that facilitate civic learning is difficult to achieve; incorporating technology adds another element of complexity. Acknowledging multifaceted dimensions of context appears to be a key step in understanding how to measure and address digital equity. What contextual conditions need to be in place to ensure students have equitable access to digital educational opportunities? In chapter 3, Goode, Flapan, and Margolis argue that increasing equity in computing education can only effectively be accomplished by tending to issues that have contributed to ongoing gender and racial imbalances in the field. This chapter explores how directed actions by policymakers and educators could increase the number of students who are exposed to computer science instruction while also supporting equitable access to quality and culturally relevant learning opportunities about computing. Simply exposing students to computing education without giving attention to the prevailing stereotypes—or societal context—about who belongs in computer science, or without minding the experiences of students, is not likely to lead to substantial gains in digital equity.

Given inequitable contexts for fostering digital growth, invested and caring individuals appear to make a difference. In chapter 4, Corwin and Tichavakunda, for instance, argue that individual educators who recognize unique backgrounds of students and specific institutional contexts are well positioned to assist students in building social capital through digital venues. In chapters 6 and 7, respectively, Ochsner and Martin highlight the role of mentors in this capacity. Instances when teachers and mentors act in opposition to hostile or inequitable contexts illustrate a larger need to create a level playing field across various contexts.

Kahne and co-authors caution against top-down approaches organized and mandated by districts. They instead advocate for teacher-led initiatives. Even the best systematic technology approaches are not likely to be effective if local school contexts are ignored. Chapter 2 contends that district-wide efforts can be effectively complemented by school-level focus and teacher-led initiatives that foster teachers' leadership, innovation, and collaboration. Empowering teachers ultimately has a direct impact on the contexts in which students engage with digital technologies.

Teachers can only have these impacts on student learning when there are opportunities for them to do so, however. Goode and co-authors, in chapter 3, speak to this issue from a policy perspective. Implementing computer science standards, providing uniform approaches to equity-minded teacher credentialing, and getting computer science classes to count toward college admission requirements could be critical in boosting the quality of computer science instruction in schools. These changes do not pertain to the computing content so much as the broader school contexts in which computing education is integrated. The contextual conditions must be laid before quality content can impact student experiences.

Quality of Content

The context of learning and content of instruction are inextricably related. Authors from this text have offered various vantage points into how we might assess quality content, both on a micro- and macrolevel, and illustrate that impactful content is not agnostic to gender, race, and culture. In chapter 5, for example, Watkins highlights the importance of school context in determining how meaningful learning opportunities emerge, but more pointedly, he draws attention to the implications high-quality digital learning has for students. His examination of a game design class where students developed games related to childhood obesity illustrated the potential of meaningful course content and pedagogy to foster critical thinking, civic media making, and community engagement. Students learned principles associated with design thinking, inquiry-driven processes, and civic engagement through techniques such as asset mapping. By being exposed to these high-order critical skills and through the engaging medium of game design, students learned to recognize and then articulate their civic voices.

In chapters 6 and 7, Ochsner and Martin, respectively, highlight the value of tailoring content to developmental stages. Both authors underscore the importance of ensuring that young people first encounter technologies and digital content at an early age. Data from both studies emphasize the need to foster positive technology experiences early on because empowering content has the potential to inspire young people to develop identities as technologically competent learners who can imagine themselves as professionals in technology fields. In chapters 8 and 9, respectively, Kvasny and Payton, and Leonard and Noble, show how particular content resonates with college and university students in ways that take into consideration their particular developmental milestones.

Content that is brokered by individual educators invested in their students' well-being has the potential to reach students in meaningful ways. Students frequently face institutional barriers that erode their ability to sustain their initial interests or connect their interests to concrete career trajectories. Martin's research shows that exposure to computer science tools like *Scratch* can enable youth to begin to imagine careers in coding and that support from adult mentors is critical to support sustained engagement. Ochsner's chapter shows that educators themselves often perpetuate stereotypes about who belongs in or can excel in technology industries, and these stereotypes sometimes deter certain groups of young people from taking more advanced coursework in technology disciplines. Corwin and Tichavakunda assert that critical educators can serve a vital role in sharing resources, in this case course content.

The Value of Connections

A prevalent theme throughout the book is that connected and collaborative efforts across stakeholders and contexts hold potential to increase equity for underrepresented student populations. Tierney and Kolluri's introductory chapter provides a framework for considering how individuals and groups use technology in ways that enhance various forms of capital. An understanding of how connections—especially those now afforded through digital channels—connect to resources has implications for how we operationalize digital equity.

No one single person or policy can make substantial impact on the same scale that coordinated efforts from multiple groups can. The book begins with chapters that focus on wide-scale, systemic efforts to make a large-scale impact. Chapters 8 and 9 focus on the experiences of Black students in higher education and demonstrate that supportive people do not always even need to be co-located where students are to have a substantial impact on their college experience and overall well-being. Whereas chapters 2 and 3 focus on formalized efforts to improve access to technology, the concluding chapters highlight a more organic, informal approach to building connections through technology—one that capitalizes on social media.

While the digital practices outlined by Kvasny and Payton are not introduced to students in formal education contexts, their chapter demonstrates that the unique position of being an African American student at a predominantly white college creates a need—in this case advice about mental health and self-care practices—that digital communities are uniquely situated to address. The immediate physical contexts in which these students live often offer little access to socially similar peers or mental health providers who are able to offer culturally sensitive care. Social media sites like Tumblr, then, are uniquely positioned to provide information and support to students who otherwise would not be able to connect to peers experiencing similar challenges. Online spaces like social media sites are able to support African American students in ways that they previously would not have had access to. These online communities might not offer the same benefits or address the same needs for students who have access to these kinds of resources in their immediate physical surroundings, but for some African American students, they play a critical support role.

Leonard and Noble explore how Black students use social media to amplify their voices, foster community, and circulate counternarratives that challenge the dehumanization of Black bodies, voices, and experiences on university and college campuses. Social media is particularly effective in reaching students across campuses, enabling student activist movements that begin on one campus to spread to students at other universities. Chapter 9 argues that hashtags like those popularized on Twitter, "represent an emergent language" that serves to "bind student movements together." Warning that social media is not a catchall and noting that it does not comprise the "substance of social media movements," the chapter nonetheless shows how social media enables the building of bridges between faculty, students, and staff at public and private campuses across the country and opens up the potential for deeper critical engagement with the issues faced by Black college students.

Like Kvasny and Payton, Leonard and Noble show how Black students use social media to document their shared experiences, establish solidarity, and build community. Both chapters 8 and 9 highlight creative uses of digital and social media by students to find resources, advocate for themselves, and bring broader awareness to their experiences. In these cases, the risks they face in their immediate lives—including mental health issues, feelings of isolation, and daily experiences of microaggressions and racism—are actually countered by their use of media. Even though the chapters are not in explicit conversation with one another, Watkins's focus, in chapter 6, on a high school course that facilitates civic engagement and the development of students' "voices" provides an interesting possibility for how to prepare students for postsecondary digital experiences. Teaching *high school* students how to effectively utilize digital means for expression and persuasion will perhaps allow them to enter college better prepared to navigate the tools mentioned in chapters 8 and 9.

Given the broad-reaching approaches outlined above, what happens when individuals find themselves in educational contexts that do not support digital equity? Challenges around technology tend to be more pervasive in low-income schools. These include outdated devices, rigid rules around technology use, Internet filters, and limited professional development opportunities. This rule- and restriction-based approach to digital media often seen in schools located in lower-income communities is the same type of approach that Blum-

Ross and Livingstone's outline as problematic in their report. Corwin and Tichavakunda do not see these challenges as insurmountable, however, and argue that educators are in a strong position to broker access to digital resources and to help students cultivate digital literacies.

Moving Forward: Digital Equity and Educational Opportunity

Given the significant challenges outlined and the wide array of potential solutions, how do organizations and their constituents move forward? In the introductory chapter, Tierney and Kolluri underlined the fact that the book would not aim to document practices that currently exist but rather put forward ways to think about how we address digital equity and consequently elevate educational opportunity for all groups of students. Lessons to be learned from the scholars who contributed chapters to this text focus on the roles taken on by people participating in social networks and emphasize structural contexts that enable the flow of resources from positions of power to students.

Policymakers play a nuanced role in creating the conditions for digital equity. District policies, including allocation of resources to particular programs or schools, can have significant implications on the day-to-day activities of low-income students. In the case of technology, who is funded, what types of classes are incentivized, and support given to the professional development of teachers all play into how educational opportunities evolve. Organizations constrain or enable digital equity by how they allocate resources. The systems they set in place influence teacher training and determine how students are able to use technology.

Practitioners are positioned to cultivate skills necessary for students to build social capital. When effective, practitioners can broker digital resources that enable students to develop digital literacy skills and cultivate relationships that allow them to expand their social networks. This role in helping students understand how to use the power of technology to forge relationships and access resources can also create conditions for increased empowerment.

Information has always been a valuable resource but is now more easily accessible than ever via the Internet. In some regards, opportunities for students to build social capital through social media and technology place youth in a greater position of empowerment more than ever before. Students can reach out beyond their immediate networks, connect with other students with similar experiences, and bond with adults in a different capacity than ever before. Yet, as several chapter authors mention, assuming that today's youth are "digital natives" and proficient in tech use is dangerous. Without the contexts for accessing quality content and forging meaningful connections, it remains difficult for low-income youth to effectively use technology to build social capital.

Looking forward, we believe it is vital to continue to open up pathways and forge opportunities for youth to critically engage with digital media. A key challenge will be to develop policies and practices that enable youth to build social capital and allow them to develop critical civic mindsets. As scholars and educators invested in digital equity and educational opportunity, we strive for a world where all youth are empowered to challenge the status quo of their local and global communities. We believe that digital media, when integrated thoughtfully, has the potential to afford youth opportunities to build connections, amplify their voices, and engage in critical dialogue with peers from around the world.

REFERENCES

Blum-Ross, A., & Livingstone, S. (2016). Families and screen time: Current advice and emerging research. *LSE Media Policy Project, Media Policy Brief 17.* London, UK: The London School of Economics and Political Science. Retrieved from http://eprints.lse.ac.uk/66927/.

boyd, d. (2014). *It's complicated: The social lives of networked teens.* New Haven, CT: Yale University Press.

Freelon, D., McIlwain, C. D., & Clark, M. D. (2016). Beyond the hashtags: #Ferguson, #Blacklivesmatter, and the online struggle for offline justice. *Center for Media and Social Impact.* Washington, DC: American University, School of Communication. Retrieved from www.cmsimpact.org/sites/default/files/beyond_the_hashtags_2016.pdf.

Hopf, W. H., Huber, G. L., & Weiß, R. H. (2008). Media violence and youth violence: A 2-year longitudinal study. *Journal of Media Psychology, 20*(3), 79–96.

Ito, M., Gutiérrez, K., Livingstone, S., Penuel, B., Rhodes, J., Salen, K., . . . & Watkins, S. C. (2013). *Connected Learning: An agenda for research and design. Digital Media and Learning Research Hub.* Irvine, CA: Digital Media and Learning Research Hub. Retrieved from dmlhub.net/wp-content/uploads/files/Connected_Learning_report.pdf.

Livingstone, S. (2006). Does TV advertising make children fat? *Public Policy Research, 13,* 54–61.

Rideout, V., & Katz, V. S. (2016). Opportunity for all? Technology and learning in lower-income families. *The Joan Ganz Cooney Center.* Retrieved from http://www.dwp.gov.uk/docs/strategyandindicators-fullreport.pdf.

Snow, B. (2016, January 19). The potential for game-based learning to improve outcomes for nontraditional students. *Muzzy Lane.* Retrieved from http://www.muzzylane.com/2016/01/game-based-learning-and-nontraditional-students-a-report/.

Strasburger, V. C., Jordan, A. B., & Donnerstein, E. (2010). Health effects of media on children and adolescents. *Pediatrics, 125,* 756–767.

YOUNG WHAN CHOI is manager of performance assessments for Oakland Unified School District (OUSD) and has been a public school teacher in New York City, Providence, Rhode Island, and Oakland, California, during which he developed expertise in culturally relevant classroom instruction, curriculum design, and work-based learning. He developed a national online ethnic studies curriculum, directed the Educating for Democracy in the Digital Age initiative, and has a master's degree in social studies teaching and instructional leadership. His writing has appeared in various publications including the *Washington Post*'s AnswerSheet, *East Bay Times*, *EdSource*, and UCLA's *Xchange* journal. Currently, he leads OUSD's ethnic studies program and supports the development of high-quality performance assessments in high school.

ZOË B. CORWIN is associate research professor with the Pullias Center for Higher Education at the University of Southern California. She is co-editor of *Postsecondary Play: The Role of Games and Social Media in Higher Education* (Johns Hopkins University Press) and *Preparing for College: Nine Elements of Effective Outreach* (SUNY Press).

CHRISTINA EVANS is a researcher with the Civic Engagement Research Group at Mills College, a member of the Youth Participatory Politics Survey Project research team (a project of the Youth & Participatory Politics Research Network), and an Oakland-based artist.

JULIE FLAPAN is the director for the Computer Science Project at UCLA's Center X, where she conducts research on opportunities for teaching and learning high school computer science. She is also the executive director for the Alliance for California Computing Education for Students and Schools (ACCESS), leading a statewide effort to support computer science education that is meaningful, equitable, and sustainable and ensures access for girls, low-income students, and students of color. She works to facilitate several National Science Foundation grants related to broadening the participation of underrepresented students in computer science.

JOANNA GOODE is an associate professor of education at the University of Oregon. Formerly a high school computer science teacher, she focuses her research on how school systems and teachers can create opportunities for more diverse students to learn about computing in school. She is the lead developer of the Exploring Computer Science high school curriculum and is a co-author of the award-winning book *Stuck in the Shallow End: Education, Race, and Computing* (MIT Press).

ERICA HODGIN is the associate director of the Civic Engagement Research Group at Mills College and the research director of the Educating for Participatory Politics project (a project of the Youth & Participatory Politics Research Network). Her research focuses on the educational implications of youth civic and political engagement in the digital age.

JOSEPH KAHNE is the Ted and Jo Dutton Presidential Professor for Education Policy and Politics at the University of California, Riverside. His research and writing focuses on the influence of school practices and new media on youth civic and political development.

SUNEAL KOLLURI is a PhD student at the University of Southern California. He researches college readiness for high school students from historically marginalized backgrounds and how pedagogies and school structures in high schools might hinder or enhance college-going for these students. In particular, he focuses on how culturally relevant pedagogy, advanced coursework, and technology are incorporated into high school academic programs to impact college outcomes. He intends for his work to inform practice such that more students from diverse racial, ethnic, and socio-economic backgrounds engage meaningfully with their schooling and prepare adequately for their college-going futures.

LYNETTE KVASNY is an associate professor in the College of Information Sciences and Technology at The Pennsylvania State University. Her research uses critical social theories to examine the ways in which historically underserved groups appropriate information and communication technologies to improve their life chances. The results of her research have been published in over 75 peer-reviewed journal articles, book chapters, and conference proceedings including *The Information Society, Information Systems Journal, Communication Research,* and the *International Conference on Information Systems.*

DAVID J. LEONARD is a professor at Washington State University, Pullman. He is the author of *Playing While White: Privilege & Power on/off the Field* (University of Washington Press), *After Artest: The NBA and the Assault on Blackness* (SUNY Press), and *Screens Fade to Black: Contemporary African American Cinema* (Praeger). Dr. Leonard also is co-editor of *Visual Economies of/in Motion: Sport and Film* (Peter Lang) and *Commodified and Criminalized: New Racism and African Americans in Contemporary Sports* (Rowman and Littlefield).

JANE MARGOLIS is a senior researcher at UCLA's Graduate School of Education and Information Studies. Her research focuses on equity in education and how fields become segregated. She is the lead author of two award-winning books about how these issues are manifested in computer science education: *Unlocking the Clubhouse: Women in Computing* (MIT Press) and *Stuck in the Shallow End: Education, Race, and Computing* (MIT Press). She was awarded as a 2016 White House Champion of Change for her work on equity and computer science education.

CRYSTLE MARTIN is a postdoctoral research fellow at the Digital Media and Learning Hub at the University of California, Irvine. She is author of *Voyage across a Constellation of Information: Information Literacy in Interest-Driven Learning Communities* (Peter Lang). Dr. Martin's research focuses on youth learning in informal contexts, specializing in information literacy and connected learning, and how those skills, if valued in academic settings, can create a more equitable education system. Along with this, she researches how libraries can support teens connecting their informal and formal learning environments.

SAFIYA UMOJA NOBLE is an assistant professor in the Department of Information Studies in the Graduate School of Education and Information Studies at UCLA. She also holds appointments in the Departments of African American Studies, Gender Studies, and Education. Her research on the design and use of applications on the Internet is at the intersection of race, gender, culture, and technology. She currently serves as an associate editor for the *Journal of Critical Library and Information Studies* and is the co-editor of two books: *The Intersectional Internet: Race, Sex, Culture and Class Online* (Peter Lang), and *Emotions, Technology & Design* (Elsevier).

AMANDA OCHSNER is an assistant professor of education at the University of Findlay in Ohio. She researches how well-designed and thoughtfully implemented experiences with games and digital media influence youth's learning pathways. Through her work, Dr. Ochsner aims to identify opportunities to increase equity and opportunity for groups traditionally underrepresented in technology fields. Her recent projects examine the experiences of women who work in the video game industry, efforts to engage girls in learning to code, and a digital initiative to increase college access for underserved youth.

FAY COBB PAYTON is a professor of information technology and university faculty scholar at North Carolina State University. She has published over 100 peer-reviewed journal articles, book chapters and conference papers covering topics, such as health IT, user design, analytics / data management and underrepresentation in tech. She was named the 2016 North Carolina Technology Association Tech Educator of the Year and participated in the 2016 White House Summit on the United State of Women. She is the author of *Leveraging Intersectionality: Seeing and Not Seeing* (Richer Press), an anthology of her research on STEM education and experiences in both academe and corporate environments.

ANTAR A. TICHAVAKUNDA is a dean's fellow in the Urban Education Policy program at the Rossier School of Education and research analyst for the Pullias Center for Higher Education at the University of Southern California. Prior to his studies, Mr. Tichavakunda taught high school English in Washington, DC, Public Schools. His research focuses on increasing college access, Black students' experiences at Predominantly White Institutions (PWIs), and digital equity. His recently published work includes a case study of the challenges Black students face with regard to college costs and financial aid, as well as a critical review of the use of digital media by Black youth. He recently completed a study of how Black students in STEM majors experience the campus racial climate and foster a sense of engagement.

WILLIAM G. TIERNEY is a university professor, Wilbur-Kieffer Professor of Higher Education, co-director of the Pullias Center for Higher Education at the University of Southern California, and past president of the American Educational Research Association (AERA). He is author of *The Impact of Culture on Organizational Decision-Making: Theory and Practice in Higher Education* (Stylus) and *New Players, Different Game: Understanding the Rise of For-Profit Colleges and Universities* (Johns Hopkins University Press), among many other books and articles. He is looking at issues of privatization, academic freedom, access to higher education for low-income students, institutional quality, and academic corruption.

S. CRAIG WATKINS studies young people's social and digital media behaviors. He is a professor in the Moody College of Communication at the University of Texas, Austin. He received his PhD from the University of Michigan. Dr.

Watkins is the author of three books, including *The Young and the Digital* (Beacon Press), which explores young people's dynamic engagement with social media, games, and mobile platforms. His forthcoming books, *The Digital Edge* (2018) and *Rethinking the Innovation Economy* (2017) explore some of the key shifts in technology, equity, diversity, innovation, and education. For updates on his research and projects visit his websites, theyoungandthedigital.com and doinginnovation.org.

Note: Page numbers in *italic* indicate figures and tables.